The Boys from Hicks Drive
Vienna, Virginia

Game 7 Publishing
https://www.game7publishing.com/

Ordering Information:
Sales on demand. For details, contact the publisher at the address above.

Printed in the United States of America

Copyright © 2018 by Game 7 Publishing
All rights reserved. This book or any portion thereof may not be reproduced or used in any manner whatsoever without the express written permission of the publisher except for the use of brief quotations in a book review.

Printed in the United States of America

First Printing, 2018

ISBN: 978-1-7327523-1-3

The Boys from Hicks Drive
Vienna, Virginia

*True adventures of growing up during the 1960s and 70s in
The Best Small Town in America*

By
Rick Speight

*"Sometimes you will never know the value of a moment
Until it becomes a memory"*

Dr. Seuss

Hicks Drive's (aka Chapel Hill) first residents, Catherine and Stephen McCarthy, circa 1953. Catherine posing on Lot #19, where she lived about sixty years. HERNDON 480 is a phone number. Builder and prior landowner is Edith V. Hicks.

Contents

Prologue   1

Part I-Building the Foundation One Adventure at a Time

Moving Day, 1961	7
New Kid on the Block	18
He Was All Teeth	24
The Legend of Dinky Grey	27
Army Family Invades Hicks Drive, 1962	34
Kennedy Assassination, 1963	41
The Search for the Dead Goat, 1964	44
Bicycle Death Plunge, 1965	51
The Blizzard of 1966	60
Roger Takes A Dip In Todd's Pond, 1966	66
Dale and the Telescope, 1966	71

Part II-Juvenile Delinquents

Don't Wanna Look, Can't Turn Away, 1967	79
We Didn't Know You Were a Cop, Officer! August 1967	84
Cherry Bombs and Private Bathroom Moments, 1967	89
Sass Your Mother, I'll Beat You for That, 1968	95
Teacher, Mentor, Lifelong Friend, Mr. Alfred W. Richardson, 1967-2000	101
A Day at the Pool, 1968	105
Todd's Farm and the Old House, 1968	111
Has Anybody Seen My Tractor? Fall 1968	116
Rush Hour Mayhem, 1969	122
Kehoes Under Attack, 1969	131
Wine Making and Poison Ivy	135
One Week Before Freshman Year of High School, 1969	

Part III-Girls, Girls, Girls

First Girlfriend, Make It Count, 1970	145
The Girl from Ipanema	152
A Pretty Girl Moves Into the Neighborhood, 1970	158
Get Out of Here, You Tramps! 1971	163
Deja Vu Summer, 1971	168
Take a Picture, It'll Last Longer, Spring 1972	174

Part IV But What If I Don't Want To Be A Responsible Adult?

Eddie the Pimp	183
Bourbon, Spring 1972	189
Grave Digging, Halloween 1972	194
Roger Gets Another Lesson, Spring 1973	201
The Grim Reaper Let Us Get Away, 1974	208
The Bridge, Spring Break 1975	213
Jaws and Aunt Fran's Wig, 1975	221
Hard at Work December, 1975	226

Part V-It's Never Too Late

So What Happened to Everybody?	241
Every Picture Tells A Story	247

Undated postcard from Pinterest. Submitted by Patti Bentley.

Prologue

I've met many people who have expressed the desire to write a book. Typically, they had given it much thought for many years. Yet, there was always something holding them back.

I have had those ambitions, as well. And I think it started after I received an *A+* on an English Comp paper at George Mason University, and the professor decided to read it to the class. Fortunately, for me and everyone else who was there that day, it was only a page or two in length.

For more than half a century, lifetime friends of my Vienna, Virginia childhood and I, have frequently gotten together for fun and adventure. And, of the hundreds of times at least, we tell and re-tell the same stories over and over again, about growing up together, in the sixties and seventies, and reliving the outrageous and sometimes dangerous things that we did as kids.

Repeatedly hearing and re-telling the same stories, for over fifty years, makes it really difficult to forget the best details.

So, sometime in 2009, I made the commitment to write down a few of the most vivid memories my buddies and I were a part of, while we lived on Hicks Drive. And once I had recorded two or three stories, I did a few more. After a while, I'd finally accumulated a sizable collection of tales that others might appreciate—perhaps, even enjoy.

I knew, then, that in me somewhere I had a book. And somehow, I was going to figure out a way to get it out and share it.

So, here we are.

As one can imagine, many thoughts were running through my mind, as I revisited and recorded the past—my past. I had a head filled with people I once was really close to, and I began to better appreciate that they are still significant players in my life.

While I was recreating each memory, sufficiently enough to write them down, the details of everybody contained in each story, suddenly began to come back into focus. That motivated me to eventually reach out to all of them, many of whom I hadn't seen or talked to in decades. And every time I spoke to them, it was like we'd been suspended in time; I instantly recognized the tone, excitement, and passion in their voices, from conversations that ended a long time ago. The years had passed, but the memories were intact, as lively and vibrant as ever.

So this latest adventure has been much more than the process of writing a book. It's been the realization that everyone I know, particularly if I formed a friendship with them as a child, is now and forever, part of me.

Part I

Building the Foundation, One Adventure at a Time

Ricky Speight in the Stroller, Front Yard of Trap Road Home
Rt. 1, Box 508 Vienna, Virginia, 1956.

Moving Day—June, 1961

"Come on (come on let me show you where it's at)
Ah, come on (come on let me show you where it's at)
Whoa!, come on (come on let me show you where it's at)
I said the name of the place is I like it like that"[1]

Fay Whetzel and I, five year old best friends, were playing at her house one afternoon, when an unexpected civil defense air raid siren went off. Her mother, a very tall and attractive woman of about thirty, frantically ran across the hardwood floor to the room where we'd built a fort out of blankets and duct tape.

"You need to go home right now, Ricky," she stated, walking toward where we were playing, skillfully hiding whatever she was feeling inside. But I could see something in her face that I hadn't seen before, as her eyes narrowed slightly, brows furrowed with determination, cheek muscles taut as she spoke.

It was the look of fear.

Fay and I'd heard the siren, but neither of us knew why it went off, nor did we understand the significance of it. But rather, we continued playing *house* in the little blanket-home we built all by ourselves. We had been the best of friends and next door neighbors since we were toddlers, often seen running together through the grass in the warm summer sunshine, or playing with our toys as our mothers chatted over coffee.

She even taught me how to tie my shoes.

But as soon as we looked up from our fort and saw Mrs. Whetzel towering over us, hands on her hips and slightly out of breath from her dash through the house, we knew this was different. And the unwavering blast of the siren suddenly seemed to get louder.

I opened my mouth, but couldn't speak. I could move, though.

I leaped up from the floor like I'd sat on a wasp, before hurrying for the front door without crashing into furniture or slipping on the newly waxed floor. I actually ran *through* the screen door, its steel mesh and wooden frame seemed to move out of my way, as I entered the threshold. I didn't bother with the remaining two stairs. I was at top speed with the second stride. My destination home seemed elusive, though right there in front of me, only about a hundred yards across the pasture that separated the Whetzel's house

---

1   Chris Kenner and Allen Touissaint, "I like It Like That", 1961

from ours. That day it seemed like miles away. So I forced myself to move my arms and legs faster, motivated by the sudden sensation of hair rising up on the back of my neck.

Fay's mom was someone I trusted, and for her to get so rattled by the sound of that never-ending siren, I knew it was something serious.

When I opened the front door, my mom was waiting for me inside, cradling my sleeping little sister, Robin, who was still an infant. Mom didn't say a word as she took me by the hand and led me into the bathroom, which was more or less in the middle of the house. I don't think she really understood what was going on, or she chose to ignore it as a means of managing something over which she had no control. She slowly closed the bathroom door behind us.

We remained there until the siren stopped. I doubt if it lasted more than a few minutes, after we'd tried to get comfortable by sitting on the bathtub rim and toilet seat. My mom still hadn't spoken, yet. Suddenly, she stood up, opened the door, and then went straight to the telephone. I didn't want to sit in the bathroom by myself, so I followed her. She grabbed the phone and sat in the adjacent chair in one motion.

I could only watch as she placed her index finger into the first phone number digit and make a clockwise motion on the rotary dialer, with my sister sleeping soundly. She just sat there for a moment when she was finished dialing. My dad must have finally answered the phone, because that's when she started to cry.

Geopolitical tension between the world's only super powers, the Soviet Union and the United States, officially began as soon as World War II ended. And this confrontation without battlefield casualties was immediately given a name: *The Cold War*. By the late fifties, it was a constant and repetitious feature of all three major television broadcast networks. Especially after communist forces in 1959, led by Fidel Castro, staged a successful coup in Cuba. Now Communism, which started in Russia and quickly spread to China, Korea, and Vietnam, had reached to within a ninety mile boat ride from the coast of Florida.

Preparations to survive an imminent Soviet intercontinental ballistic missile attack began slowly, but with determination. Air raid drills, like the one that intruded upon Fay and me, soon became weekly occurrences. Even in kindergarten, we would practice lining up and proceeding in an otherwise orderly fashion into the hallway. And once there, we were instructed to face the wall, get on our knees, and tuck our head between our legs.

Official government propaganda films and commercials provided the animated versions, intended for children, of this silly, worthless procedure called *duck and cover*. They should have called it *kiss your ass goodbye*.

And those who possessed the means and knowledge to do so, went well beyond *duck and cover* and built bomb shelters in their basements. Typically, these structures were no more than cinder blocks and mortar erected next to the washing machine and utility sink. Canned food and water were neatly stored inside, on shelves built to look like grandma's pantry. Doors were optional.

But despite the threat of nuclear annihilation from communist aggressors who had most of their arsenal aimed at Washington, DC, my future parents, Irene Ramsey and Bruce Speight, left Appalachia coal-country Virginia and share-cropping North Carolina, in search of a better life in our nation's capital. There, they married in 1947 and eventually moved to the suburbs on Trap Road, and next door to the Whetzels.

Our Trap Road home was a little, white, two-bedroom cottage, with a breezeway between the carport and side door. It didn't have a basement but was built on a crawl-space foundation. It is currently owned by the Wolf Trap Foundation for the Performing Arts.

We were surrounded by farmland; both of my parents were raised on farms, but neither became farmers. That's probably no coincidence. Farming is hard work and doesn't pay very well.

However, my dad *did* raise chickens. Why we had those large birds on our country estate of half an acre, I wasn't quite sure.

But the weasel who snuck into their quarters one night and ate the heads off three of them knew that chicken meat was delicious.

Despite the threat of a Russian missile attack, bomb shelters, air raid sirens, and headless chickens, Fay and I seemed to grow closer together with time. There weren't many children our age that lived nearby, so, often it was just her and me.

In addition to friendship, there was something else we shared, something neither of us asked for, or wanted.

I came home with a fever after a full day of kindergarten at the Holy Comforter Church. At first, it was merely a lethargic sensation, accompanied by a loss of appetite. But by morning, I convinced myself and my mom that I was feeling better, so I went to school. But when one of the other student's moms brought me home, later in the afternoon, I was feeling much worse. And I was developing a rash in areas of my body I was too embarrassed to show my mom. But she already knew. Fay had the same symptoms and stayed home from her kindergarten class that morning.

She and I'd shared the so called *red measles*. Along with it, came the misery of high fever, red splotches everywhere, and eyes so sensitive to light that we were banished to darkened rooms in our little houses; windows blacked-out with sheets and towels thumb-tacked to the frames.

Within days of the symptoms, I really missed my friend, but was too sick to think much about it. But Fay always seemed to appear in the strange, fever induced dreams I had nearly all day, every day.

She and I got the mumps and the other measles, the *German* variety, together as well.

Eventually, my best friend and I developed immunities to most childhood diseases, and we'd achieved it the hard way—actually, the only way available at the time.

A few weeks before our final Trap Road Christmas, I heard a knock on our front door. And through the large window adjacent to the door, I could see Fay tightly bundled in her winter coat and matching scarf. I quickly ran to the door and opened it so she could come inside.

"Ya wanna' play?" she asked. "My mom's going to the store and I don't want to go." She removed her cold weather gear and then tossed it on the couch before I could take it from her.

She'd just made herself at home.

Robin was crying again, so I knew my mom would be distracted by that, and Fay and I could get into just about anything we wanted.

It wasn't long before we began to jump up and down on my bed, slowly at first, then faster, while we laughed at each other's attempt to avoid falling off and crashing onto the wooden floor.

"Ricky! Stop jumping on the bed!" my mom yelled, above the din of my crying sister.

With the realization that our fun was interrupted, Fay and I jumped off the bed and scurried into the hallway.

But as I turned the corner at the door and headed for the living room, I stumbled and fell forward. My hands instinctively went out in front of me for protection against the hard floor, but ended up on the hot furnace grate. We didn't have central heat in the home, just this huge floor furnace that kept the hallway and grate blazing hot, and the living room freezing cold.

I landed firmly, with both hands palm-down, immediately followed by Fay landing on top of me, before she rolled off to the side. Luckily, she had narrowly missed the grate, but contact with her had forced my body to the floor and the hot metal.

I instantly let out a guttural scream that sent my mom into a panic. I heard her running to me through the house, at my side in an instant. Ignoring Fay, she picked me up and carried me into the kitchen, where she quickly turned on the stove. When the burner was hot, she held my seared palms and fingers over the heat, in some old mountain wives' tale procedure about holding burnt flesh over a hot stove burner to *pull the heat out*. The only thing that made her stop was my screaming directly into her ear. She was deaf on the left side for two days.

I was still crying, my bandaged hands pitifully extended in front of me like a begging dog, when I finally went back to Fay, who was sitting quietly on the sofa, hands folded neatly in her lap.

"Does it hurt?" she asked, with an empathetic expression of pain on her face in anticipation of my answer.

"Yeah," was all I could say, as I made extra effort to stop crying in front of her.

"You were yellin' pretty loud, especially when your mom took you into the kitchen," she continued, her eyes focused on my bandaged hands as she spoke. All I could do was sit there and think about how much it hurt.

We sat together in the living room until her mom returned from the grocery store. Although I was a little embarrassed from crying in front of my best friend, I was glad she was there. And the longer she stayed, the better I felt.

Eventually, life returned to normal at our home; my bandages came off, and Fay and I went back to playing, and Christmas presents were wrapped and placed under the tinsel decorated tree.

But, as my sister Robin and I got older, it was becoming more obvious that our growing family had made our tiny home impractical. My sister was still sleeping in my parents' bedroom, since we had only two, I had limited space to play inside that didn't include flesh searing metal, and traffic in front of our house was just starting to increase, in response to the residential growth surrounding us.

So, we began the weekend ritual of family house hunting.

The four of us went to a few open houses, but one objection or another had prevented my parents from making an offer. Then the realtor took us to a red brick rambler on a cul-de-sac, in a neighborhood full of kids and trees, on nearly an acre of land. The subdivision was called Chapel Hill and it contained but one street, Hicks Drive.

Suddenly, it was time to move.

My dad, possibly the world's first do-it-yourself-no-matter-what kind of guy, would never have considered hiring a moving company to relocate his wife and two children a quarter mile away. Instead, the tireless search for discarded grocery store cardboard boxes began.

Every trip to the A&P, which usually started as a routine gathering of produce, canned beans, and animal parts, now ended by excavating The Empty Box Bin, where previously filled containers of all kinds were stored before their trip to the landfill. After just a few visits, everyone at the store, from the manager to the cashiers, ran for cover when they saw DIY Bruce Speight striding through the front door.

We planned to pack everything we owned, one item at a time, into the "free" cardboard boxes we had scrounged—we carried them outside, one by one, and stacked them in the bed of a pickup truck. Filled up the truck, drove, unloaded, rinse, repeat.

Finally, with the last of our family belongings rattling around in the back, our old truck whined through all four gears, as it climbed the hill on Trap Road across from Todd's Farm, to our new home.

My dog Chico, a terrier mix of some sort, ran behind the 1950 Ford F1 with little effort. Dad was driving, of course. My mom was on the passenger side while I "rode the hump" in the middle. No seat belts.

As my dad shifted through the gears, my mind shifted through all the emotions an almost-six- year-old-boy would experience, making his first move into a new neighborhood: fear of the unknown, excitement of having a bigger and better bedroom, as well as nervousness of having to make new friends—while leaving my best one behind. And, although the back-yard of our new home almost touched that of the lot we were leaving, it seemed miles away due to the circuitous route we had to take, from one driveway to the other.

Our truck slowed down to a crawl, as we made a right turn onto the street I would live for the next sixteen years: Hicks Drive. It would be my sanctuary through childhood. It would be my financial refuge when I run out of money in college and be forced to move back home. It would be where I grow up a lot faster than I should have. Where I'd come to the realization that I alone am responsible for what happens to me in life. It would be the foundation of more adventure than any individual could have in one lifetime, and still be alive to talk about it. It was the place I would forever call *home*.

My dad down-shifted the truck, as we made our way up the initial incline on Hicks Drive. There was a large holly tree at the edge of the road on the right. It was full of red berries that were so numerous they were causing the limbs to sag, touching the ground around the periphery. Soon I'd find out that the entire neighborhood's child population would seek shelter under that tree whenever it rained, so as to stay dry while we'd wait for the big, yellow school bus to pick us up at the bottom of our street.

Now, as we proceeded a little farther up the road, I saw a group of about a half-dozen kids running around in a neighbor's yard playing a game of tag. We made our way to the third house on the right, 1635 Hicks Drive. It seemed like a mansion, all twelve hundred square feet of it; it had a full basement, partially above ground and visible from the road, which made the structure appear twice as tall. It was much bigger than our old two bedroom house.

Aerial of Trap Road home (top, center), Todd's Farm (lower right corner, note long tree-lined driveway) and Hicks Drive (slightly left of center).

Large holly tree at Trap Road and Hicks Drive. McCarthy's house to right. 1635 Hicks Drive (new home) left. Photo by Eileen McCarthy Grant.

My dad slowed the loaded truck, as he positioned it in the street for backing into the driveway. He wanted to get as close to the front door as possible. I sat upright in the seat and looked around, wondering where Chico was, since I didn't see him in front of the vehicle once it came to a stop. But when I looked down from the passenger side window, I could see the top of his tail wagging furiously in appreciation that the journey had finally come to an end.

We remained in the middle of the road, as my dad searched for *reverse* a couple of times by engaging the clutch pedal on the floorboard. Eventually, we began to move backwards, my dad ever mindful to take his time.

"Dad, why are we going so slow?" I asked, ready to jump out of the barely moving vehicle, so I could run into the house and see my new room.

"What's your hurry, Ricky? Can't you see I'm trying to drive?"

He always made an elaborate procedure out of everything he did, while meticulously attending to every detail.

"I want to see my room and climb one of those trees in the backyard," was the best I could do to state my case.

Ever so slowly, our truck made its way closer to the house, while Chico ran circles around us, barking loudly and with much enthusiasm. As my dad cautiously glanced between the side and rear- view mirrors for any hazard that might suddenly pop up out of nowhere, we finally approached the end of the gravel driveway.

Once we came to a halt, my mom opened her door, turned in her seat, and slid out of the truck and onto the driveway. I nearly pushed her, as I climbed out right behind and firmly planted both feet on the driveway.

I sprinted along the short sidewalk and up the steps to the front door. I tried to open it, but it was locked. I glanced back to the truck, where I saw that my dad hadn't moved an inch since we arrived. His eyes seemed to be fixated on something on the street in front of our house. Then I saw him slowly reach across the truck seat for the glovebox on the passenger side. He opened its door and began rummaging through its contents like he was searching for something. His hand stopped moving for a moment, until it finally emerged holding a flashlight. He brought the light close to his face, flashed it on and off several times, before he finally opened the driver's side door.

I couldn't get into the house without a key, and my dad didn't seem to be in a hurry to bring it, so I sat on the top step in frustration.

The afternoon sun seemed to be setting while I waited for my dad. *I'd seen snails move faster than him*, I thought, as the minutes passed. I had already chewed up four of my fingernails, when he finally reached the foot of the stairs, to begin his step-by-step methodical climbing. I waited until he'd reached the top, before I jumped up and held the wooden screen door, so he could let us in.

When I was about eye-level to his waist and close enough to get a good look, I saw that he wore a jumble of keys attached to his belt. There must have been hundreds of them. One by one, my dad examined the keys in succession, looking for the perfect match. I couldn't take it anymore, so with a disappointed sigh of complete surrender, I sat back down on the stairs.

But this time, as I looked across our front yard, I saw a very tall, cross-eyed boy staring at me as he was casually leaning on the hood of a car. I couldn't really tell which eye was looking at me. I glanced back over my shoulder and saw that my dad was still key-searching and it would undoubtedly be dark soon. So, I again turned toward the boy next door, who hadn't moved, but continued to stare at me. Finally, I couldn't wait for slow-poke-dad to find the matching key, nor stare at the kid next door any longer, so I started to walk toward my new neighbor. As I approached, he didn't smile or seem to care what the outcome of our initial meeting would be.

After an awkward few seconds, though, I learned the kid's name was Roger Martin. He would be my next-door neighbor until I got married and moved away, and my good friend for the next fifty years. He was, and remains to this day, the most unique person I have ever known.

Hicks Drive's new kid. Photo from Speight family album. 1961.

New Kid on the Block, 1961

*"Hit the road Jack and don't cha come back
No more no more no more no more
Hit the road Jack and don't cha come back no more
What'd you say?"[2]*

"Why don't you go over to that nice boy's house next door and see if he can play?" my mom asked me before she had unpacked a single box of our furnishings.

"But don't go anywhere else" she added, as I went out the front door, slamming it behind me. Message received: Get out from under my feet, but don't stray more than a few yards from the property line.

I ran over to Roger's, but before I reached his sidewalk, I saw him coming out the front door. I wonder how he knew I would be there.

At first, I was somewhat apprehensive about my new next-door neighbor, after I'd apparently won the staring contest the previous day. But we seemed to quickly become friends, as children typically do.

He had two older sisters, neither of whom was in our peer group.

His parents were from Portsmouth, Virginia. At least his mom was, and I think his dad ran those roads, as well. Neither one was particularly friendly.

I suspected this attitude almost immediately upon my arrival on Hicks Drive. And from that day onward, whenever I was in the company of either of Roger's parents, I couldn't escape this feeling of discomfort, knowing that whatever I said or did might result in a frown or elicit a negative comment from the elder Martins.

And in later years, I confirmed this observation because Roger, always willing to share the private conversations he had with Mommy and Daddy, told me all of the unkind comments they made about the members of my family, especially me. The reasons were never clear.

So, I lived next door to a good buddy for many years, along with his not too warm and fuzzy mom and dad. I simply avoided the parents, occasionally found sitting in their darkened living room with the curtains pulled tight, slumped in a favorite over-stuffed chair, puffing a Kent cigarette, while sipping a medium-priced bourbon.

But, despite the odds against him, Roger could be a decent and often

---

2   Percy Mayfield, "Hit the Road, Jack", 1961

caring individual. He had his good moments. Actually, he had some great moments.

Nevertheless, in spite of his successful attempts to be a regular guy, often he was intentionally intimidating and belligerent. And he was frequently a bully. It appeared that he just couldn't help himself. But his friends, like us, had tolerated it. Others didn't, so Roger became famous for stopping many fists with his face.

But through it all, he was one of us, one of The Boys from Hicks Drive.

"Let's go across the street to David's house. His mom always gives us Popsicles," Roger said authoritatively, while flashing a large, mostly toothless grin of a seven-year-old kid in the midst of a dental transformation.

I stopped at the foot of the stairs, as Roger began to descend, and we both pivoted in the general direction of SomeWhereElse, the destination my mom seemed to be suggesting I should visit for a while.

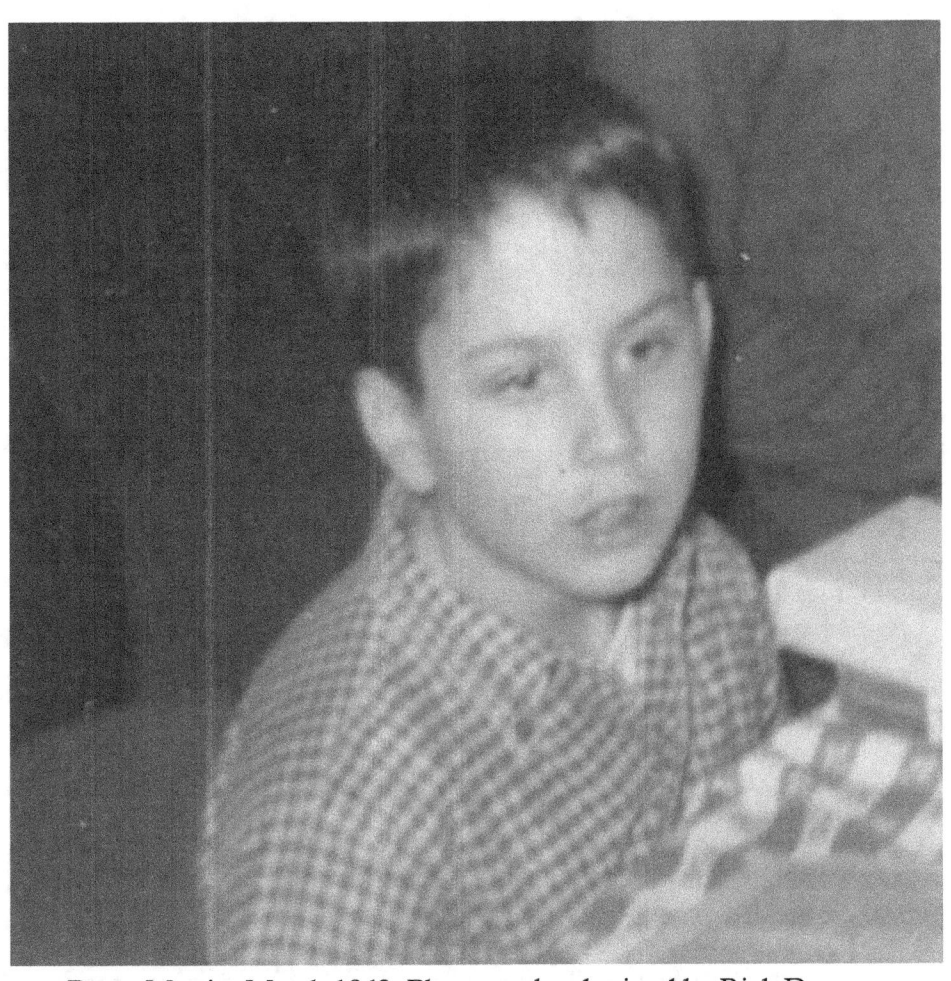
Roger Martin, March 1962. Photograph submitted by Rick Duncan.

I would soon learn that David Finch was one of three children in a Catholic family that lived directly across the street from me. The Catholic distinction was notable for several reasons: they wore uniforms and rode to school in retired DC Transit buses, went to church on Saturday, and they tried their hardest to convince all non-Catholics that we were going to hell. That was a heavy load for a child. No wonder so many had bailed out and went to public school, once they were able to complain loud enough to convince their parents.

On this day, I forgot all about my temporary eviction from my new home as I followed Roger between the forsythias in our yard, across the street and into the Finch's driveway. A few leaps up the front steps, and Roger loudly banged on the door to announce our arrival.

Mrs. Finch opened the door and I was initially shocked at how pretty she was. I thought all grown up women were big. My mom was definitely hefty, along with all three of her sisters. My grandmothers were big, too. And all these extra-large ladies smelled kind of funny. Sort of a sweet, sweaty sort of odor that I had gotten used to, because I thought it was normal.

Mrs. Finch looked like an angel and smelled like flowers. She gracefully stepped back and invited us into her living room.

"And who is this young man, Roger?" she inquired, as her whole face seemed to light up in a smile.

"What's your name again?" Roger said, as he tried in vain to recall the conversation we had about ten minutes earlier.

"Ricky, Ricky Speight," I replied, while still mesmerized by Mrs. Finch, in her colorful, flowery house dress so popular in the fifties and early sixties.

"How about a Popsicle while David helps his father repair his bike in the basement?" she asked, while already knowing the answer to her question. With that, she began to walk toward the kitchen in the back of their house. Roger and I were already salivating right behind her, in anticipation of a brightly colored sugar rush.

I never had a real Popsicle before, just the ones we'd made out of Kool-Aid poured into those plastic forms that went into the freezer. The real ones were ready to eat, right out of the box.

Mrs. Finch handed me the frozen treat wrapped in white paper, and it seemed too big to hold in one hand. I opened it up and caught a glimpse of brilliant red, with not one, but two wooden sticks at the bottom. A Double Popsicle!

"These will melt pretty fast," Mrs. Finch said, as she handed us our treats with one hand, while deftly opening the spring-loaded screen door out the back with the other. I had guessed it was her polite way to say, *you can't eat those messy things in my house.*

"See! I told you she would give us a Popsicle," Roger firmly stated, as we went down the steps into the back yard. I heard what must have been David clomp-clomping up the wooden stairs of the basement, quickly followed by him throwing open the back door so hard that it hit the wall behind it. He then made the three-foot leap off the porch.

"Hey, where's mine, mom?" David whined, seeing Roger and I devouring our delicious frozen confection, as I tried to figure out the best way to eat it without allowing any of the rapidly thawing child-meal to hit the ground. Mrs. Finch suddenly, magically appeared with another Popsicle for David, and the three new friends ran for the woods behind the house to find that secret, hidden place to get away from everybody over the age of seven.

"This is the new kid, Ricky Something," Roger said, to nobody in particular, as yellow Popsicle juice ran all over his dirty hands. He had already forgotten my name again.

We devoured our flavorful snacks, temporarily ignoring the brain freeze.

"Wanna build a fort?" David asked, as he started to run toward the woods. Before I could follow, his dad came up from the basement and into the back-yard with a glass of something in his hand.

"My dad really likes beer," David spoke over his shoulder, rather nonchalantly, as he began to slow down and wait for Roger and I to catch up to him.

"Beer?" I asked.

"It's what grownups drink, stupid!" Roger shouted in that how-many-times-do-I-have-to-tell-you voice. He was about three inches from my face and sprayed me with enough spit to wash it.

This new adventure on my inaugural day in the neighborhood was my first exposure to at least two things: the neighborhood bully, and that not all parents were teetotalers like mine.

David's idea to build a fort started to gain some momentum. The three of us hiked into the forest behind the house, until we came to a hole in the ground. It appeared to be an excavation effort to build a fort.

"We started this yesterday. My dad used to own the world, and he gave us this area to build a fort. So, I'm President," Roger said, as I awaited instructions for what came next. I was the new guy, after all. For years, Roger would continue to proclaim that his Dad owned the world. I believed him.

Roger quickly gathered a handful of sticks, just long enough to reach across a three foot wide trench, about three feet deep. It seemed like the window to the middle of the Earth. He haphazardly arranged the sticks across the width of the hole, climbed out and defiantly put his hands on his hips. David and I sat along the edge of the crevasse, with our feet dangling over the side.

"Okay, Finch, walk across this and see if it'll hold you." Roger gave David little choice but to obey. David just sat there looking at the makeshift bridge, wondering if it was a good idea or not. Finally, he stood up and walked around the hole, to where Roger's bridge seemed to begin. He cautiously took one step, which was instantly greeted with the crack of twigs under his foot. Then he took another, then two more, until he was almost to the middle of our fort's subterranean foundation. Suddenly the whole structure snapped in half, plunging poor David toward the ends of the Earth. It all happened so fast, that it took me a moment to process the entirety of what I'd just witnessed.

As I saw David begin his descent, I heard the sticks shatter under him. Upon his impact with the bottom of the hole, I heard a louder *crack*, maybe David's bones, and the thud from his body with the *whoosh* of air quickly forced from his lungs.

Then it got quiet.

He had come to rest on his back, so the first thing I saw was a facial expression of intense pain and anguish, as David seemed to desperately process the damage that had just incurred. That look was quickly followed by one of panic, when he tried to breathe, but couldn't. Then he started screaming. I thought he would never stop.

A short moment later, his mom and dad came running into the woods with the look of terror on their faces, anticipating an unknown, but certain danger, to their oldest child. David's father reached us first, with Mrs. Finch scurrying right behind him. The father stepped into the hole and picked David up, as his screams got louder, peeling the bark off all the trees in the vicinity.

David's leg was in an unnaturally awkward position, turned to the side, as Mr. Finch looked at his wife and then said rather stoically, "I think he broke it."

David must have known what that meant, because his screams reached a new level, and my ears began to ache from the volume.

Dad rushed inside, carrying his screaming baby boy, with mom right behind him. Roger and I sat and stared into the hole, without saying a word. After a few moments, Roger stood up and walked over to me, sat uncomfortably close, and then said, "If you tell anybody, I'm gonna knock your teeth down your throat."

I believed it, as I unwittingly ran my tongue over my teeth, as a sort of subliminal reality check on my chompers.

We got up and slowly started our walk home. As we proceeded past the Finch house, I could still hear David screaming from the pain, his mom and dad arguing over whose fault it was, and his little brother crying due to all the commotion.

When we finally reached the street, I started to re-process the events that had occurred all within the last hour; I moved into our new home with my own bedroom, I met two kids in the neighborhood, one was the bully, and the other broken his own leg—Mrs. Finch looked like an angel, Mr. Finch drank some grown up beverage called *beer*, and real Popsicles had two sticks.

What a great start to a new life.

He Was All Teeth

"Oh, the shark, babe, has such teeth, dear
And it shows them pearly white
Just a jackknife has old MacHeath, babe
And he keeps it, ah, out of sight
Ya know when that shark bites with his teeth, babe
Scarlet billows start to spread
Fancy gloves, oh, wears old MacHeath, babe
So there's never, never a trace of red"[3]

David didn't stay in the hospital very long. He had broken his ankle in three places that required surgery to install metal pins to hold it together and allow it to heal properly. In his absence, I helped my parents unpack boxes to move into our new house. And just when I was getting bored with that, I heard my mom in the kitchen say,

"Ricky, someone's at the back door to see you."

I raced through the house, savoring the echoes of my running feet on hardwood floors, appreciative of someone at my door who wanted to play. There was Roger standing on the back porch, peering in through the screen door. He was with some shorter, other kid who also appeared much younger. But as I got closer, something told me to slow down and not open it just yet, to proceed with caution because of imminent danger.

"This is Allen Armstrong. He bites," Roger said, in a threatening tone that would soon be his trademark. I froze and stared at this strange, new creature.

As I looked closer at Allen, I immediately saw that he was flashing a lot of teeth. Perhaps many more than he actually needed. I imagined that it was surely human flesh wedged into the spaces between his incisors, as Roger's warning continued to resonate. Without hesitation, I quickly reached for the little latch to lock the screen door to initiate a sense of security, without actually providing any whatsoever. Screen doors don't keep anything out except bugs, and even that was iffy at best. It didn't help that *Mack the Knife,* a song that sounded like it was all about a shark, was playing on my mom's AM radio, which was always tuned to WEAM in Arlington. All I thought about was this toothy kid sinking his canines into me.

I wanted to move back to that safe place we left just a half mile

---

[3] Kurt Weill and Bertold Brecht, "Mack The Knife", 1928

around the corner and away from this monster on my porch.

"I can't come out. My mom says I have to help," I somehow managed to say through the screen door. Suddenly, I heard a deep, almost gravelly voice coming from the direction of Roger's house next door.

"*Rahja*, time to come in," the voice commanded, in a distinctive Tidewater pronunciation of *Roger*. It rolled off the tongue without a hint of emotion, but delivered succinctly and to the point.

A feeling of relief washed over me, as Roger led Allen back down the steps and off to terrorize someone else. But, as The Shark was leaving, he kept glancing back over his shoulder with an exaggerated grin, undoubtedly confident he had me right where he wanted. At that moment, I think I threw-up a little bit into my mouth.

Later that afternoon, I had two choices: I could either stay home and listen to my sister endlessly whine about nothing, or knock on Roger's door and risk running into the shark again. I chose the latter and sprinted out the back-door, thinking I could outrun any potential danger in the one hundred fifty yards or so to Roger's house.

As I approached our neighbor's back-door, my momentum must have caused me to knock a bit louder than I'd planned. A moment later, I heard that same voice again, "Rahja, get the door and tell them not to knock so loud. We're not *deaf*."

Roger arrived and opened the door for me to come into his home.

Roger's house was exactly like mine, but with more stuff hanging on the walls, and a *lot* more furniture. I opened my mouth to speak, but the overpowering odor of cigarette smoke burned my nose when I inhaled.

He led me through the kitchen and dining room, and then into the living area, a room that was much darker than it should have been, where his mom was seated in a comfortable-looking chair.

Mrs. Martin, iced tea in one hand, burning cigarette in the other, set her beverage aside and demanded to know who I was.

"Rahja, who is this?" she growled, while exhaling a deep, lung-full of smoke. But before Roger could reply, she quickly stuffed the cigarette back into her mouth and took another drag. The tip burned bright red and reflected off of the plastic covered lamp shade on the table next to her.

"And stop running in the house, Dummy," she added, while sizing me up.

"This is Ricky, the new kid next door," Roger carefully introduced, in fear that he might mispronounce a syllable or two.

"Tell your mother to come over when she can," Mrs. Martin offered, as she again blew out a cloud of smoke, but this time, in my direction.

"Okay, Mrs. Martin. I will," was the best I could do, as Roger and I looked for an escape route.

Once we were safely outside, I asked Roger about Shark Boy.

"Mommy says Allen and his little brother are spoiled cuz' they have every toy ever invented," he said. "I used to have every toy, but I gave most of them to the Armstrongs. He bit me once and I punched him, so he stopped."

In about an hour, we'd gone from "He bites" to "He bit me once and I punched him." Perhaps Allen wasn't what I had imagined.

We then ran as fast as we could around his house and a hundred yards up the street.

"There's Allen's house," Roger said. "His dad is an astronaut or something. That's why they're rich."

Roger and his encyclopedic knowledge of everything were useful, after all. But, it took me about six months to learn that there were limits to this constant flow of unsolicited information.

On that day it didn't matter. Instead, we explored the bridle path, a forest highway of sorts, which cut through the woods from Beulah to Trap Road, behind five houses at the top of our street.

And that path remained a major transportation route for The Boys over the ensuing decade.

The Legend and Tragedy of Dinky Gray

"I hear the train a comin'
It's rollin' 'round the bend,
And I ain't seen the sunshine
Since, I don't know when
I'm stuck in Folsom Prison"[4]

When we moved to Hicks Drive in April 1961, we had already known and associated with the Gray family that lived diagonally across the street from our new home. The respective moms had somehow connected when we lived around the corner on Trap Road and their friendship endured for many years.

They seemed like an ordinary, nineteen sixties middle class family; the dad, like my own, was blue-collar, the mom, a stay-at-home wife, two absolutely beautiful daughters several years older than me, and two sons Michael and Dinky. They lived in "the house with the pool", the only one in our neighborhood. Heck, it was the only house with a pool for several miles around. Getting an invitation from them to come for a swim was a rare and welcomed treat.

With the exception of Dinky, all of the Gray family members exhibited what seemed to be normal social behavior. The mom and dad were like regular moms and dads, the daughters were nice to us little kids, and the younger brother was always getting in the way like a little sibling is supposed to.

Before and after we moved to Hicks Drive, our moms would make us tag along on trips to the grocery store or occasionally the local five and dime, Wright and Hunt's. That usually entailed one or more of the Gray children plus me and my always whining and crying sister. We got to know each other quite well.

While the rest of the Grays seemed typically average, Dinky was special. He was smaller than most kids his age, but never did I see him back down from a confrontation. And there were many of those. In fact, he was the consummate bully to most kids, but strangely, very friendly to others—like me. For whatever reason, I always got along with Dinky Gray, and while

---

[4] Johnny Cash, "Folsom Prison Blues", 1955

I wouldn't call him a true friend, he was okay to hang with from time to time.

One of those occasions, Dinky and I were playing in the woods behind the Finch's house next-door to his, when we came upon a large bird nest underneath, behind a thick cluster of some sort of bush. And in the nest was the largest egg I had ever seen. We figured from its size and the occasional sighting of a reclusive water fowl in the area, it must have once belonged to a mother goose who, for some mysterious reason, had abandoned it.

Dinky made the decision right then that the egg belonged to him. He picked it up and examined it from one end to the other.

"Look what I found—a damned goose egg!" Dinky said, displaying his early utilization of colorful language.

"It's gigantic. Wonder if it's got a goose still in it," I mused, while watching Dinky hold the egg up to the bright sunrays that shone through the pine needles in the trees just above our heads.

"Can't see anything. Let's go show it to Finch," Dinky said, as we headed for the street and a short walk around the front of David's house. He tucked the egg into his arm like it was a small football, and we walked out of the woods together.

When we got to the road, we saw Roger and David Finch riding their bikes. They didn't seem to be going anywhere in particular.

When we got closer to them, Dinky didn't waste any time announcing his discovery of the treasured goose egg. "Hey stupids," he called out to Roger and David collectively. "Look what I found."

"What is it?" David asked, while keeping a safe distance from Dinky. He knew from previous experience that saying the wrong thing, while standing too close to Dinky Gray, could have deleterious consequences.

"What's it look like, dummy?" Dinky said.

"Looks like an egg," chimed in Roger, who had already ridden his bike too close to get away if he had to. Roger's vision was never 20:20, so he got within inches of the egg, as Dinky held it out in front of him on display.

"Yeah, it's an egg, genius. And it's mine," Dinky said, while giving Roger a shove into the chest with his left hand, still cradling the egg in his right. The shove didn't hurt Roger, but he clearly didn't like being pushed by the little runt from across the street.

And with that, Roger wheeled his bike around the driveway circuit.

"Where ya' going?" asked Dinky, who was left standing alone, egg in hand.

Dinky reached back before hurling the egg in a perfect spiral in the direction of Roger, who was riding away on his bike, with his back turned to us. The egg seemed to float majestically, aimed directly for Roger's head. The goose egg missed Roger by about six inches, crashing to the ground beside him.

Dinky immediately turned to me and said, "I can't believe I missed that cross-eyed freak."

I couldn't believe he got that close. It had to have been about thirty yards in the air.

But at the exact moment of impact, a horrible stench exploded from inside the now destroyed egg. The horrific smell seemed to engulf all four of us in such a way that we couldn't escape. For that matter, we couldn't even breathe. It was like a chemical warfare agent.

"Oh, jeez! It's rotten," I yelled, as loud as I could. I knew it right away, because we'd discovered a rotten chicken egg back at the old house, after a hen got loose and started laying eggs under, what she thought was a private bush in our back-yard. My dad didn't find it until it was too late. He'd stepped on it while trimming the limbs one autumn afternoon.

Now there was that putrid, foul smelling, rancid, rotten egg splattered in a four-foot diameter pattern on the Martins' driveway sending all of us retching to our knees. It was worse than Finch's socks when he forgot to take them off for about a week, earlier in the summer. It was worse than the time my dog accidentally pooped in the house, sending all family members gagging and heading for an open window. The stench was ten times more potent than the worst fart ever emitted by any animal on planet Earth!

Dinky ran home, sensing the impending blame for the smell that knocked all of us senseless. David and I began yelling for someone, anyone, to come outside and witness this once in a lifetime event.

"Mom! Dad! Come quick," we hollered in the direction of our homes.

Roger chimed in with a barely audible: "Mommy, help me." Some of the egg, just a little green chunk or two, stuck to his leg, and he was deciding whether he was going to die on the spot, or a slow agonizing death.

First, one, and then another, neighborhood kid heard our cries and began to move in closer, ever so cautiously, approaching the bomb site. Most adults couldn't get within fifty yards before running back into the house and closing all of the street-facing windows. But every child in the neighborhood between the ages of four and fourteen soon gathered around to share in The Event of the Summer of 1962.

I was convinced now that I had moved onto the coolest street in the whole world.

Soon after the Goose Egg Incident, Dinky and I began to go our separate ways. We seldom played together after that, and on those rare occasions when we did, Dinky would usually get into a fight with one of the other neighborhood boys.

His anti-social, attention-seeking behavior seemed to escalate.

One of the fathers on the street, Mr. Hall, saw him throwing rocks at the family car that was parked in their driveway. Suddenly, the man heard the sound of shattering glass and immediately afterwards, saw Dinky running down the street. Mr. Hall followed Dinky to his house and knocked on the door. Mr. Gray answered, with an out of breath Dinky standing directly behind him. After Mr. Hall shared what he had seen, including the fleeing boy, Dinky's father turned around and asked his son whether he'd thrown the rock that had broken the car window.

Dinky denied ever leaving the house that day and Mr. Gray believed him and closed the door.

He continued his torment of Roger, beating him up several times, using various objects such as a full book bag, marbles shot from a slingshot, acorns strategically thrown at his face, and his fists delivered in succession toward multiple body parts.

He intimidated countless others with his aggressiveness and abusive behavior, perhaps foretelling what Dinky was becoming.

His grades in school were abysmal and he seemed to spend more time in the principal's office than in the classroom.

Eventually, and to the relief of many on Hicks Drive, he and his family moved out of the neighborhood.

They remained in Fairfax County, as Dinky's life continued to spiral out of control.

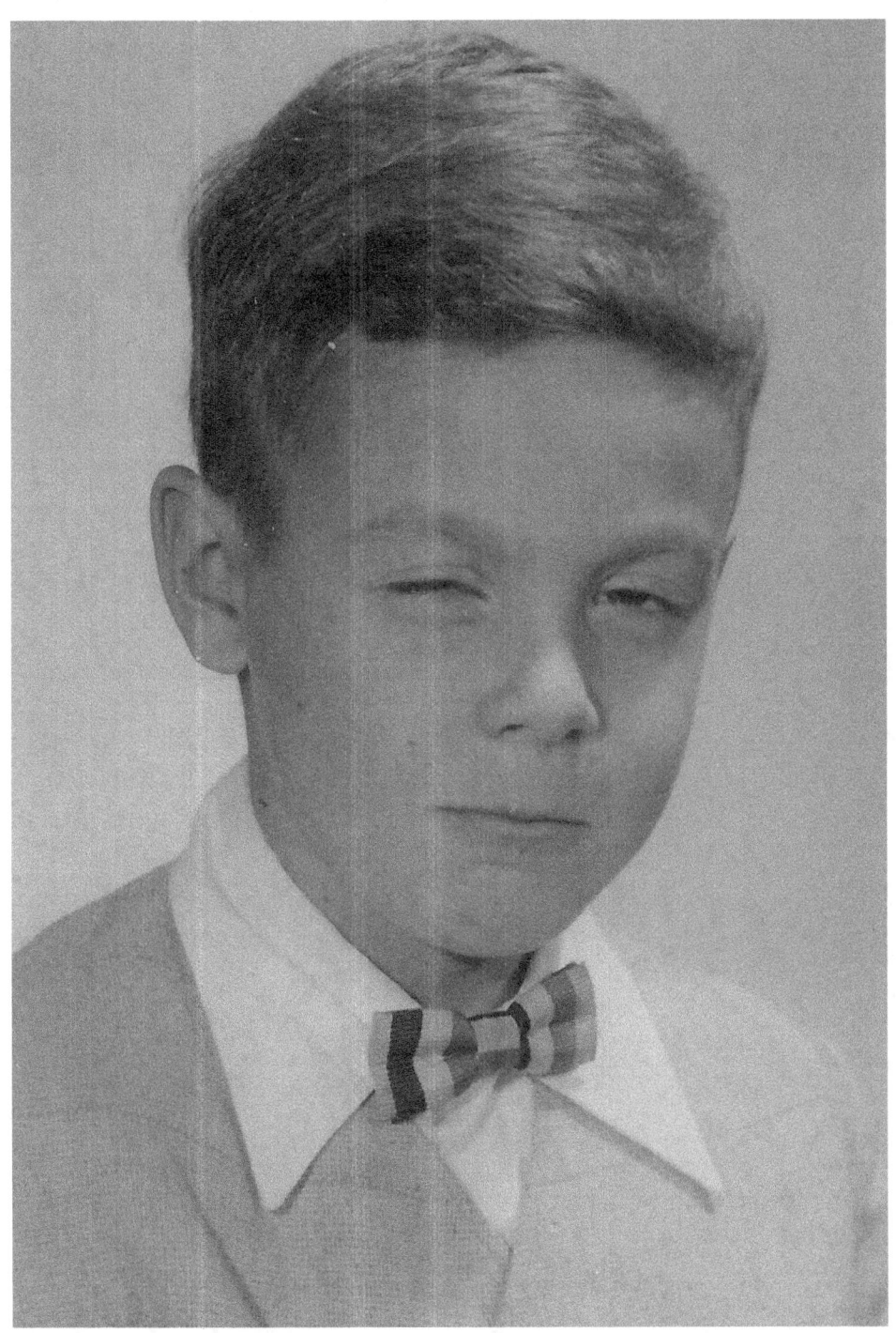

Peter Canciglia, circa 1962. Photo provided by Peter.

Army Family Invades Hicks Drive, 1962

"March along, sing our song, with the Army of the free
Count the brave, count the true, who have fought to victory
We're the Army and proud of our name
We're the Army and proudly proclaim"[5]

It didn't take more than a few weeks for me to realize that Allen's appetite for human flesh was greatly exaggerated and soon he and I were hanging out together.

One particularly hot, humid day in the summer of 1962, we were in his bedroom playing with the myriad of really cool toys he had readily available. Not only did he have the best stuff around, he had them in duplicate. More precisely, Allen and his younger brother, Buck, always received the same toy for Christmas, birthdays, Easter, and no reason other than their parents wanting to buy them a gift. So, they had two of everything made by Mattel, Hasbro, and Parker Brothers.

And on this day, plastic World War II German soldiers were poised, ready for attack, behind a large pillow that Allen and I had decorated with a few trees we borrowed from his train set. Their mission was to annihilate the advancing GIs and their armored escort, before they could reach The Fatherland-Germany.

But the Germans hadn't anticipated being flanked and overpowered by General Patton's Third Army, who rapidly approached the enemy from under Allen's bed.

When I stood up to drop a hail of bombs on the Germans from oversized B-17s we'd found in the basement, I glanced out of the window and down to the house next-door, which had been for sale several months. There hadn't been much sales activity there up to that point, and when the lawn grew up so high that we could barely run from one side to the other, it was unofficially off-limits for a play area. I suspected that was because the last time I ran through it, I had three tick heads embedded into my skin.

That day, when I gazed outside the window, a large crowd was viewing the property. There seemed to be too many of them for just one family. But, I saw a diminutive mom-type and a muscular dad sort of guy

---

5   The Army Goes Rolling Along, Edmund L Gruber and John Philip Sousa, 1908 and 1917

with fifteen or twenty kids of various sizes and ages running around the yard, screaming and yelling like it was a playground. I didn't think to raise the window and yell out a warning about the tick infestation. I was just a kid.

But they certainly looked different, and behaved in a manner, unlike any I had seen before. Our prospective new neighbors all had dark wavy hair, sun-tanned skin, and none were particularly tall. And, as I said, they were very loud. Everybody was shouting. It was quite a scene.

My world, up to that day, had been 99.9% White Anglo-Saxon Protestant. Quietly pale white of English/Irish/Scottish descent.

I hadn't yet seen an Asian, anybody from the Mediterranean area, and very few of African or Eastern European origin.

I watched intently, as the rolling gaggle made their way around the end of the house, closest to my observation point and then into the back yard. And, since all of the children were running and screaming at each other, the movement seemed more like a human hurricane—a stable center, or the eye, which was the mom and dad, with kids literally running in circles around them. Then an occasional straggler would join the group, like a feeder band, and the whole mess was moving in a particular, but unknown direction. Soon they were out of sight, and just as quickly, out of my mind.

About a month later, a moving van slowly made its way up Hicks Drive and then headed straight to the house that was for sale. It was the biggest truck I had ever seen up close. But once it had parked on the street in front of the house, the eighteen-wheeler began moving again, from the end of the street, somehow turned around in the cul-de-sac, and then parked in the same spot, but this time in the opposite direction from five minutes earlier.

And driving up Hicks Drive, right behind the moving van, was a car filled to the brim with occupants. It was the screaming mega-family.

Before the car came to a complete stop, a stream of kids exploded out of it, like a thumb over the lip of a shook soda bottle. The kids all ran inside the house, while the movers climbed out of their eighteen-wheeler, before opening the doors to their van.

It took nearly two days to empty the truck of its contents. This, of course provided forty-eight hours of entertainment to bored boys on bikes, like Roger, Finch, and I—kids with nothing else to do, as the summer waned. The children, now seeming like a manageable dozen of them, were organized as an army of mini-movers, emptying the contents of their automobile and *helping* the professionals un-load the van, while the Dad shouted detailed instructions, waving his arms about wildly.

After a few minutes of watching from a safe distance, I focused on a kid about my age, who was regularly getting in the way. So, I rode my bike over to him and offered a lame, "Hi, wanna play with us?"

"I'm Pete and we just moved from Germany," replied the new kid.

He was the youngest boy in a large, military officer-led family, seven in all: Pete, two parents, three sisters, and an older brother. They lived the global army life, before finally making their fort on Hicks Drive.

"Well, do you wanna ride bikes?" I said, thinking maybe he hadn't heard me the first time I asked.

"Hunh? Can't, gotta help my dad unpack," he replied, as he returned to the car and moved yet another box inside their home.

"When you gonna be done?" I asked, while watching Peter poke around in the car, as if he was busy.

"Hunh? Probably never. My dad has a list of chores for all of us when we empty the car."

I gestured in the general direction of my house, while asking my new friend to stop by, should he ever complete his work.

Then the three of us hopped on our bikes and coasted down the hill toward home.

It was several days before I ever saw our new neighbor again, so I'd guessed he wasn't kidding about the chores.

But, once Peter had been released from family servitude, he joined us in an all-day bike ride to nowhere in particular. We didn't need a destination.

Roger, Finch, Peter, and I headed for the creek, down by the "S" turn on Old Courthouse Road. It was a short five minute ride from Hicks Drive.

Soon after we got underway, Peter continued to ride his bike in the middle of the road, while the rest of us queued up single-file on the edge. Within minutes, a car approached from behind and blew the horn. It scared me enough to temporarily swerve off the edge of the pavement and onto the adjacent narrow strip of gravel.

"Why do you ride your bike in the middle of the road?" I asked Peter, after the approaching car had passed, and I was back in control of my own wheels.

"Wasn't anybody coming," he said.

"What about that car that blew its horn?" I reminded him.

"Hunh? I moved out of the way."

I could see that I wasn't getting anywhere with this kid, so we pedaled on until we reached our destination with limited chit-chat.

"Let's see if there's any crawfish over here," Roger said, as he got off his bike, dropped the kick stand, and approached the bank of the creek.

Since it hadn't rained in more than a week, the flowing water was crystal clear, but the crawfish weren't waiting around to be caught. They were usually hiding under a rock in the creek.

"Here's a big one!" Finch shouted, as he attempted to grab the crustacean from behind to avoid its painful claws.

"Got one!" Peter yelled, as he held it up for display while standing in the water. Peter was obviously skilled at catching crawfish with his hands, because he naturally held it firmly from the tail to avoid the claws snapping wildly.

After an hour of catch and release, we jumped back on our bikes before heading home.

Soon, Peter was once again in the middle of the road while riding next to me, before we started up the hill.

"So, why did you move here?" I asked him.

He stood up while pedaling, to better climb the hill.

"My dad's in the army and we moved from Germany."

"Oh," I said.

"I've got a brother and three sisters," he added, after pumping his legs several times on the bike.

"I've got a little sister," I said in what sounded apologetic. I couldn't imagine having three of them.

"Most of the time, they're okay. But my younger sister, Mary, is a pain in the neck. She's always bossing me around, and she's younger than me."

We all got a little winded by the time we got to the top of Old Courthouse Road, just before hitting Four Corners.

"Hey, Roger. You got any Coke at your house?" I asked, because I knew we didn't have any at ours.

"I think so. I'll grab one to share, and go out the basement door. My mom will never see me."

With a cold, refreshing drink now awaiting us, we picked up speed on our bikes.

Immediately upon our arrival at Roger's, Peter, Finch, and I parked by the back door. It was so hot.

"What kinda toys you got?" Finch asked Peter, as both of them peered through the glass window, hoping Roger was in sight.

"I got lotsa guns, roller skates, uh, and Monopoly, but I don't know how to play that—some army stuff of my dad's, you know, that kind of junk. My brother Hank has some cool stuff, but he'll kill me if I mess with it."

"And get *caught*," I added for clarification.

"He *always* knows. Hit me with a stick the last time. My dad was pissed, at him and me."

It wasn't long before Roger came through the basement door with not one, but two opened bottles of ice-cold Coke.

Pete and I shared one, while he and Finch shared the other, as we all shared stories.

I learned that Pete's dad was an officer, stationed with the conquering and now occupying United States Army in Germany. They moved back to Northern Virginia, where they had lived a few years earlier, before his most recent assignment in Europe.

I tried to make my family sound more exciting than they actually were, but there was no way I could compete with Peter's.

Even Pete's bike looked different—yet another clue that there was something very strange about these people from Germany. Later, I would notice his dad spoke in a Brooklyn accent, which I had never heard. His mom created some of the most delicious aromas I had ever smelled, all of it Greek food straight out of the kitchen. The three sisters were very friendly, and the oldest brother, Hank, was a commanding, but very gregarious and accommodating boy at least five years older than me.

But, perhaps the biggest surprise was learning that there were only five children, not fifteen to twenty that I'd estimated earlier. I guess each of them occupied four times the space, and made at least ten times the noise of a normal kid.

The Canciglia family began with the marriage of the father being a Brooklyn Sicilian and a Washington, DC Greek mother, who begat five high energy and very successful children, all of whom brought a new world to our little enclave on Hicks Drive. Their impact was immediate and everlasting, providing a new and very different culture, lifetime friendships, and family values, all of which made a positive impact on everyone around them. They were loud, fought amongst themselves constantly, bought fifty bags of groceries at a time from the Ft Myer PX (On one occasion, I counted them), they constantly talked about Germany, and always had at least three old Mercedes in their yard and driveway, all in various degrees of drivability. But, perhaps, most important of all, they demonstrated to me that people from cultures and backgrounds that were distinctly different from mine, was a good thing.

No, it was a great thing.

Stories of Mr. Canciglia's Brooklyn upbringing taught me that New York City was a cool place to call *home*. I heard from him and his kids, what it was like growing up in a poor, immigrant family in the place that accepted everyone: New York City. He also told us war stories—endless war stories. Our favorite one was how he taught monkeys on some semi-deserted, but Japanese-occupied island, to drop coconuts on the heads of the enemy soldiers when the GIs ran out of ammunition.

Mrs. Canciglia's Greek heritage introduced me to the most wonderful cuisine on the planet. But, since Mrs. C had to feed five children and one always-hungry husband, the invitations to their table were few and far between. That didn't stop Pete and me from raiding the refrigerator, often devouring all of the leftovers.

Peter's endless clamor about living in Germany convinced me that it was more than the epicenter of the only wars with Roman numerals. It was a vibrant country, filled with industrious people trying to re-assimilate themselves back into the rest of world, who had just kicked their asses. Again.

The sisters introduced beauty, grace, and intelligence to adolescent boys, too young to appreciate it until they were older.

And the brother, Hank, before his eventual acceptance into West Point, showed us that chemistry sets could be fun and explosive, while providing an academic lesson. We blew up a lot of stuff.

The Canciglias had the greatest impact on my life of any family I'd ever encountered. We lived on the same street at the same time for more than fifteen years. That meant we all grew up together. Relationships formed with someone from childhood can never be duplicated.

Peter's family was also the most interesting on The Drive. They were everything right out of a Hollywood script about the immigrants who arrived on Ellis Island with nothing but strong family bonds, and even stronger work ethics. And they all became something special.

They were also loud, argued constantly, and everybody talked at the same time, while nobody appeared to listen to a word the other was saying. Total chaos, seven days a week.

Peter was, and remains to this day, the best of all of us. He was the kindest, most forgiving, most astute at reading the feelings of others, and the person most likely to care about the most people.

Walter Cronkite, November 22, 1963. Courtesy of CBS News.

Kennedy Assassination, 1963

"From Dallas, Texas, the flash apparently official, President Kennedy died at 1 p.m. Central Standard Time, 2 o'clock Eastern Standard Time, some 38 minutes ago."[6]

John Fitzgerald Kennedy created the earliest Presidential images and memories for most baby boomers.

But, few know, even today, that fifty percent of the voters did not choose the handsome man with the funny Yankee accent, perfect hair, gorgeous wife, and adorable children. But I, and everyone else with a Zenith black and white television, would soon learn about his life story, military career on PT-109, back problems, book-writing achievements, and reading capability. The Kennedys were everywhere. Everyday.

If the Nixon-Kennedy debates were the infants of the modern television age, then the Kennedy presidency was the toddler, because the day after the 1960 presidential election on November 8, all media attention was devoted to the man, myth, family, and legacy of the thirty-fifth President of The United States. And rightly so.

There were just four television stations in the DC metro area in the early sixties: CBS affiliate WTOP, NBC had WRC, ABC's WMAL then WJLA, and a local station WTTG on channel five, which aired an odd assortment of mostly cartoons and reruns. So when something presidential was happening, three of the four available broadcasts were all over it. There was no escape.

That was particularly true in November of 1963 as Air Force One headed to Dallas, Texas.

The buildup to that trip was extensive and comprehensive. While President Kennedy won Texas' eight electoral votes, he did not carry the conservative Dallas metro area. And this trip was in combination, a victory lap and concession to a strategic political base moving forward.

Friday, the twenty second day of November was particularly warm in Washington, upper sixties for a high—and as an extremely fashionable second grader I probably flashed around the playground in my Buster Browns with the top button fastened on my way-too-hot, long-sleeved shirt.

But everything changed after lunch. First, the news had arrived that the president had been shot while traveling in his motorcade. That announcement was quickly followed by cautious optimism that the

---

6   Walter Cronkite, CBS News, November 22, 1963

"wounded" president was rushed to the hospital. Soon, we found ourselves, every student in every classroom at Freedom Hill Elementary, glued to the television screen, which was typically only used for learning French on PBS.

Then the announcement was delivered, as Mr. Cronkite struggled to contain his emotion on national television. The camera seemed to stay focused on him for a long time, watching as he put his glasses on, before just as deliberately, removing them.

I looked away from the television in search of my teacher, Mrs. Barufi, who stood quietly off to the side of the classroom. Though the room was darkened to better view the broadcast, I saw her wipe a tear off of her cheek and quickly turn away from the class to cry in private.

I had never seen a teacher cry.

Immediately, reality became so overwhelming that school was cancelled for the rest of the day, and everyone was sent home to the comfort of their families.

Nobody said a word during the entire bus trip. Not a sound could be heard, except the squeak of the brakes on approach to the next stop.

We lived three miles from school, and the bus ride seemed to take an eternity.

When we reached our stop, all of the children in the neighborhood stepped off the bus and quietly walked home.

It's likely that all of the kids on Hicks Drive, perhaps across the country, had experienced death through the loss of an elderly family member, or perhaps a friend of the family. But none of us, before the Kennedy assassination, had ever gone through a national crisis like the murder of our President.

It has since been written that America lost its innocence that day in Dallas, when President Kennedy was assassinated. Maybe that's true. But what is certain, is that every citizen in the United States born after the mid-1950s, remembers where they were, what they were doing, and with whom they were doing it, on November 22, 1963.

And then, when our attention was still wholly focused on Kennedy, the assassination of the alleged assassin, Lee Harvey Oswald, right on national television, was surreal, to say the least.

Timing is everything, and the way those events collided was unprecedented; advances in television technology, the explosion of media coverage, a politically savvy and attractive couple in the White House, and a determined assassin, all met in the same place at the exact same time.

The ensuing days of dissecting Dealey Plaza seemed to all run together—slow-motion footage of the president's motorcade, and the First Lady climbing over the car seat. I sat with my family, in front of the television screen in our living room, reliving the moments over and over and over. We were numb from it all. And we mourned all weekend.

By Monday the 25th, the slow parade began of soldiers and dignitaries surrounding the horse drawn carriage to Arlington National Cemetery. Indelible images began to emerge of Mrs. Kennedy, standing strong with her children at her side. Likely, the most poignant of all, was three-year old John Jr, wearing a winter coat over short pants, and alone in front of the adults, standing at attention, and saluting his father in the casket as it passed.

But, perhaps my most vivid memory of that time, straight from the mind of an eight-year old boy, was the jet fly-over to follow the twenty-one-gun salute at the cemetery.

Displaying their most professional precision at the perfect moment, just when the graveside saluting gunfire had ceased, we all witnessed from the comforts of our living rooms, a formation of jets flying directly over the ceremony.

Immediately, I heard the jets directly over my house, for I lived less than ten miles from Arlington. I ran to the front door and looked up, where I saw the planes pass directly over me. And it was loud.

One of the reasons growing up in the DC area was so great was that, unlike anywhere else in the US, local news was national news. And that had never been truer than the four days President Kennedy was assassinated, mourned about, eulogized, and buried.

The Search for the Dead Goat, 1964

"A-well-a ev'rybody's heard about the bird
B-b-b-bird, b-birdd's a word
A-well, a bird, bird, bird, bird is a word"[7]

We had spent the previous hot and humid July afternoon playing baseball in our front yard. Home plate was near the driveway, first base between the forsythia bushes, second near the Martins' driveway, and third was a hill climb up to our front porch. Then it was downhill, all the way home.

A homerun was any ball not retrieved from under a bush before the batter could touch 'em all.

But the following day, we had bigger plans than sandlot ball.

Some kid from another neighborhood told me he'd found a dead goat, located just on the other side of the Dulles Highway, a four-lane expressway built in the early sixties, between the respective properties of the Shouse and Todd families. The highway was a short walking distance from Hicks Drive, and used only for ground transportation to Dulles Airport. This airport was unique in that it had its own nine- mile-long, tax-funded highway that could not be used by commuters for any other destinations—at least for another twenty years, or so.

Like most summer days before I was old enough to get a job, I had slept late. When I woke up, I called Peter and Mark and went into more detail about the goat than I had the previous day. I told them we'd have to cross the Dulles Highway, and I didn't know the exact location of the goat.

I didn't have to convince either of them that it would be an adventure, so we agreed to meet at my house after lunch.

Mark had moved into the neighborhood somewhat later than the rest of us, about 1963. And his dad must have misread the compass a little bit, because he bought a house on Trap Road and not Hicks Drive, about a three-minute walk up the hill for his son to join us in our misadventures. Ironically, it is located next door to the house my family lived in until we moved to the neighborhood in 1961.

His home was brand new when he arrived, with central air-

---

7 Surfin' Bird, The Trashmen. 1963.

conditioning and a finished basement. None of the other houses on The Drive had those features. For further comfort, the Woods had an above ground pool, to which they invited the whole neighborhood to swim on one of the hottest days on record. It's the little things that seem to make the biggest impressions.

His family came to us from Annandale, now another suburb in the DC Metro sprawl. But in the sixties, it seemed way out there in the country. And when they would reminisce about life in The Big A, it seemed distant and foreign—except when it came to high school football. Thank you, Coach Ed Henry, who would become more famous for his role in *Remember the Titans* at another school.

While the reporting Goat Spotter had given us a general description of its location, we reasoned the exact coordinates were really not necessary. Just a directional finger point and we'd figure it out.

The more direct goat-route was simply through a few backyards and down the hill from the top of our street to Trap Road, cross the bridge over Dulles Highway, and then walk another mile to the location. But that wouldn't have been adventurous enough for us. We'd already run out of things to do by mid-summer and needed more.

We'd ridden our bikes to every known location a half-dozen times. We played baseball nearly every day that it didn't rain, and there were only half a dozen rainouts all summer.

The Washington and Old Dominion Railroad that connected Alexandria to Round Hill, was still operable in 1964. Walking on foot or pushing our bikes along the wooden cross ties of the track was very scary indeed for nine-year-old boys, so we had saved that risky adventure for the weekend before Labor Day. In case one of us was squished by a train, that unfortunate individual wouldn't miss any summer vacation in 1964. A lifetime sick-note out of school would then be issued.

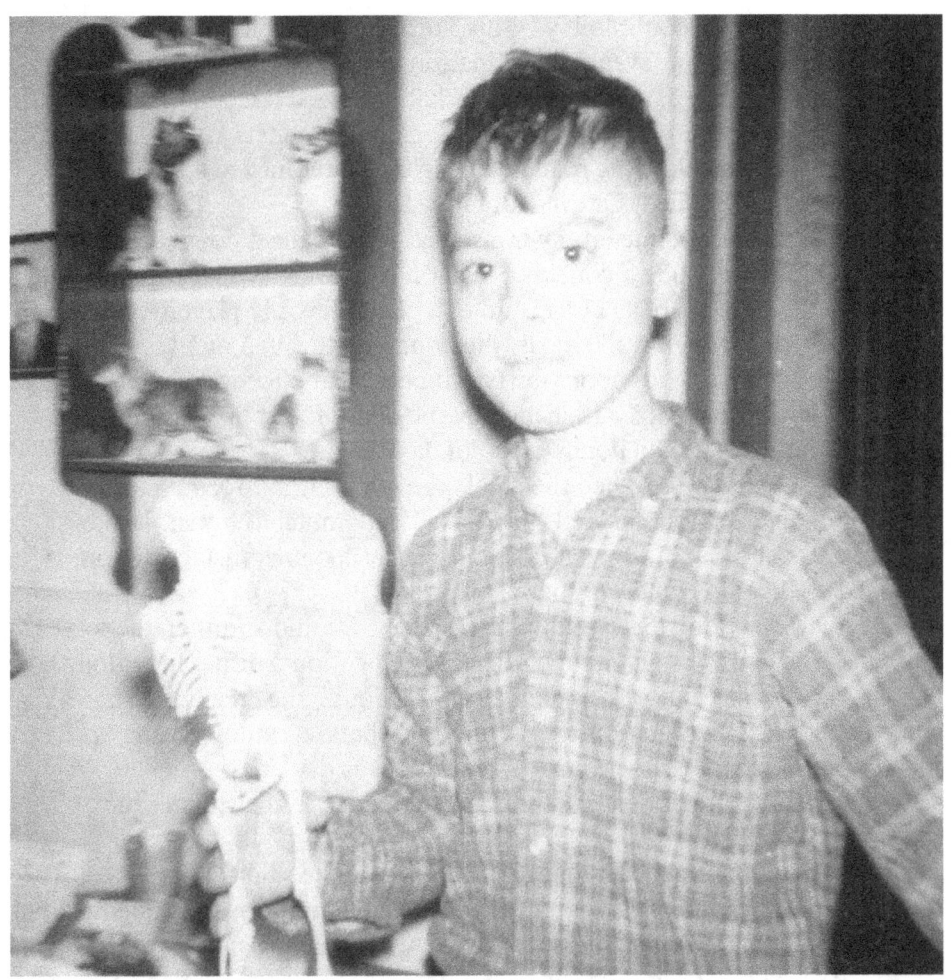

Mark Wood and a skeleton from his closet, 1964. Photo by Rick Duncan.

We knew we could follow Wolf Trap Creek from Old Courthouse Road all the way to our eventual destination, but we had never attempted that route before that day. Previously, we had followed the creek as far as the Dulles Highway, where it split into three separate channels, then disappeared into total darkness below the road. Chasing the water into that abyss had never been accomplished. Or even attempted.

The three of us met at my house and soon walked down the street. At the last minute, we made a course correction by cutting across Todd's field, located at the foot of Hicks Drive, and one of our favorite play areas in the neighborhood. We then walked past the pond and through the woods to the creek. That would save us about thirty minutes. And once we'd reached the pond, the rest of the walk was shaded by the dense forest in a canopy over the horse trails. An added bonus on a hot day.

As soon as we reached the creek, the temptation to search for crawfish under every submerged rock was just too much to resist. It didn't take long to collect about fifteen or twenty unsuspecting crustaceans, but it provided challenging entertainment.

Walking along the creek was never easy. By mid-summer, the weeds and grass had grown high enough to create navigational difficulties along its banks. And despite our rock hopping efforts through the creek bed, to avoid some of the excess vegetation, falling into the shallow running water was inevitable. Wet, heavy shoes didn't travel as fast as dry ones.

Mark was the first to spot the three concrete tunnels under the highway.

"There it is. Just past that big tree," was all he said.

We knew if we followed the creek, we couldn't miss the aqueduct, but seeing it from that distance reassured us we were going the right way.

As we got closer, the tunnels got darker. The water seemed to vanish into nothing. And it wasn't until we stood on a rock in the deeper middle channel, that we could see even a trace of light reflecting from the other end.

The floor of the left channel was completely covered with sand and rocks, so it was relatively dry, but the space up to the ceiling was too short, without us having to bend completely over. And it would be a long walk.

The channel on the right seemed the most navigable, so we picked that one to tunnel under the highway.

I went first. I walked ever so cautiously into the first fifty feet or so of our chosen path, allowing my eyes to adjust to the diminishing light.

"It's not as dark in here as I thought." I spoke in a brave tone, while hoping it wouldn't get any darker.

But my confidence grew and so did the length of my strides as I marched on, trying to stay on the dry areas.

Peter and Mark were maybe five feet behind me. The tunnel was so narrow that single-file was the only option. And it was really, really dark, so I picked up the pace.

Suddenly, a scream pierced the darkness. It was just Mark trying to scare us—and it did.

I now found myself starting to run, while slightly bent over. Mark and Peter were at least half a football length behind, as I then ran as fast as I could. I wanted the hell out of that tunnel.

Once I reached the other side, I sat down on a large boulder to catch my breath, and wait for the two stragglers to emerge from within.

"I'm glad there wasn't a rabid fox in there," Peter mustered out, in an attempt to talk before he caught his breath from running.

"Yeah!" Mark and I answered in unison, as I thought to myself about what we might have done, faced with that encounter.

Soon, we were on our way once more, hopping rocks, falling in, and occasionally splashing each other in the creek. By the time we had reached the cliffs on the Shouse property near Trap Road, we were no longer distracted by crawfish, minnows, or tadpoles, which inhabited the water. We were now in a hurry to see the goat.

Once we reached the one lane bridge at Trap Road, we stopped to get our bearings. And just above the tree line, off in the distance of perhaps a half mile, I thought I saw a large bird gliding about.

"Buzzard!" I shouted, and we all leaped up from our resting spots and began a slow trot toward the circling bird.

Within minutes, we saw two more. Then five. There had to have been ten buzzards doing the buzzard thing, all soaring in a tight loop just above the trees.

We were getting close.

Immediately, we started running as fast as we could go, breathing in that humid summer air.

When we had reached the woods underneath the buzzards circling above, we could hear them voicing their displeasure at our arrival. And they began to retreat farther away from us.

But the avian squawking was quickly replaced by an overwhelming stench. Perhaps it was that of a dead animal, our goat.

"Gawd, do you smell that?" Peter asked, already knowing the answer.

"I think I'm gonna puke," was Mark's only words. His grin of anticipation had been replaced by a sickly smirk, revealing that he wasn't kidding about the potential spew.

"Well, aim it that way." I pointed, allowing no sympathy for Mark's queasy stomach.

Just ahead, I saw one buzzard on the ground. It must have been the leader, or the hungriest, for no others were nearby.

"There it is," was all I had to say.

A mere twenty yards was all that now separated us from the low buzzing of the blow flies, those found only on dead things, twenty yards from the gawdawfulest smell ever, twenty yards from the little goat horn pointing defiantly into the air, at nothing in particular. The ground buzzard was long gone.

We could not get any closer than about ten feet, no matter where we stood. There was nothing very attractive about a rotted goat when we were up close and personal. The reward would come later, when we'd tell others about our adventure. But for now, we had to stand there and take it. Take it all, because we sure as hell weren't coming back.

First Peter, then Mark and I began a hasty retreat from the scene, soon in a full gallop toward fresh air.

We'd had enough.

And like many adventures, toward destinations that do not end quite like you would expect or want, it's all about the journey.

Schwinn (Approved) Bicycle Speedometer-Fifty Miles Per Hour!

Bicycle Death Plunge, 1965

*"Dead Man's Curve is no place to play
Dead Man's Curve you'd best keep away
Dead Man's Curve I can hear 'em say
'Won't come back from Dead Man's Curve'"*[8]

Much like the previous summer, in 1965 we must have played sandlot/front yard baseball nearly every day. But we were just starting to scare my parents, whose picture window was in danger of being shattered into a million pieces by our ball. Previously, they didn't seem to worry about it, as they cheered us on from the front porch steps, an icy glass of sweet tea in hand. True Americana.

But all of us boys were bigger, a little stronger, and definitely threw and hit the baseball harder than ever before. And the games went on forever, sometimes finishing under the lights of our front porch.

While the rest of us developed into average to slightly above average players, Peter could never hit a lick, as they say. We all agreed, regardless of whose team he was on that day, to allow Peter four strikes before he was out, rather than the regulation three. Some days he'd get five or six— depending on who lobbied the loudest, I suppose.

"Come on, Pete, it's getting dark," I taunted, although it wasn't quite four in the afternoon. He'd missed five consecutive pitches, all right down the middle of the plate. A plate that wasn't actually there, but would have been if that piece of cardboard wasn't so easy to retrieve from inside my front door.

"Throw it slower," Peter said. He was now starting to get aggravated by the multiple swing-and-misses.

"Want me to roll it to you?" chimed in Roger, who was in complete command of his slow, slower, and slowest fastball.

Peter finally hit the next pitch into the Martins' azaleas, about a hundred feet away from home plate.

"A ten-year-old Mickey Mantle never hit it that far!" gloated Peter, before he dropped the bat and began his semi-sprint. There was no way we could disagree with him: we weren't even born back then.

Peter rounded first base and was headed for second, as I attempted to retrieve the ball as quickly as I could. He didn't run very fast, so I knew I had a chance to throw him out if I found the ball before Roger's mom could catch

---

[8] Dead Man's Curve, Jan and Dean. 1963

me rooting around in her prize azaleas. Those bushes were more important to her than anything else in her yard, and she didn't mind letting us know that, with every ball we hit within ten feet of them.

By the time I found the baseball, Peter was chugging up the hill toward third, and I didn't have the arm strength to throw him out at the plate. Not for another two or three years, at least.

So, that meant we'd have to listen to Pete pontificate about how great the Yankees were. In truth, they did win the pennant the previous year, not too likely in 1965, though. The team that defected from Washington, The Minnesota Twins, was playing World Series quality baseball before the regular season was completed, and they were the favorites to capture the American League Pennant.

Peter's older brother hit next and drove the ball into the sticker bushes on the other side of Roger's yard, at least two hundred feet away. The ball rolled into no-man's-land, under the hedges—which meant it would take at least several minutes and a drop or two of blood to get it.

None of us volunteered to crawl into the thorns, so we decided to let *rock, paper, scissors* make the selection. I lost.

I grabbed the only bat that had been brought to the game, and started chopping toward the ball, a path in the vegetation. Finally, I reached into the opening I'd made, stretched out my arm as far as I could, grabbed the ball, and brought it out. This time, I didn't get stuck by one of the painful thorns.

"You guys are already ahead by ten runs. Let's call it a game," I said, as I picked up my glove and headed for my front porch.

The other kids eventually went home, but Rick Duncan, Pete, Dale, Mark, and I sat on my porch, while we talked about what we were going to do for the rest of the day. We'd already kicked around a few ideas, but none of them sounded exciting enough to pursue.

"Let's ride bikes over to Carter's Grove and see if we can hit fifty again," I said, as I jumped up and headed to our basement door to get my two-wheeled chariot.

I had reached the basement door and attempted to turn the knob, but it was locked. My dad always locked every door, even when he was standing next to it, so I ran around to the back-door to get inside the house.

"Don't slam the door," my dad demanded from the kitchen, before I'd attempted to close it. Dads, mine in particular, seemed to have obsessions about doors—refrigerator, house, and car. It seemed that nobody could open them correctly, close them quietly enough, or leave them open for the proper amount of time.

Once I was inside, I opened the basement door, and thundered down two stairs at a time, to the bottom. I saw my bike leaning against a wall near the basement door so I grabbed it by the handlebars, and went outside.

I'd saved my chores money for about six months and bought a shiny new Schwinn speedometer for my bicycle at the beginning of the summer.

The gauge topped out at fifty miles per hour! I tried to peg the needle every time I found a steep hill with a smooth surface. And Carter's Grove, properly named Campbell Road, was the perfect spot. While Hicks Drive was still gravel, Campbell Road was black topped, had a steep incline, shade, and no traffic, being a cul-de-sac.

Mark, Dale, and Rick Duncan were already waiting for me when I got outside.

After living on Hicks Drive for nearly four years, I'd spent more time with Dale and Rick than I had in the past.

Rick, his two older brothers, and parents were Legacy Settlers on Hicks Drive. Mrs. Duncan was, by unanimous vote, the best mom in the neighborhood. She was everything to all of us: transportation provider, fun maker, Cub Scout Den Mother, adult adventurer, and sometimes confidant. She was educated, and while on Hicks Drive continued that effort by taking college-level classes. Nobody else in the neighborhood was doing that. She was perhaps one of the nicest people I'd ever known.

His dad, The Colonel, was distant and aloof—and, as far as I could tell, had few friends. But, on the plus side, he was a non-factor to all of us except his family. A lot to be said for that, I guess.

Rick was the most introspective and introverted of all of us. He often provided unsolicited advice (speeches) which, in retrospect, was probably accurate but a little ahead of its time. He never meant any harm with his monologues. Instead, I believe he had some deeper, perhaps more mature thoughts than the rest of us did, and he wanted to share. He was very generous.

He was also a good guy, extremely dependable and usually willing to go along with whatever mischief or adventure we had concocted for the day. He and I were the same age and grade level, but rarely in the same classes together. But, most important of all, we were childhood friends.

"We'll take the bridle path from Pete's, out to Beulah," offered Duncan, in a clear reference to the best short cut to the top of Campbell Road.

Mark, Dale, and I had three-speed bikes, each capable of traveling nearly fifty miles per hour—while Duncan had a Schwinn Sting Ray, with twenty-inch wheels and a stick-shift on the crotch bar. His machine was built for luxury, not speed. That said, it was by far, the best-looking bike in the neighborhood.

Before we could begin our journey, we had to wait for Pete. Again. It seemed impossible for Peter to find whatever it was he needed in his house, and be back in less than half an hour.

After we rode in circles for fifteen minutes, I decided to go inside his house and get him.

I hopped off my bike, bolted to the door, and then knocked. Then I knocked again. I heard a voice coming from somewhere inside.

"Come in," the voice faintly said.

I opened the door and stepped into the kitchen. Again, I heard the same voice, but much louder, yell out, "what?" from the living room. It was Pete's dad.

"Can Pete play?" I asked, as I walked toward the living room where I saw Mr. Canciglia kneeling on the floor, holding a saw in his hand.

"He's not here. He's playing ball down the street," he said, as he turned his attention away from me and toward the hole he seemed to be cutting in the floor.

"We finished and he came home," I said, as I continued to watch Pete's dad, while I wondered why he was destroying their living room floor.

"Well, where is he?" his dad asked, as if *I* should know the answer.

"Maybe he's in the basement, Mr. C. I'll check." I turned away to find Peter, but stopped suddenly and faced his dad again.

"What are you doing?" I asked, just before Mr. Canciglia began to saw.

"Cutting a hole over the wood stove in the basement, so the heat will come upstairs."

"Oh", was my only reply.

Then I walked away and toward the basement steps. The light in the stairwell wasn't on, so I turned the switch a couple of times. I finally gave up and carefully descended the stairs in darkness.

When I got to the basement, I saw light coming from the workshop, so I walked in that direction, where I found Peter pumping air into a flat tire on his bike.

"Both were flat and I couldn't find the pump," volunteered Pete before I asked.

"Well, hurry up. Duncan has to be home for dinner at seven, else The Colonel will declare World War III on all of us."

After a few more pumps of air, both tires were ready to go.

I opened the basement door for Peter to push his bike through the opening and into the side yard. He thanked me by running over my foot that somehow got in his way.

"You drive like an old lady," I teased, as we went up the hill in Pete's back-yard to join the other bikers.

"Hunh? You shoulda moved your foot."

After I joined him on my bike, we hurdled down the well-worn trail behind Peter's house, heading for the aptly named bridle path toward our eventual destination. Horses often used those paths to get riders where they wanted to go, between Beulah and Trap Roads, while avoiding any vehicles. It was our favorite route to nearly everywhere.

Mark had an early lead, and soon had made the ninety degree turn to the left, before Peter, Duncan, and I had made much progress.

Finally, we all were perched on our bicycle seats at the trail head on

Beulah Road. And in single- file we took off, knowing we would soon arrive at the top of the hill at Carter's Grove.

"I'm gonna hit fifty today," I yelled out, as we brought our bikes to a halt with the screeching of metal on rubber brake pads.

Pedaling our bikes down Campbell Road offered a thrill like no other street. It was steep, with limited to no traffic, and it was fairly close to Hicks Drive. But it was extremely dangerous.

Rick Duncan (l) and Roger Martin, Halloween 1965.
Photo provided by Rick Duncan.

Plummeting downhill on a bike I had pieced together from spare parts, no helmet, on an asphalt roadway surrounded by large oak trees on all sides.

What could go wrong?

"I nearly wrecked the last time I did this," added Peter, with just a hint of hesitation in his voice.

"You nearly wreck every time you get on your bike, Poot," responded Duncan, with uncharacteristic aggressiveness.

"No shock, Sherlock. He almost got run over going to Vienna yesterday," I added, as we all laughed at Pete's refusal to ride on the side of the road like everyone else.

"Nobody hit me."

"No. They just blew the horn for about forty five minutes." Mark saw an opportunity to rub it in and he took it. That car horn scared the crap out of all of us.

"Since I'm the one with the speedometer, I should go first. You guys can follow me to the bottom," I suggested. But I had already made up my mind I was going first, while the other guys were still picking on Pete.

Dale had vanished after we took off toward the bridle path, but I now saw him slowly pedaling toward us along Beulah Road.

"My mom called me to mow the stupid lawn, but I got out of it," puffed Dale, nearly out of breath as he slowed down on approach to where we had stopped

"You always get out of it," we all answered in unison, as if we'd practiced our response. Then all of us started laughing at the unlikely synchronized chorus. Even Dale.

"I'm about to break the sound barrier, Dale, so you better cover your ears," I warned, as I got into position to speed down the hill.

I started pedaling in first gear, shifted to second, and then clicked the handlebar mounted gear-shifter to third. I was accelerating rapidly. I quickly glanced down at the speedometer. I was already going thirty five. I yelled over my shoulder, "thirty five!"

I kept pedaling faster and faster. But soon I couldn't increase my speed to more than forty five miles per hour. The road was leveling off, and I knew the ride was over.

"One more time," I yelled, as I turned my bike around and started pedaling back up the hill. Peter and Mark had reached the bottom of the hill and were slowing down. I waited for them so we could pedal up the hill together.

At the top, Dale hadn't moved at all.

I was out of breath by the time I reached him.

"Forty five," was all I said.

"I'm going down, too," said Dale, as he adjusted his seat for the descent.

Peter, Mark, and Duncan were nearing the top from their climb up the hill, so I waited for them before getting myself ready to go back down.

"I'm gonna start farther back this time. Maybe I can go faster, before I reach the bottom." It was the only plan I had.

I didn't wait for anybody to fall in line this time, either. I saw an opening between the three bikes and took off.

I immediately started pedaling as fast as I could, quickly shifting to second, once I reached where I had started the first time. I made the final shift to third and accelerated with each pump of my now tired legs. But I kept going.

I was now getting a little afraid, as trees, driveways, and bushes rushed by me much faster than the previous downhill plunge. I quickly glanced down at my speedometer.

"Fifty-one," I yelled as loud as I could. But my enthusiasm caused me to steer slightly to the left. I wasn't going to make the long driveway at the end that allowed us to decrease our speed without losing control. Instead, I was speeding straight toward a long cluster of mailboxes.

I squeezed the front and rear brake handles as hard as I could, which immediately caused the back tire to lock up and skid. The front wheel's deceleration caused me to lurch over the handlebars more than I wanted. But soon I regained my balance and slowed enough to regain control and avoid the mailboxes.

When I'd come to a stop, the guys finally caught up, while I tried to catch my breath.

"How fast did you go?" Dale asked, as he steered his bike next to mine, and came to a stop.

"Fifty-one," I proudly breathed out, secretly grateful I hadn't crashed at the end.

"Did you see me heading for those mailboxes?" I asked.

"I thought you were dead meat for a second," Peter answered, as my mind drifted toward the image of me crashing at fifty-one miles per hour.

"I'm glad I put on new brake pads last week", I said, in a voice filled with a mixture of concern and relief.

The sun had set and it was starting to get dark, so we slowly pedaled our bikes up the hill and headed for home. And along the way, I knew I wouldn't come back to Campbell Road for a while.

I didn't need to come back—until I was ready to go fifty-two miles per hour.

Unknown people in WT Grants Parking Lot, Blizzard of 1966, Vienna, VA
Photo from Facebook Group Vienna Kids.

The Blizzard of 1966

"Here they come again, mmmm-mm-mm
Catch us if you can, mmmm-mm-mm
Time to get a move on, mmmm-mm-mm
We will yell with all of our might"[9]

I had just finished a hearty Pop-Tart breakfast, and was looking for ways to annoy my sister without getting into too much trouble, when the first person that morning to climbing our snow-covered front porch steps, banged on the door. I knew it was Pete before I opened it.

"Make sure to stomp your feet before you come inside," my dad commanded, as I opened the door but before Pete could step inside. Pete's grin was from ear to ear. He was covered in an assortment of winter clothes that looked like they'd just emerged from a box in the attic.

"I will, Mr. Speight," he said while jumping up and down in the snow on the area just outside the door. As a result, more, not less, snow seemed to gather on his feet before entering. But the attempt still seemed to satisfy my dad.

"Come in and warm yourself by the fire," my mom offered, as Pete tracked snow across the carpet with every step.

My father looked on in mock frustration but didn't speak further about it, as Pete walked toward the roaring fire at the far end of the living room.

For some reason, we used the fireplaces sparingly, though we had one upstairs in the living room and another in the basement. But that day we had a blaze that often hissed and popped, sending sparks in random directions.

"Everybody's going up to Kehoe's hill in about an hour," announced Pete with the confidence that he'd obtained some inside-information from a well-placed source.

"Can I go up to Kehoe's?" I pleaded to nobody in particular. I knew that, somehow, I was going, regardless of the response to my question.

"Well, all right. But first you have to clean your room," my mom replied. Getting permission from her was always conditional. Never *yes, have a good time*, or a simple nod of the head. I had to perform some random task to justify her agreement to let me off the leash.

"I cleaned my room last week, mom," I whined, despite knowing it <u>wouldn't help</u> me get out of her manual labor camp for the morning.

[9] "Catch Us If You Can", Dave Clark and Lenny Davidson, 1965

"Come on and help me." I said to Pete." It'll take just a minute."

I went into my room, threw the dirty clothes under the bed, pulled the covers over the pillow, and then *presto!*

Pete and I quickly ran out the back door while my mom was reading her most recent copy of *The National Enquirer*. I think she mostly just looked at the pictures, since reading was not her best skill—but too late for her, even if she was engrossed by the words on the page. We were gone and trudging through the fresh tundra, pulling my sled in our tracks up the short walk to Kehoe's hill.

Except for the crunching snow under our feet, we had complete silence as we walked. There are few things as quiet and peaceful as walking along a snow-covered landscape.

The Blizzard of January 1966 ranks as one of the all-time biggest, most crippling, and, definitely most fun, snow storms in the long history of Fairfax County. We had returned to school for only four weeks after the Christmas and New Year's holiday season, when the area was slammed by the winter weather system. The Christmas presents that Santa so graciously delivered to our homes still had the new toy smell, so we were still playing with Chatty Cathy, GI Joe, Easy Bake oven, or perhaps a shiny new Huffy bicycle.

My favorite gift that year, maybe even all-time greatest, was the Secret Sam Attaché Case. This awesome assortment of all the plastic spy equipment, which any deep undercover prepubescent boy would require, included an assault rifle disassembled to fit into the case, and a built-in hidden camera. The latter had real film, capable of capturing clandestine operations surely happening in the basement of the neighbors we really didn't know very well. James Bond movies, as well as the TV shows *I Spy* and *Get Smart*, were very popular during the mid-sixties, as Madison Avenue tried to integrate children's toys into the very adult reality of The Cold War. And it worked.

Many kids on the street who got new bikes for Christmas that year received the ultimate in youth transportation, an "English Racer." Usually there wasn't anything English about them, at all. Made in Japan, more likely. But these two-wheeled wonders had three speeds rather than one, like our starter bikes with training wheels had. The Racers also might have included a front and rear light assembly, speedometer, and a plastic, fake engine that made plastic, fake motorcycle noises; we'd hit the road in the morning and not return until called for dinner. The occasional warm spring-like days in January of 1966 made all of this possible. And the endless array of country roads, bike trails, and the recently decommissioned Washington and Old Dominion Railroad line all offered a terrain that begged to be explored by adventurous pre-teen boys with a lot of time and energy.

But outdoor life began to dramatically change on Sunday night, January 30th. The old timers, the dads, always claimed in retrospect, that flurries had been predicted as a light end of January dusting to merely complicate the Monday morning commute—and not much else; everything was to be melted by noon.

The predictions were not even close. The temperature began to drop early Sunday evening, along with a steady snowfall. It snowed and it snowed some more. By the time the storm had passed, two to three *feet* of snow had smothered the entire mid-Atlantic region. The wind, with gusts up to thirty five miles per hour, then pushed some of this wintry heaven into giant drifts ten feet high, or even more in some places. It was beyond awesome.

School closings were immediately announced. By daybreak, roads were not just closed, but hermetically sealed, as the snow continued to accumulate throughout the night.

At least a foot of it had accumulated by the time most of us woke up on Monday—and then it was still snowing.

The Kehoes lived at the top of the street, in a home with a huge backyard that steeply sloped from one end to the other. It was the perfect sled run of about three hundred yards, offering plenty of speed, sharp turns, and a few obstacles like trees and shrubbery, to make it challenging. And most of the time we just showed up with sleds or toboggans in tow, ready to use their property as if it were our own. Usually they never complained, but tolerated us with parental understanding. More often than not, this was our snow day hangout.

A crowd was already gathering by the time Pete and I arrived.

"What took you so long?" Dale asked, as he made the final steps up the summit of the sled run.

"I had to clean my room before I could come out," I replied, announcing it to everybody within earshot. As I got my sled into position to make my first run of the day, I could see Roger near the bottom of the hill pulling his sled nicknamed *Pokey*, along with Mark, who was trying to catch him from behind so they could walk up together.

I picked up my sled and walked away from the hill's initial descent so as to get a running start when I hit the slope. I sprinted as fast as I could, quickly positioned my Flexible Flyer on the ground, and made a diving belly flop, head-first lunge onto the moving sled.

The snow hit my face, as the sled accelerated down the hill, with a couple of stragglers scurrying a few steps to either side of the path, to avoid getting their legs amputated at ankle height by my now rapidly moving sled.

I hit the turn with maximum speed, narrowly avoiding an edge that would've launched me into an oak tree. The entire time I squealed like a little girl.

We enjoyed sledding for days on end, alternating Kehoe's hill with Hicks Drive, and the much steeper, Campbell Road.

But after a few days of fun, families became stranded without fresh groceries, and help was not on the way any time soon. We lived two miles from the nearest grocery store and away from the Town of Vienna and the major commuting roads, so we had to improvise.

My dad was the first to attempt plowing Trap and Beulah Road all the way to Vienna. By himself. He got the snow chains out of the basement and attached them to the rear tires of our old Ford pickup and slowly backed out of our driveway, with me in the passenger seat. We uneventfully plowed the first tire tracks down Hicks Drive, then slowly rounded the turn onto Trap Road, and saw there was a giant, eight-foot high, snowdrift in the middle of the road.

But my dad had to try to plow through it.

He shifted the transmission into reverse, and slowly backed up several feet on Trap Road so he had a straight line into the snowdrift.

"Hold on," was all he said, as he downshifted into first gear, then quickly into *second*, once he realized he had enough traction to avoid a spinout.

We were instantly snow blind when we hit the drift that sent crystals into the air and directly into our windshield. Then we came to a sudden stop and the wheels started spinning. We backed up and tried again.

After three or four collisions with the snowdrift, my dad conceded defeat. He backed up the truck a final time, turned into Hicks Drive, and headed for home.

The next day, one of the moms assembled a sled caravan to march into town and get essential groceries for the neighbors.

"Where's your sled, Pete," Roger asked as he pulled Pokey behind him on a very long rope.

"Hunh? I'm putting stuff in this army backpack my dad gave me," Peter replied, while making a three-sixty rotation to show Roger his gear.

All of the Hicks Drive boys were part of the caravan for a variety of reasons—fulfill our civic and neighborhood duty, fun and adventure, or our parents made us do it.

A four-wheel drive vehicle of some sort had made two tire tracks all the way into Vienna. And that was it. In some areas along the way, snow had drifted so high that we disappeared into the banks, before coming out the other side. None of the kids complained it was too cold. Nobody whined they were too tired. We were on an adventure through the greatest snow storm any of us had ever experienced, and there wouldn't be any school for days, maybe even weeks.

The adult chaperones were smart. They knew that if hot cocoa and leftover Christmas cookies were the provisions, we'd march all day. And we nearly did.

We didn't see one vehicle during the entire time it took us to walk to Vienna and back home, sleds filled to capacity, boys filled with sugar.

About a week or so after the storm, two road graders, operating side-by-side, plowed the snow that cleared the roads from Hicks Drive to Vienna.

Soon after that, life quickly returned to normal.

However, mountainous piles of plowed snow seem to linger in the Giant and A&P parking lots until spring. School buses kept the chains on their tires for so long, we could hear them approaching from far in the distance, and still have plenty of time to scurry to the bus stop before their arrival.

There have been other major storms that continue to keep fond memories alive of how everything changed for a brief moment in time. But to the boys from Hicks Drive, and countless others in the DC Metro area, The Blizzard of 1966 ranks as the all-time greatest snow storm to ever come to town.

My Fifth Grade Class, Westbriar Elementary Vienna, VA.
Ms. Dinsmore, my teacher and Mr. Nolan P. Arritt, Principal at top right.
Three boys from Hicks Drive were in this class.

Roger Takes A Dip In Todd's Pond, 1966

"Life is very short, and there's no time
For fussing and fighting, my friend.
I have always thought that it's a crime,
So I will ask you once again."[10]

It was a beautiful, but chilly spring day, as Roger, Peter, and I headed for Todd's Pond after spending several hours catching crawfish in Wolf Trap Creek behind and below the Todd property, near the old spring house.

We walked along the path, where past generations had stored their food in the cool environs of the enclosed spring.

Throughout the years of our childhood, we made regular visits to the small pond on the Todd Estate that we called, appropriately, Todd's Pond. It was no larger than an eighth of an acre, fed by a spring somewhere in the vicinity. Its original purpose was purely recreational, serving as a swimming hole for the children, Elizabeth and Therese, with plans to expand its volume for other uses—but the dam couldn't hold enough water for it to be developed further.[11] So it remained a fun, little pond for decades.

It didn't appear to have the necessary food sources to sustain large fish, but little minnows and tadpoles were abundant. During the hot days of summer, scum formed on the surface of the slow moving water. It even smelled funny, like anaerobic pond scum growth is supposed to smell, I guess.

So, for those and other reasons, none of us were eager to get our feet wet in that nasty stuff. But despite, or maybe because of the water quality, we went there often. It was surrounded by trees and accessible only by narrow paths from four directions. The seclusion was very attractive to adventurous little boys with plenty of free time to explore. As an added bonus, the pond was really just a large mud puddle, and therefore always attractive as a source of children's entertainment.

When we arrived at our destination, there was a kid, Wynn, who lived in a nearby neighborhood, with some other guy named Corey, skipping rocks in Todd's Pond. We all knew and liked Wynn, so we immediately

---

10   "We Can Work It Out", The Beatles, 1966
11   From a conversation with daughter, Elizabeth on September 26, 2018

joined in on the fun.

The exercise soon turned to one of competition to see how many skips a thrown rock would take before it hit the bank on the other side of the pond.

Wynn was about three years older than us, had a strong throwing arm, and was very skillful in the art of skipping rocks on water. It didn't take him long to establish his supremacy that day at the pond.

Roger, despite his superior size and strength to us little guys, was never a very gifted athlete. His clumsiness often elicited giggles and smirks that usually resulted in his retaliation. All of us on Hicks Drive were intimidated by him, so we used extra care when Roger exhibited his all-too-frequent gaffes and goof ups. And that day was no different.

After Pete and I made a couple of successful attempts at rock skipping and appeared to be keeping up with the two older boys, Roger reached down and found a rock much larger than typically used for skipping. And it was round, not flat. He went into a Don Drysdale-like wind up and threw the rock at the pond with all of his strength. He missed the water completely, while the rock made a loud *thud* on the other side.

"Roger, the pond is over here," I said sarcastically, as everyone started laughing at the worst display of rock skipping in the history of Hicks Drive.

"Yeah, well, my rock was bigger than those you wimps are using."

"Why don't you try something smaller, like your pecker," chimed Wynn, as we all howled at the crude reference to Roger's pride and joy.

Roger immediately retaliated.

He dropped the rock he'd been holding and ran over to confront Wynn, who was still laughing at his own joke at Roger's expense.

Some things never change. That was certainly the case of Roger getting beaten up, time after time, for the same reason, throughout his entire life. It seemed like he always had to prove how tough he was, even though he wasn't. And when faced with a potential confrontation, he wasn't able to turn it off and walk away, like the rest of us could. And often did.

I can't count the number of times I saw or learned of Roger starting a fight, only to emerge on the losing end, due to his aggressive belligerence, shameless ignorance, or negative condescending attitude.

Every winter, it was snowball fights that escalated into violence—but only for Roger.

In the fall, it was acorn battles that always started innocently enough. We typically self-divided ourselves into teams, collected a cache of large acorns, and lobbed them back and forth until we got tired. Or bored. But invariably, Roger would cross that invisible line that the rest of us wouldn't. And one of the older brothers would beat the crap out of him, sending him home crying. Again.

And in the summer, it was everything imaginable that would provoke Roger into a confrontation that never ended well for him.

"You got something you want to say to me?" Roger asked, with his hands on his hips, standing directly in front of Wynn.

"I think I just did, Four Eyes," Wynn replied, as Peter and I tried to stifle a snicker of laughter. Corey wasn't so considerate and began a hysterical, hyena laugh that seemed a bit intentional.

Roger struck the first blow, as his right fist glanced off Wynn's cheek. Then all hell broke loose.

Suddenly Wynn shoved Roger in the chest and knocked him completely off-balance and backwards into the pond, where he landed flat on his back.

Now, Roger was really mad.

He stood up and slowly emerged from the soggy, smelly pond and approached Wynn with a daze, climbing up the embankment with a determined look in his eyes through glasses that sat askew, making him look even sillier. Peter and I couldn't hold back our laughter any longer, as Roger's mud-covered face turned bright red. Our laughter infuriated him even more.

Roger ran full speed toward Wynn, in an attempt to tackle him and bring him down into submission.

But Wynn was much quicker than Roger, so he grabbed the would-be-aggressor by the back of the neck, and forced him to the ground.

But Roger didn't give up.

He jumped to his feet, took a couple of steps toward Wynn and took another swing at Wynn's face.

But this time, Wynn ducked, quickly stood up and punched Roger in the face so hard that his glasses went flying into the pond.

Roger groaned loudly from fist-to-face impact, but remained standing close to Wynn. Too close.

In an attempt to finish him off, Wynn grabbed Roger by his shirt and flung him once again into the pond. The combination of mid-calf water and ankle-deep ooze underneath him, trapped Roger in full display, right in front of all of us. He couldn't move.

Peter and I weren't laughing anymore. Roger was clearly wounded and defeated.

His lip was cut and swollen, glasses were lying somewhere at the bottom of the pond, clothes soaking wet and covered in muck. It required every ounce of his effort to keep from crying.

It took him at least two minutes to take three steps out of his trap. As he slowly approached the shore, Pete and I ran home, knowing Roger would come after us first. But as we were running away, nearly side-by-side on the trail out of the woods, I glanced over my shoulder and saw Wynn push Roger back into the pond. Now Wynn was taunting Roger with Corey joining in the humiliation of someone who never learned his lesson.

"We gotta go rescue him," Peter said, as we stopped in the middle of the trail and started feeling guilty we were running away.

"Yeah, we do. Let's go back, Pete."

We'd returned to the pond just in time to see Roger making another attempt to extract himself from the water.

"Wynn, he's had enough. Save some for next year," I said, in reference to Roger's annual beat down.

I walked around the pond to where Roger was now standing motionless in the water, as if that were better than trying to climb out, only to be pushed back again by the dominating Wynn. I reached out to him, grabbed his extended arm, and pulled him out of the mud.

"I coulda' beat him if we'd wrestled," sniffed Roger, through tears he was struggling to contain.

"Yeah, I know," I said.

It wasn't the first time I'd heard that.

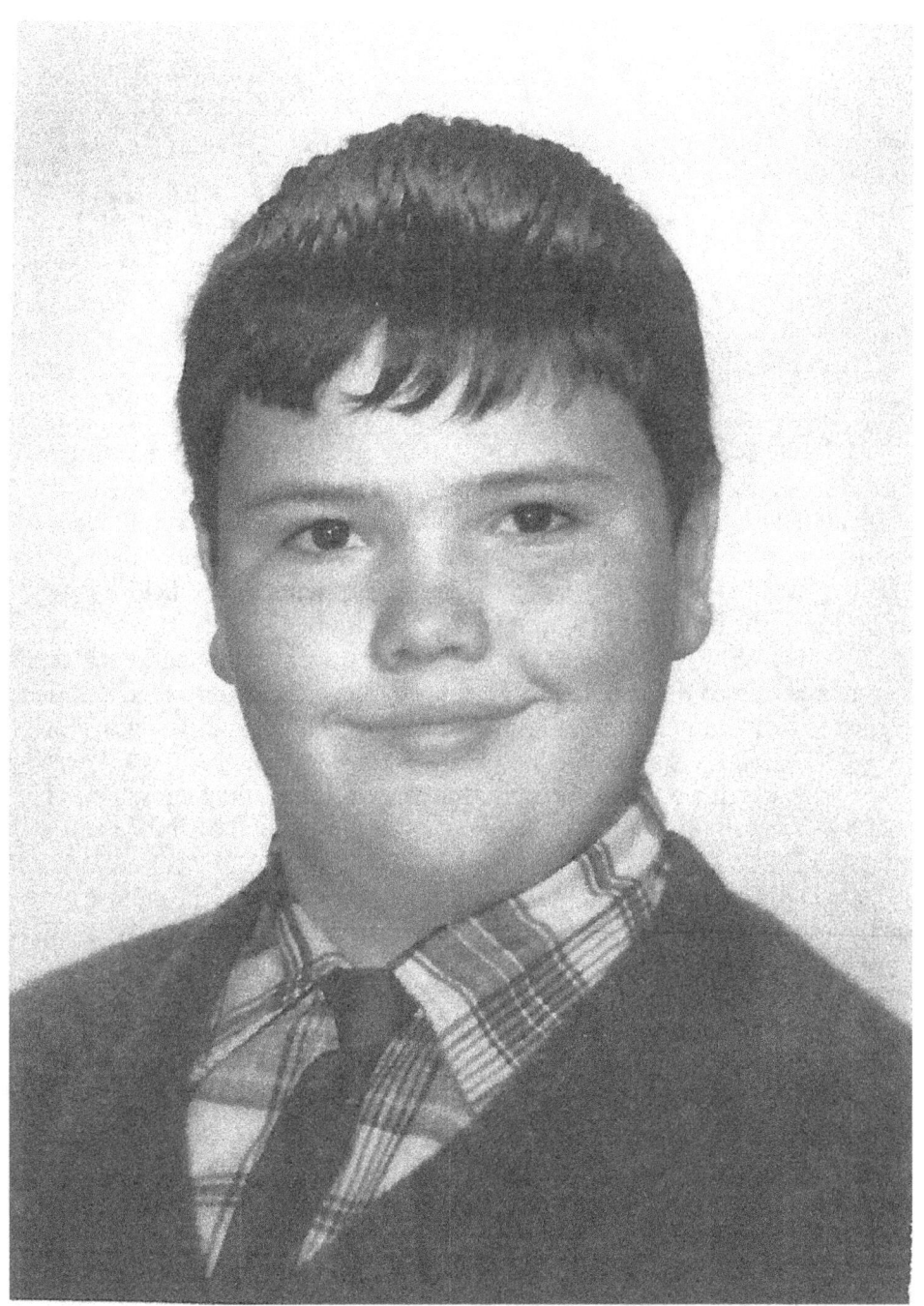

Dale Hall, circa 1966. Photo submitted by Dale Hall.

Dale and the Telescope, 1966

"I ain't gonna work on Maggie's farm no more
No, I ain't gonna work on Maggie's farm no more
Well, I wake in the morning
Fold my hands and pray for rain"[12]

Peter was late in arriving for our daily chores and ball game, at the pasture we'd claimed from the Todd family, and where we'd built a real baseball field, we sometimes called Todd's Stadium. After we'd completed our routine grounds-keeping, we picked teams and started to play a game.

"Wanna' know why Dale is never here to work on the field?" Pete asked, as it was his turn to bat and lead off the inning.

"No. Why?" I responded, without giving it much thought. Peter then swung and missed the first pitch. He stepped out of the batter's box, and then turned to me. "Remember that telescope he got for Christmas last year?" he asked. "The one he said that he used to look through neighbors' windows."

It suddenly became apparent that Peter was unveiling a mystery, one that had been on the minds of all the boys who played ball on our newly acquired field.

Daily games of sandlot baseball were ingrained into the culture of all the boys on Hicks Drive. The tradition began on my front yard, soon after we'd moved into the neighborhood. And it continued until 1966, at which point we had grown in stature and strength enough to endanger the windows of our houses. While we never broke any glass, we started getting closer and closer. However, most of us could hit the ball into the outfield at the far end of the Martins' yard, under the thick growth of thorny hedges. This presented another obstacle.

It was game over until we found the ball. That could sometimes take thirty minutes or more, as we hacked our way with bats and gloves into deep crevasses of baseball-eating vegetation.

Sometimes we never found it, and play was thereby suspended until somebody ponied up for another ball.

After my parents evicted us from my own front yard, somebody got the inspiration to start playing baseball in the large field at the end of the street. It was flat and wide open and we never saw anybody use it, except in late summer when a local farmer named Fremont Day would send his boys

---

12   Maggie's Farm, Bob Dylan. 1965

to cut and bale it for his cattle. That usually took about a week. So, the other fifty-one weeks out of the year we figured it belonged to us.

We carved out a spot in the field adjacent to Trap Road, close to the bottom of our street. And that was our home turf for the next two years.

But the summer of 1968 was when it all came to an end. The owners, Clarence and Elizabeth Todd, had sold the property to Dupont Developers, Inc. on March 18, 1966. It was subsequently developed by The Lerner Companies, who built nearly two hundred homes on the seventy-eight acre spread.

But, for that brief period of time when it was ours, we spent many hours building a regulation pitcher's mound, mowing the infield grass, generally keeping the field playable. We even built a backstop out of two-by-fours and chicken wire. With all of this stuff to take care of, before we played, we usually did some maintenance-related task for about an hour.

Peter stepped back in the batter's box, as his question about Dale remained lingering. He then swung at the next pitch before sharply hitting the ball through the hole between shortstop and third base. I knew that I had to wait until he scored, for him to finish the story.

He came around and touched home plate, after one of the older brothers hit the ball in the tall outfield grass for a homerun.

"Finish the story about Dale's telescope," I pleaded, while trying to hide the desperation in my voice.

"He watches all of us through his telescope until we finish the work, and *then* he comes down to play."

"How do you know that?" I asked, with much skepticism. The world through Peter's eyes didn't always match with everybody else's.

"Hunh? Cuz I saw him, that's how I know. Just a few minutes ago, when I was late. I saw he had his telescope out on his front porch, pointed in this direction. His mom ratted him out and told me when I saw her out in the yard, as I was leaving."

This was something I had to see for myself, so I began to hatch out a plan to catch Dale in the act. I thought about it the entire time we were playing ball; I couldn't wait to get Pete alone, so I could reveal my stealthy strategy.

Playing ball and/or working on the field all day, three days a week, for an entire summer, naturally bonded us together. Some of us more than others, though.

For the first two or three years on Hicks Drive, it seemed that the kids who lived at the top of the street hung together, while those of us at the bottom did the same. I guess it was because relationships had already been established, and our short legs made the distance seem greater between the top and bottom sections of the street.

Those boundaries were broken as soon as we played ball.

Dale Hall was one of the kids in the neighborhood I really didn't know that well in 1966. He was a year older than me, and hung with the kids at the top of the street. I saw him occasionally during the summer, in winter when we all met to go sledding, and, of course, at the bus stop every morning, nine months out of the year.

Dale's family lived next-door to Peter, near the top of the street. Another legacy family, Dale's had an older brother and sister, too far beyond our age to be in our peer group. But his family was unique to the neighborhood, having lost their husband and father to cancer when Dale was young, about eleven years old. After his siblings moved out, Dale and his mom lived alone on Hicks Drive for about a decade.

Though we lived only two hundred yards apart, Dale and I didn't become the close friends we are today until middle and high school. In the early years, the kids at the top of the street mostly played with those living at the same altitude, likewise for the bottom feeders like Roger and me who lived closer to Trap Road.

But once we started to bond, we spent as much time together as anybody. And as a consequence of that, he and I likely had more high school hijinks than the rest of the group.

Dale and I usually had similar tastes and interests, and his never-ending enthusiasm for thrill seeking made him an easy candidate for best friend. But it was more than that, too. He was generous of his time, always was concerned about what others thought of him, and had an enormous and surprising amount of empathy, even as a child.

He was a good guy and a decent ball player. But it was his determination to compete that made me want him on my team.

He was also extremely polite, especially around adults. Dale put us all to shame when it came to manners and elocution—always with the "yes, sir" and "no ma'am" replies. But he really excelled in one area above all of us: avoiding manual labor.

I always wondered why Dale would show up, baseball glove in hand, right after we had mowed the grass or some other field duty chore. When the work was done, Dale would miraculously appear. He'd claim he had chores to do, or some other excuse.

Future site of Todd's Stadium, our ball field,
Trap Road in front of hedgerow mid-photo, Circa 1956.
Photo by Eileen McCarthy Grant.

"Hey, Pete. Wait up," I said, while grabbing my bat, glove, and ball before the walk back home.

"Call Dale tomorrow and tell him we're gonna mow the field at eleven o'clock, before playing McGuire Court when we're done." I spoke to Pete in a low voice so nobody else could hear. We always looked forward to playing the boys on McGuire Court, because we knew all of them from school, and they never beat us. And I knew Dale would want to be there—*after* we worked on the field, of course.

"I'll be at your house when you call. He should have his telescope out at about noontime and we'll nail him," I proudly predicted, like we were going to catch some criminal.

Dale Hall (l) wearing his game face, Rick Duncan (r), 1966.
Photo supplied by Rick Duncan.

"Well, okay," Peter said—reluctantly, though. He was probably uncomfortable setting the trap for his next door neighbor.

"We won't tell the others. Just mess with Dale a little," I offered in a negotiating tone.

It was a go. I walked up the street to Peter's about ten thirty, thinking the entire way about catching Dale slacking off with his telescope, but feeling just a bit guilty that I was taking so much pleasure in the whole affair.

When Pete called Dale, as soon as I walked through his kitchen door, the trap was set.

We dragged the kitchen chairs over to the door so we could remain unseen, while comfortably sitting, watching out the window.

We'd been at our posts for about fifteen minutes when Pete's younger sister, Mary, walked into the kitchen.

"What're you guys doing? Spying on the neighbors, again?"

"Shhh… Yes," Peter said. "Now be quiet and move away from the window, so he won't see you." His voice was louder than necessary.

"Who?" she asked.

"Dale, that's who," I said in almost a whisper. "We want to catch him with his telescope."

"He has that thing set up on his porch every time you guys play ball. Didn't you know that?" Mary announced in a matter-of-fact tone, too knowledgeable for our comfort. Obviously, she had figured out this scam well before we even had a hint.

Peter just hushed her before excitedly squealing out, "There he is!"

Dale methodically unfolded the telescope from its tripod, made a few adjustments with the focus, and then aimed it down the street, directly in line with the ballfield.

Busted!

It was so simple; watch the worker bees from the comfort of your own home until they are finished with their appointed tasks—then join in during the fun part.

Though Pete and I had agreed to keep our discovery a secret, word quickly spread about Dale's advanced skills to avoid manual labor. While none of us were particularly happy about it, a wedgie might have been the worst punishment we'd have applied in retribution. And I don't think we even did that. Perhaps because his scam was discovered, Dale occasionally joined us when we worked on the field.

Catching Dale in the act of avoiding a chore that was expected of all of us, but failing to punish him for doing so, might well have been the beginning of what's kept the boys from Hicks Drive together for so long; the ability to not just overlook, but accept the faults of each of us—all while we didn't cut each other any slack for screwing up. In fact, teasing and taunting was a ritual and we enjoyed hours of entertainment at the expense of others.

It's that we never judged one another nor held a grudge.

Part II
Juvenile Delinquents

Don't Wanna Look, Can't Turn Away, 1967

*"Pardon the way that I stare
There's nothing else to compare
The sight of you leaves me weak
There are no words left to speak"*[13]

At the age of twelve or thirteen, I doubt that any of us knew much about the finer points of a lady's body, except what we saw in a Playboy magazine that our dad or big brother hid-not-too-carefully under the socks in the top drawer of their dresser. But ignorance never prevented us from looking. And looking was quickly followed by wondering and then wondering led to even more looking.

My neighbor was Mrs. Johnson, a rather plain looking woman, probably in her late thirties or early forties. She lived in the home with her husband and daughter, Amber who was our age, but always attended schools other than ours.

Faithfully every week, Monday through Friday, Mrs. Johnson came home from work at exactly the same time.

We quickly recognized the sound of her car as she made the turn onto our street from Trap Road. She would slowly accelerate up the hill, so by the time she hit maximum speed of about twenty one miles per hour, she would have to slow down again on final approach to her home.

One of our favorite neighborhood places to congregate and discuss sports, world events, girls, gossip, or nothing at all, was located directly across the street from the Johnsons' driveway that led up to their house. We called this gathering spot, appropriately enough, *The Gossip Fence*. Structurally, it was the tail-end of a decorative split-rail fence, offering the ideal height for sitting, perfectly placed under a large oak tree for shade. We regularly congregated there twelve months a year for over twenty years.

And from the Gossip Fence we could watch the entire world go by, at least the world on Hicks Drive. All cars that turned onto the street could be and were carefully examined from the top rail of the fence. Anyone that drove by where we sat, received an inquisitive stare, followed by a wave; slow and casual if we didn't know you very well, rapid and enthusiastic if we did.

---

13   "Can't Take My Eyes Off of You", Frankie Valli, 1967

But since the Gossip Fence was directly across from the Johnson's place, that meant we were perched directly across the street from their mailbox, since all mailboxes on our street were at the end of the driveways. And, after work, Mrs. Johnson always stopped her car and retrieved the mail before making final entry into her driveway. That's when the show began.

A summary of these, at this point, random events is necessary: typically, two to four adolescent boys, hormones oozing from every pore, idly sitting on a split-rail fence, waiting for something—anything. The boys have a 360 degree view of everything that happens in their neighborhood, anticipating the arrival of a plain-looking woman to drive up the road just to see her get out of the car to get the mail.

Why go through all that trouble?

The answer was the method in which she consistently used to extract herself from the car.

Like most women in the 1960s, Mrs. Johnson wore a dress or skirt to work. It was not only the fashion for that time, but many places of employment used it as part of their dress code.

And Mrs. J followed the rules.

While the mechanics of wearing a dress might have seemed rather straightforward, there was more to it than I'd have considered before witnessing plenty of women making adjustments, or pulling down on this or that.

Getting out of a car in a dress was very likely, something Mrs. Johnson had to really focus on to get right. After a long day at work, who'd have the energy to concentrate on anything but getting home in one piece just to start dinner?

When Mrs. J opened the car door, she typically looked straight ahead, almost in a trance. The door would open rather quickly. But then, ever so slowly, the left leg, the one closest to the door, would separate from the right. The top of her stockings would come into view. Farther and farther her leg would open like a silent, rusty gate. The garter belts, with those snappy things that held the stockings in place, would appear, and so too the fair skin of her thighs. Her leg would pause in midair, before slowly reaching the ground. The right leg anchored to the floor board of the car.

"Here she comes, Mark," I more announced to the group than just Mark. I was the first to see Mrs. Johnson turn onto Hicks Drive, less than a quarter mile straight down the hill.

"I'm not lookin," Mark said, as he turned his head away, with a face emphatically distained.

"I'm sure as hell gonna look," shouted Peter. "I missed it the last time you guys were out here."

"Well you didn't miss much," I volunteered, while trying to act like the disinterested expert.

"Are you gonna look, Roger?" Peter whispered, just as Mrs. Johnson was slowing down to approach her mailbox.

"What do you think?" Roger said with a mischievous grin that he shared with all of us.

I glanced over at Mark, out of the corner of my eye, so as not to miss anything Mrs. Johnson might do. He was slowly, almost imperceptibly turning *his* body to get a better view.

"Look! Look! Here it comes. It's show time," I whispered to nobody in particular.

"I'm still not looking," Mark said, probably more so trying to convince himself than any of us.

And it *was* like a train wreck; we didn't want to look because she was someone's mom, but we couldn't look away. The anticipation of seeing something private, something naughty was overpowering.

Most times we compromised by closing one eye.

We all knew exactly what we were about to see because we'd seen it countless times before.

And good ol' Mrs. Johnson never disappointed.

The car door opened with a "Hi, boys." greeting from Mrs. Johnson, as she turned off the ignition.

The left leg moved away from the right with almost painful, glacial speed.

Left foot touched the ground, as I try to gaze without being caught. I let my eyes quickly wander to the side just in case she's looking directly at me.

"Hi Mrs. Johnson," I said as I made eye contact for the first time. My greeting was followed in close succession by the others.

It was impossible for me to look her in the eye for very long, as my stare fixated on her white, mom thighs. I quickly glanced back again and I saw a smile on her face.

The right leg began to move, rising from the floor board, and then slowly to the left.

Like an eclipse, it would be gone, as quick as it had shone, so we had to be rapt.

I instantly glanced at the others to confirm what I'd suspected—all of us were staring directly at Mrs. Johnson, while she seemed oblivious to anything but retrieving the mail.

She finally had both feet firmly planted on the ground before getting out of the car.

The show was over.

We pretended to return to what we were doing a mere sixty seconds ago by continuing some conversation that never existed, or haphazardly looking around in search of something that wasn't there.

Mrs. Johnson retrieved her mail then walked back to her car.

Once she had gotten in and shifted the car into *Drive*, she pulled safely into her driveway, out of earshot.

We burst out laughing as quietly as we could, while accusing each other of watching the longest.

"This is the last time I'm lookin', you guys. She's old as my mom," Mark said, an observation that none of us wanted to hear.

"You'll look." Roger said. "And you'll keep lookin'. We all will." It was the most sensible thing any of us had said.

We knew we'd look again. We always did. And Mark was always the last to look away.

We Didn't Know You Were a Cop, Officer, August 1967

"Breakin' rocks in the hot sun
I fought the law and the law won
I fought the law and the law won
I needed money 'cause I had none
I fought the law and the law won
I fought the law and the law won"[14]

When Parkington was built in 1951, it was a phenomenal innovation. Located in Arlington, Virginia at the intersection of Wilson Boulevard and Glebe Road, it was the largest suburban retail shopping center on the East Coast. And it was the first of its kind in the United States to be built around a parking garage.[15]

By the 1950s, many people were moving out of the inner cities and farm country to become suburban commuters. But if you commuted from the burbs, you needed a car. And if you were fortunate enough to afford one of those, you had to park it somewhere when you went shopping. Parkington filled that need. Even the name removed all of the guesswork.

Like nearly every parking structure that followed, Parkington contained a multi-level garage, capable of temporarily storing hundreds of two-ton vehicles at any given moment. And on a busy shopping day, like those *Back to School* specials or Christmas, the lower parking levels would quickly fill to the brim with fake wood-paneled station wagons. These classics were soon to be followed by chrome appointed, fin-equipped beauties, with factory air conditioning and two-tone paint jobs.

Fortunately, the designers of these concrete parking behemoths included even more vehicle spaces on the roof, to be utilized once the lower and more convenient levels had filled up.

Mark, Duncan, and I tagged along with Mrs. Duncan, who drove us to Parkington with the promise of stopping at Gifford's Ice Cream Shop

14   "I Fought the Law", Sonny Curtis, 1960
15   Eno Transportation Foundation, "Parkington Shopping Center Design," Transportation Quarterly(1952, vol. 6, no. 4, pp. 440–456.)

in Falls Church on the way home. That late August morning, the four of us piled into their light blue, '66 Dodge Dart one late August morning and then off we went.

And although we arrived at the parking garage about eleven o'clock, it was already packed with bargain hunter shoppers. Mrs. Duncan kept driving around, in one of those never-ending circular patterns, to reach another level that looked exactly like the one before it. Up and up, and around and around, climbing toward the top with each revolution of the interior of the building. This continued until we lost track of the number of floors we'd climbed. Three queasy stomachs later, we found that we'd run out of levels; we were on the roof.

The view from the top was fantastic. We could see all of the taller buildings in Washington, like the U. S. Capitol and the Washington Monument, as well as the campus of Georgetown University. And a little farther on the eastern horizon, in full view was the Masonic Temple in Alexandria.

After Mrs. Duncan finally came to a stop and parked the car, assuring us she would return in an hour, we had to go exploring. It didn't take long for me to find a ledge with a perfect view straight down, about five levels below, even though it seemed like much more. Mark was afraid of heights, so he and Duncan decided that the stairwell would be an interesting place to find trouble.

They opened the door at the top of the stairs, before heading down. But just like they'd been shot from a cannon, they burst right back through the door, pinching their noses.

"Gross, man. Somebody pissed in there. You can smell it," Duncan yelled, as he and Mark were laughing and gagging at the same time. I ran over to investigate, since anything that smelled bad usually had tremendous entertainment value to a twelve-year-old boy.

I opened the stairway door. Trash was scattered everywhere. I then spotted an old sleeping bag in the corner, unrolled, as if someone planned to return.

"I think hobos have been sleeping in here," I said.

My nose was burning from the pungent aroma of piss, turned ammonia, so I left the stairwell to join Mark and Duncan.

"Do you think those bums live in there?" Mark asked, as if the reality of their living conditions had just sunk in.

"Hell, I don't know, but it sure as hell smells like it," Duncan replied, as we quickly walked away. Near my feet were a few small pebbles, scattered about the concrete floor of the parking garage, so I bent down and picked up a handful.

I considered how cool they'd look when dropped over the high ledge to hit the pavement below. I collected about a dozen small rocks, carrying in my left hand, while foraging with the right. The rock hunt led me straight to the ledge, before I cautiously looked over the side at the exit to the parking garage below.

I dropped the first tiny rock and let gravity do its thing.

"Wow, cool! Did you see that rock bounce?" I asked Mark and Duncan, who were peering apprehensively over the ledge beside me.

"Try one of the bigger ones," said Mark, who seemed braver by the moment.

"Bombs away," I shouted, while dropping the biggest stone I had, about the size of a dime. It struck the pavement below and ricocheted at an angle that caused it to strike a metal sign adjacent to the road. The clang of rock to steel reverberated around the inside of the garage below, and the echo soon reached us on top.

"Damn, did you hear that?" Duncan said. "Try something else," he continued, as we scurried about, looking for more objects.

It wasn't long before we were tossing more than pebbles: a couple of Bic pens, and then a chunk of concrete the size of a golf ball. Every time they hit the ground, we'd yell in celebration at the destructive force of gravity. We were doing this bit twenty years before David Letterman even thought of it.

Suddenly, Mark was standing next to me, holding a paper cup full of sand.

"Where'd you find that?" I demanded, frustrated it wasn't me holding the cup.

"Over there by the hobo home," he said.

"Well, pour it over the side," Duncan suggested, as we all stood shoulder-to-shoulder, staring down below, watching automobiles drive into and out of the garage.

Mark reached out his hand with the paper cup full of sand, and slowly started to pour over the ledge. Then he stopped, as if waiting for something, then poured a little more—and while he was doing this, all of us were looking over the ledge to see what was happening below. It was then that I saw a tiny sliver of a front bumper, sticking out from the ground level of the garage. Mark started pouring sand at the same time the car started moving, and it drove right into the line of fire. Some of the sand started blowing in the wind currents, but most of it went straight down.

Our accidental target was a convertible.

When the driver looked up, receiving sand in the face was his greeting. He quickly pawed his face and eyes, put the car in reverse and then peeled backward into the garage.

Back to school at Parkington.
Photo from WalkArlington brochure, Arlington Central Library.

We started running, but we were fleeing the scene in the wrong direction. The exit stairway through Peeville was between us and the ramp coming up from below, too far to run with the convertible in rapid pursuit, so we turned around and went the opposite way. But before we got to the other end of the roof, the car had reached the top level and was hot on our trail, tires squealing with every turn. As we were running, the driver pulled up next to us before slamming on the brakes.

There was nowhere to go.

We stopped our getaway attempt, as the driver got out of his car. As soon as his feet hit the ground, he reached into his pants pocket and pulled out a leather wallet or money clip, reached inside of it and pulled out a badge.

He was an Arlington County cop.

"What the hell do you think you're doing?" shouted the cop, spittle flying out as he spoke.

"We were just messin' around, sir," Duncan said, as Mark and I kept our eyes searching for another escape route.

"Don't you even think about running, boy," the officer said, when he saw what I was doing.

"Did you ever think you might have hurt someone dropping debris on top of cars?" he asked.

We all mumbled a "no" in unison, while shamefully looking at the ground.

"Where's your mother?"

"Shopping in there." Duncan pointed in the direction of the nearest store.

"If I ever catch you little turds doing this again, you're all going to jail. You hear me?"

"Yessir," came out from all of us.

The officer turned around before storming back to his car. He sped off, likely aggravated not being able to collar us because of our age.

When the coast was clear, each of us looked at the other, first in embarrassment, but then followed by enlightenment: we started laughing as loud as we ever had.

"*Man*, that guy was pissed," Mark cackled, as we started walking in the direction of the Duncan's car.

"Why'd you have to pick a cop?" asked Duncan, after he'd quelled some of his laughter.

"Why'd you have to pick one driving a convertible?" I added, as we again shrieked out with laughter.

Cherry Bombs and Private Bathroom Moments, 1967

"People try to put us d-down (talkin' 'bout my generation)
Just because we get around (talkin' 'bout my generation)
Things they do look awful c-c-cold (talkin' 'bout my generation)
I hope I die before I get old (talkin' 'bout my generation)"[16]

Peter, Dale, and I had finished riding our bikes, past the horse farms along Clark's Crossing Road, to the old Washington and Old Dominion Railroad tracks. There weren't any more trains on this discontinued line, but we liked to use it for easy access to play in the water of Difficult Run, as well as an alternate route into Vienna. We were sitting on my front porch, drinking sweet tea after the long ride on a warm summer day, as we flipped through the *Washington Post* sports page. Every day during the summer we did this sports page routine on one of our porches, mostly poring over the box scores of all the baseball games, while focusing most of our attention on the hometown Baltimore Orioles and Washington Senators. Peter was a Yankee fan.

Suddenly, in the middle of calculating how many home runs Frank Howard would hit this year, I made the sudden announcement: "I got two cherry bombs from my dad," I whispered very softly to Dale and Pete so that my parents wouldn't hear me through the open windows. Peter immediately looked at me and smiled that mischievous grin he often used, while Dale, without averting his gaze at *The Post,* seemed to be thinking about the possibilities.

"What do you plan to do with those?" Dale asked me, after he finally looked up from the printed pages.

"I was thinking we should scare the crap out of Mr. Martin," I replied, in a voice louder than I intended. I hand motioned for all of us to leave the porch, and then proceed into the yard, where we could talk in private. From that vantage point, the Martins' house was in plain view.

As detached and unfriendly as Mrs. Martin could be, her husband and Roger's father, Carl, was even more so. His tone of voice, at times, could be a little condescending. And it always seemed like he was unhappy about something.

---

[16] My Generation, Peter Townsend, 1965

Roger made matters more uncomfortable by forcing us to go out of our way to say *hello* to him every time we came inside.

Most of the time, when I went over to Roger's house, I would wait outside on the front porch just to avoid contact with Mr. Martin. His surliness was often directed at Roger, when he'd utter the confusing statement "Rahja, you're contradictin' yourself," using his Tidewater pronunciation of *Roger*. I didn't even know what he meant, but Roger would get very quiet every time he said it.

I had wanted to pull a prank on Mr. Martin ever since that time he told me I would never amount to anything, and I would never go to college. It took me many years to fully comprehend the amount of resentment, anger, and general frustration with life, his hurtful comment contained. But for now, I knew he simply didn't like me or my family—and I didn't like him, either.

Every year, around the fourth of July, my dad would come home with a paper sack full of firecrackers. Since firecrackers were illegal, I always wondered where he got them. And these weren't the rolled up Chinese newspaper filled with a pinch of gunpowder variety; these were genuine cherry bombs and M80s. The kind of firecrackers that would quickly remove a finger or two, if you didn't throw them before the fuse burned all the way down.

And, as one would expect, they were extremely loud.

They emitted a resonating *boom* when detonated, rather than the gentle *crack* like the tame versions. They also left a gaping hole in the lawn when placed on the ground for detonation, as if to remind us what they could do to our hands.

I was nearing my twelfth birthday, the summer of 1967, when my dad came home with his annual bag of bombs. I knew that if I could somehow acquire just two or three of them, not enough that he'd notice, there was no limit to the fun I could have. So, I came up with a plan.

Every afternoon, about five o'clock, Mr. Martin would begin his afternoon bathroom routine. I knew this. We all knew this. We could see him close the curtain in the bathroom window immediately after he turned on the overhead light—and during the summer, in a house without air conditioning, we could see cigarette smoke billowing out of the open window. And we all knew what cigarette smoke in the bathroom meant.

The Martins' house was designed exactly like ours and nearly every other house on Hicks Drive, with the toilet adjacent to and approximately six inches from the window. The sink was between the toilet and the door, with the tub on the opposite wall. These were tiny, but functional rooms.

I pointed my finger at the house. "Every day about five o'clock, that old grouch, Mr. Martin, uses the john," I said with extreme confidence.

"He stays in there about a year," Peter stifled a laugh, seeming to know where I was going with my idea.

"Let's wait until he gets real comfortable, then I'll light one of these right outside his window." I tried not to laugh as I said this, and reached into my pants pocket to retrieve a cherry bomb. I proudly held it up for Pete and Dale to view, as Peter reached out his hand to touch it.

"Is this real?" he asked while petting it.

"Yeah, it's real. And loud as hell. These things will blow your fingers off."

"Jeez. Mr. Martin will shit a brick," Dale added, while laughing hysterically at the thought.

"That's the whole idea," I continued, as the three of us kept laughing so loud that I saw my mom's bouffant hairdo peeking out the picture window in our living room, trying to figure out what was going on outside. She wasn't very energetic, and if she couldn't determine what all the commotion was about from her stationary position, we were quite safe.

We retreated to the drainage ditch that ran along the road, in front of ours and the Martins' house. It would give us a cat bird's view of the bathroom window and Mr. Martin's evening ritual. We were giggling like little girls, as we shared our imagined scenarios of Mr. Martin going to the bathroom and being suddenly and violently interrupted.

We must have waited about thirty minutes, when all of a sudden, I saw the Martins' bathroom light come on, quickly followed by our intended victim's Grinch-like visage quickly appearing in the window before the curtain closed.

"Let's go," I said and we crept along the cars parked in the driveway toward the house. Peter and Dale hid behind a clump of Mrs. Martin's prized azalea bushes, while I continued toward the front steps. I reached into my right pants pocket and then pulled out the cherry bomb.

But, Peter had the lighter. I reversed course and found Peter and Dale wondering if they should run.

"Gimme the lighter, Pete. And after I light this thing, haul ass and keep running," I said while grabbing the Zippo from Peter's hand.

I crept back toward the house again and up the front steps. Now, all I had to do was climb the guard rail at the top, hold on to it to keep from falling, and then place the cherry bomb on the window ledge, light it, then run.

I made it over the railing while clutching the cherry bomb, and then quickly placed it on the window sill. I listened for a moment, a radio playing through the open window, with some fast-talking DJ saying something about Texas Ted Britt Ford and the new Mustang. The radio would provide adequate background noise to mask any I'd create. I reached back into my pocket for the lighter.

I rolled the ignition wheel on the Zippo, creating a healthy flame, gripped the handrail and leaned out toward the window. On the first try I caught the tip of the cherry bomb fuse with the flame of the lighter. It started to hiss, while sending sparks out in all directions. I didn't bother to climb the handrail to escape, but instead jumped down the six feet or so to a soft landing in the grass below the window. I then ran as fast as I could.

Although they were running away in the same direction, I managed to pass Peter and Dale at the end of the driveway. I knew it was merely seconds before all hell broke loose.

That's when we heard the *BOOM!* that seemed louder than anything I'd ever heard, certainly that I'd ever instigated. The sound of the explosion made us run even faster, as our heads instinctively lowered, and our knees slightly buckled in response. We leaped across the street and dove headfirst behind some thick evergreens, where we knew Mr. Martin couldn't see us. And still yet, we tried to make ourselves invisible by lying as flat on the ground as we could, nearly burying ourselves in the tall weeds that surrounded us.

Within thirty seconds of the explosion, Mr. Martin stood on his front porch, defiantly and authoritatively holding a rifle with both hands. His big black-framed glasses were askew on his face, and his pants were only partially buckled, with half of his shirt tucked inside his waist. He definitely didn't spend much time worrying about his appearance: he must've thought World War III had just been declared, with the first shot fired at him on the commode.

It was the funniest spectacle I had ever seen. Mr. Martin just invented the "Go ahead, make my day" posture years before Clint Eastwood famously borrowed it. We stared at Mr. Poopus Interuptus with fear and excitement, while earnestly trying to stifle our laughter, which would have resulted in certain death for us all. Despite his poor health and declining eyesight, Mr. Martin was an expert marksman. Fortunately, his hearing was rendered temporarily useless by the cherry bomb's explosion, twelve inches from his head. He was as deaf as a door.

Finally, he gave a dismissive snort before returning to the safety of his home. And then, like a scene from a B movie, a three-foot-long string of toilet paper waved from the back of his pants, as he defiantly marched away from view. We began laughing even harder.

"Man, I bet he was just gettin' comfortable when that thing went off. He must have thought the Russians were coming through his bathroom window!" Peter roared out.

"Do ya' think he saw me running away, Dale?" I finally asked, starting to worry if he did.

"Nah, I don't think so. He was probably too busy diving head first onto the bathroom floor!"

For at least another thirty minutes, we sat there behind the bushes to make sure the fully armed Mr. Martin was no longer peering out the window, lying in-wait for the perpetrators to show themselves. And, just to be sure, we crept along the forsythia bushes, up the street to Peter's place, where we raided the refrigerator in our own celebratory feast.

While scarfing down some tasty Greek dish that Pete's mom was probably saving for dinner the next day, I knew I would remember that day for the rest of my life.

Sass Your Mother, I'll Beat You for That, 1968

> *"Please allow me to introduce myself*
> *I'm a man of wealth and taste*
> *I've been around for a long, long year*
> *Stole many a man's soul to waste"*[17]

Mr. Armstrong, the "astronaut", moved his family to Australia for two years in 1967. And while they were away from Hicks Drive, they rented their house to a very strange man and his family. Mr. Tolbert was loud, abusive, and extremely resolute. It didn't take long for all the boys on Hicks Drive to conclude this guy was a nut.

His family of two young boys and a wife cowered in his presence, as he repeatedly delivered verbal and physical destruction to anyone and everyone unfortunate enough to be caught in his path. All of us had witnessed it on more than one occasion.

It wasn't unusual during their first year living on Hicks Drive, that we could hear Mr. Tolbert screaming at one of his unfortunate children, "Sass your mother, I'll beat you for that."

Then, he did.

The terrorized crying of his kids responding to his torture could be heard by anybody in the vicinity. Just imagining the sound of a leather belt on flesh makes me uncomfortable to this day. And why nobody ever called authorities to report this monster remains a mystery. Maybe the adults in our neighborhood were also afraid of him. But it was a different world back then, when outsiders didn't interfere in family business. Or abuse. But in our own extremely judgmental way, the jury of thirteen and fourteen-year-old boys interfered. We found Tolbert guilty and we sentenced him to brief torment in a method we would never forget.

One evening, Mark, Peter, and I were sitting on the split-rail fence in front of the Tolberts' next door neighbor. The fence was a favorite of ours to meet, discuss, and solve all of the world's problems in about thirty minutes; we called it The Gossip Fence. We were about to leave, after dissecting all the ways that the Green Bay Packers were superior to every other team in the National Football League, when I looked up and saw Tolbert's car coming up

---

17　"Sympathy For The Devil", Keith Richards and Mick Jagger, 1968

the street, returning home from work at the Pentagon.

He slowly drove by, glancing at us out of his open car window. The smile he displayed was an attempt to mask a headful of demons. But we had this guy figured out from the get-go, so his efforts at concealment were in vain. As he passed, I suddenly felt the middle finger of my concealed right hand extend in an appropriate salute.

He proceeded up his inclined driveway and parked his car at the top, adjacent to the house. It didn't take more than ten minutes for his family to receive all of the frustrations he had accumulated at work that day.

The open windows in his home were more than adequate for us to overhear some argument about toys left outside, caught in the rain the night before. And, as if on cue, Tolbert yelled at full volume over the timid response of his wife, who was trying in vain to interject some form of verbal protection of her children. The faint sound of a child's voice was immediately interrupted by an angry retort.

"Sass your mother, I'll beat you for that," yelled Tolbert in his now familiar announcement of what was surely to follow. I heard a child screaming, louder each time, in response to what sounded like a belt or strap, repeatedly striking his body. The mother's pleading voice suddenly got louder, as well, as she tried to stop the blows from being delivered by her maniacal husband.

Suddenly, Peter turned toward the Tolberts' house, cupped his hands around his mouth and shouted, "Sass your mother, I'll beat you for that!" as loud as he could, until he was completely out of breath. And like a thoroughbred horse bolting from the gate at the Kentucky Derby, Mr. Tolbert burst through his kitchen door in pursuit of who yelled his signature trademark. We scattered in all directions like a herd of frightened deer.

I had at least a hundred-yard head start on Tolbert, so I ran down the street, too afraid to go home, for fear that he might murder me in my sleep, if he knew where I lived. But I had just gotten out of his line of sight, when I ducked under some thick forsythia bushes in my front yard, which allowed me a clear view of the surrounding area, but kept me hidden from anyone passing by.

Pete had the shortest legs, and wasn't as fast as the rest of us, so he dived under a row of thorny bushes across the street, next-door to where I lived. It was within thirty yards of the Tolberts' front yard.

Peter hadn't been in his hiding place for more than a minute, when Tolbert ran down his driveway and began looking for him. Then he quit running and started walking very slowly, as if he knew one of us was nearby. He stopped and listened, took a couple of steps, and just stood there. If he caught Peter right then, there was no way for him to escape. He would have dragged him out from under that bush and pummeled him with his bare hands.

I held my breath, as I watched Tolbert take one calculated step after another, in search of the hiding boy, who had the audacity to mock him in front of his family. He still had his suit on, tie neatly tucked under the jacket, as he bent over to peer underneath one of the bushes. Now I was really scared. And Peter must have been catatonic with fear.

But he slowly and methodically crouched, then crept by, where I saw Peter hide; I thought the worst was over. But he then suddenly looked up to see Mark bolting for home from his own hiding spot.

"Stop! You there! Stop immediately!" screamed the psycho. But Mark had perfectly timed his getaway: He'd waited for Tolbert to be distracted as he looked for Pete, and his temporary hiding place was far enough away to avoid detection. Soon, Mark was out of sight, and his visible and daring escape likely saved Peter.

Tolbert finally turned a one eighty before heading for home. But a few times, he'd quickly turn around to see if we'd revealed ourselves from our hiding places. We didn't dare, until he was inside his house.

I finally came out from under the forsythia hedgerow and crept over to Pete's hiding place. I looked under the bush, and, although I knew he was there, it was difficult to see him, because Peter had hidden under the thickest part of the undergrowth. It took him several minutes to extricate himself, and when he stood, I saw his face was as white as a sheet. And his arms had several streaks of blood, where he'd been nicked by the thorns.

"I thought I was dead meat for a second, man," he said with his lower lip quivering, while nervously wiping at the bloody streaks.

"I prayed for the first time in months, I was so scared." He didn't have to convince me of that.

"We should walk up the street a little farther, Pete. Mark might be waiting for us and we don't want to hang around for Tolbert," I suggested. We cautiously made our way up the road, reliving the entire sequence of events, beginning with Tolbert bolting from the house. Relief and wonder punctuated the retelling of every scene. How miraculous it was that all of us escaped punishment for calling out an abusive psychopath.

Later that week, I walked up the street to Pete's house, nervously glancing at the Tolberts', fearing that somehow, the abuser would recognize my walk, or perhaps my clothing.

Peter opened the door before I knocked, and quickly motioned for me to follow him to his room.

"Mrs. Tolbert came over yesterday," Pete said in a low, almost somber voice after he'd closed the door.

I already knew this story wasn't going to end well.

"So, what happened?" I asked.

"My mom invited her over for coffee. She'd been over a few times. They always talk about moving around a lot. That kind of stuff."

"Did you talk to her?" I asked, although I really didn't want to hear the answer.

"Yeah, I talked to her. She asked me to sit next to her on the couch when my mom left the room to get the coffee cups. I saw she had a bruise on the side of her face."

"That bastard," I said in helpless resignation.

"As soon as I sat down next to her, she said, 'Peter, please don't yell at my husband like you did on Monday. It just makes matters worse.' After we'd taunted him, I think he went back inside his house and beat the crap out of his kids, again." Peter lowered his eyes to avoid looking at me.

Silence then filled the room, as I contemplated what it must be like living in an abusive family. But I'd already seen the answer, and it was right next door to where we were sitting.

"I told her I wouldn't," Peter finally said, as I stood up.

The Tolberts soon moved away, taking their family turmoil with them. But they left an indelible mark on us, as we began to better appreciate the impact of domestic violence, something we were not aware of, before the Tolbert Devil Monster.

We never knew what happened to his wife or children. But it probably wasn't good.

Mr. Alfred Richardson

Mr. Alfred W Richardson-Great teacher and friend to all.
Photo from the 1969 Joyce Kilmer Intermediate Yearbook.

Teacher, Mentor, Lifelong Friend—Mr. Alfred W. Richardson 1967-2000

"Teach the children so it will not be necessary to teach the adults."
                                                            -Abraham Lincoln

Intermediate school was weird; always had been, always will be. You start with a group of children, about twelve years old, too young to be called anything *but* children, add a couple of fifty-five gallon drums of hormones, a six-pack of pimple cream, some body hair sprouting in previously unfertile areas, a myriad of strange smells, and you've got your intermediate school kids.

So, this strange interruption of the maturing process between little kid elementary and almost-adult high school, begs the question; what would motivate someone to be a teacher there?

Perhaps desperation to grab the first job offer out of college? There's probably some of that. Someone completely deranged? A few, but not likely many. A neurotic with nothing better to do, perhaps? That's not it, either.

Or maybe someone who is dedicated, really dedicated, to education at all levels? Dedicated to education delivered to the kids that need order, guidance, stability, and inspiration more than the kids in other grade levels might need—those aforementioned creatures: intermediate school kids.

Because of, or despite these challenges, someone special comes around, maybe once a generation or so, excelling at their craft unlike any of their peers— someone like Mr. Alfred W. Richardson at Joyce Kilmer Intermediate in Dunn Loring, Virginia.

My seventh grade class in 1967 was the one that opened the doors for a brand new middle school in Fairfax County called Joyce Kilmer.

It was awesome—air conditioning, all the latest hi-fi equipment in the music room, wide hallways to accommodate a lot of kids, and it even had lockers! I had never used or seen lockers at school before entering the hallowed halls of Kilmer.

The school was pretty, too. Even many of the teachers were pretty, and I was just starting to notice that kind of thing in the seventh grade. Miss V, an art teacher, was so hot that another instructor divorced his wife and married her. I often wondered why those two spent so much time in the Art

Supply Room together.

Like most intermediate schools, we changed classes and had different teachers for each subject: a new teacher every hour. Get bored with one, suck it up for an hour, and then a change of scenery would soon appear, after the bell and a brief stroll down the hall.

And when we changed classes, everyone in the school was dumped into those halls for about ten minutes. And girls in the seventh and eighth grade were much prettier than those in elementary school. They looked like tiny grown-ups, and even some who weren't so tiny.

In Fairfax County, the intermediate schools combined three subjects together for seventh graders; English, social studies, and guidance—and they called it ESG. And ESG ran for nearly half of a day, at about three hours. So, if you had a lousy ESG teacher, you were really screwed for what would have seemed like an eternity.

But if you had Mr. Richardson, you were in for the best learning experience you would likely ever receive.

Mr. Richardson was a big man, about six feet four inches tall, and tipped the scales at about two hundred seventy five pounds. He wore black-framed, thick lens glasses that sometimes exaggerated the size of his eyes. He was married, but childless, and had about five years of teaching experience prior to the opening of Kilmer in 1967. He grew up in a little town called Selma, North Carolina, located almost walking distance from where my father was born in Wilson. Small world.

But more important than all of that, Mr. Richardson had discovered a way to light up our imagination. It could have been a natural talent, or one that he developed sometime in his brief teaching career. He didn't teach history by ramming dates and facts down our throats, before asking us to regurgitate them for the test in the following week. He challenged us to appreciate the historical significance of those events, as though we were present during their unfolding.

And often, on Saturday mornings, we actually were present. On those special days, he would take a group of four or five of us in his gigantic Buick LeSabre, and drive off to Gettysburg, Antietam, Bull Run, or Harper's Ferry. We thought we were just having fun, but all of us were learning valuable lessons literally on the field of battle, about one hundred years after the last musket round ripped through the last Confederate soldier to run in Pickett's Charge or Little Round Top. On the field of battle, where a century before, the last cannon was fired at the retreating Union soldiers at Bull Run. Twice.

Seeing all of those historical sites opened the door for all of the associated facts and dates, we now didn't have to memorize, because we had seen it. We had been there.

And from that year forward, I viewed the previously boring topic of history in a totally different perspective. Newspapers and books became the classrooms. I wondered how history would view a current event as it was developing in real time, on the front page of the *Washington Post*.

In the summer, Mr. Richardson would once again pile a group of us into his Buick and head to RFK Stadium to watch the hapless Washington Senators attempt to play America's Pastime. Although the Senators were horrible, I saw several soon-to-be Hall of Famers play against them, like Frank and Brooks Robinson, Al Kaline, and Mickey Mantle. Even the great Ted Williams managed the Senators for a while, so seeing him was quite a treat, as well.

As the years went by, our contact became less frequent, but relatively steady.

Sometime, just before I graduated from high school, Mr. R bought a home with a swimming pool. He called the first summer he'd lived there and invited me and a girl I was dating, over to his house for a swim. We stayed about four hours, very little swimming, lots of talking and catching up on what had happened ever since we'd last communicated. I always enjoyed the conversations I had with him upon entering adulthood.

He was also a traveler. Every summer I would get a postcard from him that he had sent from places like Costa Rica, Guatemala, or Panama. I think I saved most of them. The ink has now run together between some of the words, but the message is crystal clear; he was saying hello from wherever he was, thinking about me while he was touring the world.

Mr. Alfred W. Richardson touched his students' lives in ways we couldn't fully appreciate until many years later. And he was able to do this, because he had a passion for teaching, a strong knowledge of the subject matter, and an effective method to develop rapport with his students.

But his inspiration as a teacher, mentor, and friend was perhaps his greatest gift.

A Day at the Pool, 1968

"Uno, dos, one, two, tres, quatro
Matty told Hatty about a thing she saw
Had two big horns and a wooly jaw
Wooly bully, wooly bully
Wooly bully, wooly bully, wooly bully"[18]

    A brand-new swimming pool opened the summer of 1968, to the welcome relief of those who were members of the overcrowded Freedom Hill and Westwood Country Club facilities. The new pool, called Cardinal Hill, was highly anticipated by Hicks Drive residents, because of its proximity and relatively low cost. Nevertheless, I was still the only schmuck on the street whose family wasn't members at *any* of the pools, so I depended upon the kindness of neighbors to bring me along for the seventy five cent guest entry fee. And, usually, it wasn't a problem. I was able to earn my own money mowing lawns, and a brief stint delivering newspapers for the Northern Virginia Sun, and even the Washington Star, so most days I could come up with three quarters of a dollar.
    But, the main attraction at Cardinal Hill was certainly not the hyper-chlorinated water. Nor was it the high dive, a diving board so spectacular that it took nerves of steel just to climb the ladder to get to the top. It was none of that. It was girls, lots of girls, lots of itsy bitsy, teeny weeny bikini-clad girls. Especially, any girls older than the middle school dweebs we were at the time.
    And, by the summer of 1968, I was starting to put all the pieces into place, so to speak, as I began to realize that girls were just about the most alluring, and pleasing to the eyes, creatures in the universe.
    I had come to that conclusion by foraging for, and occasionally locating, men's magazines, like Playboy and some of the other raunchier ones I won't identify. And, as I entered my final year of middle school, I also started to notice how girls dressed; short skirts well above the knee, stockings, garter belts, bras, the whole nine yards. I was learning it all as fast as I could.
    And, all that anatomical education was the perfect precursor to seeing, up close and personal, the real thing at the swimming pool. It was a buffet of scantily clad babes; one entry fee, unlimited eye candy. And it was impossible to get your fill without going back for another helping on another day. Every day.

---

18   Wooly Bully, Domingo Samudio, 1965

One particular hot, hazy afternoon, typical of summer in DC, almost the entire neighborhood gang went to Cardinal Hill and spent most of the time grating the bottom of our toes raw, while standing and bobbing on the concrete floor of the pool. Fortunately, Roger had brought with him a brand-new snorkel and mask set, and he was gracious enough to share it. But one mask for five teenaged boys required patience for all participants; patience was something none of us had.

And, to properly put this tale into perspective, I should point out that objects definitely look different under water, especially when you consider the twenty-five percent magnification in water versus air. Or something such as that. Things simply looked bigger. And closer.

On this particular occasion, when it was my turn to use the mask, I inconspicuously made my rounds along the side of the pool, where most of the girls were clinging and bobbing up and down. Except for the occasional percussion from someone jumping into the water, it was silent, enabling me to focus my attention exclusively on vision.

To my delight, everything was perfectly aligned with each of the bathing beauties, as I took it all into view with my underwater stalking apparatus. It was Anatomy 101, literally from head to toe. I could see everything in relative obscurity, remaining anonymous while in plain view.

Some of the girls I was ogling, I knew from school, which made it even better. With my all-seeing mask I was able to know them in a way I previously hadn't. Some of the ladies I'd never seen before, which offered many pleasant discoveries. That was especially true of the high school girls, who were beyond pretty—they were beautiful.

I became almost hypnotized as I got as close as I dared, to see every detail of those girls. When one turned around and faced the other way, or got out of the pool before I'd completed my viewing, I'd move on to the next one. There could easily have been a hundred babes in the pool that day.

Even some of the moms were worth a second pass. Several were particularly alluring in ways that the younger ones weren't. Same stuff, just somehow a bit better.

My confidence grew with each inspection. After a while, I didn't care if I got caught spying on innocent ladies in their almost-underwear. *What would they do, throw me out of the pool for gawking?* I thought briefly, as I made my final turn and swam back to where the guys had been waiting.

My voyeuristic journey around the pool had kept me busily taking it all in during the fifteen minute time interval I had before returning the mask to its rightful owner. I'd already spent what seemed like a long time checking out a specific mom, who'd worn a particularly revealing bikini—one that the other mothers hadn't. I was nearly motionless, suspended in the water, as I passed by, inches away from her, so I wouldn't miss a single detail.

My eyes began to search for the next one in line, when suddenly, out of nowhere, I saw it—the largest pair of breasts I'd ever seen. And underwater, the bathing suit seemed to disappear.

Girlie magazines had definitely not prepared me for this.

I was out of air from my lengthy swim and the instant adrenaline rush from a surprise attack of mammary origin.

When I re-surfaced, I saw that it was Mrs. Jones, a lady who lived in my neighborhood. Suddenly my cover was in danger of being blown.

I took a giant gulp of air and immediately dived under the water.

Surprisingly, though, I hesitated for just a moment. *What if she recognized me studying her with a SCUBA mask and snorkel attached to my face?*

But curiosity soon prevailed, and I got as close as I could to the new discovery, without drawing any undue attention to myself. I then made a Mark Spitz-like underwater turn, and went back to get another look. My face was turning blue from certain lack of oxygen, but I wanted to stare as long as I could. Finally, when it felt that my lungs would burst, I surfaced, gasping for air, only to be surrounded by Roger, Peter, Rick Duncan, and Mark. The look on their faces told me I had exceeded my mask time limit.

"My turn," Roger said, as he quickly grabbed it out of my hands. I was still out of breath and couldn't speak, but held up my right hand like I didn't want anybody to leave.

"You won't... believe... what I saw, guys." I kept on gasping. "Go check out Mrs. Jones... under water... and get up real close," I challenged, as I now had the group's undivided attention.

I motioned for them to move in closer around me, so nobody else would eavesdrop on my Top-Secret revelation.

"Her bathing suit makes her look nekkid underwater, and everything's showin'," I whispered.

"What does she look like?" Duncan hysterically laughed out.

"What do you think she looks like?" I said.

Then all of us were laughing like hyenas, causing a scene in the middle of the swimming pool. There had to have been several rules broken with that many boys having that much fun.

Roger then quickly put on the mask, before diving underwater in the direction of Mrs. Jones and her spectacle. He took his time, as he paced back and forth in front of her, at a safer distance than I did.

Soon after, he returned, as breathless as I was.

"You were right!" Roger revealed, while trying to catch his breath. "I've never seen someone up close like *that* before."

Then it was Peter's turn, then Duncan's, and on it went, for the next hour and a half. How all this activity went unnoticed, I will never know, because Mrs. Jones never left the pool the entire time we were inspecting her.

During one of the required hourly breaks, when the lifeguards cleared the pool for "safety" reasons, we gathered in one of the picnic areas adjacent to the pool deck and compared notes.

"Imagine she's like an octopus," Duncan started, "stranded on a desert island, awaiting a lone sailor standing on the deck of a passing ship." He waved his hand at us to stop laughing, and just listen. "Suddenly, she spots her prey in the distance and reaches out with her tentacles and grabs the unsuspecting sailor, pulling him into her."

"Gross, man! What made you think of that?" I said, as I starting laughing so hard that some pool water that'd been up my nose, suddenly squirted onto my upper lip.

"You're the one that's gross," Peter said, as he averted his eyes from me, back to the empty pool.

"She'd wait for years until a ship passed. Then she'd grab him," Mark added. "What if she'd grabbed us?" he continued, as he made a face of disgust at what he'd shared.

"She'd have drowned us, right here at Cardinal Hill, in front of all these girls," I finally added, as I imagined our corpses drifting down to the bottom of the pool, before getting stuck in the drain, girls peering cautiously over the edge of the water.

And then, Roger said what was true for all of us: "I won't forget this any time soon."

The Trails ad in The Evening Star. March 20, 1970.
Provided by John Thompson.

FAIRFAX LODGE

This historic property is located in Fairfax County, Virginia, on 76 acres of beautiful fertile rolling land with Wolf Trap Run winding through the property.

The main house is approached over a thousand-foot, tree-lined driveway. The original part of the house was built of log and clapboard during the latter part of the eighteenth century to serve as a hunting lodge for Lord Fairfax.

On the first floor is a 10-foot wide center hall, a large living room with hand-hewn beamed ceiling, a stone fireplace and built-in bookcases. The dining room is 13½x17, the butler's pantry 10x16, and the fully equipped kitchen, 12x16. There is a downstairs bedroom 13½x16, with private bath; a large dressing room and screened porch.

On the second floor there are three large bedrooms, 13½ x16, 15½x15½, 15½x20, all with ample closet space and a tiled bath with shower.

On the third floor is a large finished storage room. Random-width flooring throughout. Copper plumbing. Oil hot-water heat.

Other buildings consist of a 3-room tenant house, a 2-room guesthouse with bath and shower, a stock barn with 4 horse stalls and 3 cow stalls, equipped with automatic drinking cups; a hay barn, chicken house, 2 tool sheds, a root cellar and a 3-car shelter. All outbuildings have water and electricity.

There are about 55 acres of cleared, fertile, fenced fields, all amply watered and 21 acres of woods.

The banks of Wolf Trap Run at the rear of the main house have been landscaped so as to provide a private park and picnic ground.

PRICED AT $50,000. A LARGE FIRST TRUST CAN BE ARRANGED AT 4% FOR 20 YEARS

Shown by appointment only.

STANLEY R. ROWLAND CO.
Realtor
118 East Broad St., Falls Church, Virginia
Chestnut 3421 Eves., FA 2842

Advertisement for property that became Todd's Farm, Evening Star November 30, 1946. Provided by John Thompson.

Todd's Farm and the Old House, 1968

"Wait a minute, something's wrong here
The key won't unlock this door
Wait a minute, something's wrong, lord, have mercy
This key won't unlock this door,
Something's goin' on here
I have a bad bad feeling
That my baby don't live her no more"[19]

Peter playfully knocked on the door of the old, abandoned Todd farmhouse, while Mark and I looked for an instrument of destruction with which to enter the premises. A rock would do just fine.

I gently tapped twice before slamming the rock against the window pane closest to the door knob, sending glass flying three feet in all directions.

"Do you always have to be so damned noisy?" Mark seriously asked.

"Only when I'm breaking into somebody's house," I replied, as I reached through the now broken window pane and turned the door-knob from the inside, while pushing up against the door from the outside. Nothing. The door wouldn't budge.

"Why don't you just break all the windows?" Peter asked, apparently not realizing that wasn't the issue, at all.

I gave the door knob another twist, this time from outside, and then drove my shoulder violently into the door. It sprang open like a jack-in-the-box lid, and after losing my balance, I nearly fell on the broken glass.

The seventy-eight acre farm at the end of our street, owned by the Todd family since 1947, was turned into a subdivision in 1969. The entire farm had been sacred territory to all of the kids on Hicks Drive, especially to the boys. As long as we didn't get too close to the house and risk being seen by the owners, we enjoyed the rest of the estate like it was ours, to do as we pleased.

Every summer, we caught crawfish in Wolf Trap Creek, which ran behind the house and barn. Year round, we played in the pond that was surrounded on all sides by trees, but easily accessible by horse trails. Occasionally, we even went horse-back riding through the network of paths

---

19   "Red House", Jimi Hendrix, 1967

that went well beyond where we'd typically play.

A level part of their expansive field was where we had played numerous baseball games during those hot summer days, when America's Pastime seemed like the perfect thing to do. The location was ideal—at the bottom of Hicks Drive.

And miraculously, nobody ever chased us off for trespassing. It was like we had a rent-free lease to use it whenever we wanted. But the owner and his wife, Mr. Clarence and Elizabeth O'Brien Todd, knew all about our stadium, choosing to let us play there, anyway.[20]

We built a pitcher's mound and backstop, and my dad furnished a real home-plate and pitcher's rubber. A home run was achieved by hitting the ball into the tall, un-mowed outfield grass, which was far enough from home-plate, that few fly balls were ever hit there. But if it got a good roll, it temporarily disappeared, as the batter circled the bases.

Not too long after the property was sold, we discovered the old Todd house up close and personal, having been too afraid to approach it when it was occupied. It was a massive old, white wooden mansion with three floors, and at least fifteen rooms, with sort of a spooky and mysterious feel about it from afar. One of the rooms in the center of the house was a log cabin, called Fairfax Lodge, named after its original owner, Lord Fairfax, in the eighteenth century, who used it as a remote hunting lodge.

The top floor of the log cabin was made into a bedroom, occupied by one of the daughters, Elizabeth, who had the same first name as her mother.

There was also a tenant house on the premises, which had served as refuge for three consecutive eastern European families, forced to flee their homes that had fallen under Soviet domination after World War II.[21]

The hay barn, a couple of storage sheds, and some horse stalls, comprised the rest of the buildings, all located close to the main house. And the entire complex was half of a mile from the frontage road, and out of sight from just about everybody without a telescope.

It was the perfect playground for adventurous juvenile semi-delinquents.

Before the house was abandoned, we'd never been inside, so we entered it with uncharacteristic caution, not knowing what we'd find; perhaps, somebody forgot to move out when the bull-dozers came rolling in. Or a pack of wild dogs had found some food left behind by the owners and decided to stay.

As we stood in the large foyer, glass crunching under our feet every time we took a step, we saw that the interior of the house was in surprisingly good shape. Each room on the first floor had ceilings so high that none of us could have reached with a running head start and a skyward leap. There were two massive picture windows: one facing the front, the other the woods and

---

20   Conversation with Elizabeth Todd Rupert, 11/7/18
21   Ibid

Wolf Trap Creek in the back.

The wooden floors soon echoed the sounds of our feet running from room to room, in search of some hidden treasure left behind. Everything was gone, except generations of someone else's memories, of a home that no longer belonged to them. And, soon, that home would be demolished.

After we had inspected every room at least once, some twice, we headed for the exit through the back door off the kitchen. It was there that we found another door. One we hadn't earlier noticed while scurrying around. I very carefully opened it, thinking about rabid bats that might fly out upon their release. Rabies had several times been in the news that summer, and my imagination convinced me that all bats were rabid, and would, if given the chance, get tangled in my hair while mauling my face with their sharp teeth and claws.

Once I cracked open the door, I instantly recognized the smell: damp, moldy cellar. But I couldn't resist the opportunity that instantly popped into my head, as Peter and Mark had very cautiously come up behind me, to safely observe what I might discover upon opening the door.

I pulled on the door, and then just like a scene from The Addams Family, it creaked and groaned with every movement—as if vocally trying to resist all of my attempts to open it.

"Oh shit, bats!" I screamed while ducking my head and stomping my feet, pretending to run. I think Mark wet his pants trying to get away, and Peter's knees buckled in terror. The fun was fleeting, but worth every moment, as I started laughing so hard that my stomach hurt.

"Damn you, Ricky. You scared the bejesus out of me," said Mark, who had gotten out of the room faster than I had ever seen him move.

By now, Peter, who had instinctively covered his frizzy hair with both of his hands, had apparently recovered enough to be the first one to go down the very dark and narrow staircase into the cellar. Mark and I were right behind him. With the cellar door open, and our eyes slowly, but steadily adjusting to the limited lighting, we could see a mattress, a kerosene lamp, and some empty cans of food scattered about.

"What the hell?" I wondered out loud, as we tried to envision what kind of activity had occurred in this dark, smelly cellar.

"It looks like somebody's been sleeping down here, maybe hobos," I said, as we finally reached the bottom of the stairs and stood on the floor.

"Or that new girl who moved onto Beulah Road has been down here messin' around," Peter argued. "She wears falsies, ya' know?"

She was the first female schoolmate we knew who developed breasts. She was gorgeous.

The enclosed area there was about the size of a bedroom, fairly large for a cellar, but small in comparison to the much larger rooms above it. The walls were made of stone, stacked one on top of the other, like in a very old fence around the numerous Civil War battlefields in the area.

We picked and prodded the various items lying about, without uncovering anything of particular interest. Just more trash, some cigarette butts, and a Zippo lighter that I quickly stuffed into my pocket, before anyone saw me.

There was a darkened area, at the far end of the cellar, indicating another room, or an alcove that we couldn't clearly see from our vantage point. I started to walk toward it, and as I approached, my eyes became more and more adjusted to the limited light, so that the bottom of another staircase came into view out of the darkness.

I finally came to an abrupt, but apprehensive halt, standing at the foot of those mysterious new stairs. It was only then that I could see that they went up to the ceiling, or the floor of the room above, depending on point of reference.

"Mark, Pete, over here," I called out in a conversational tone. As Mark made his way across the room, I saw a sudden beam of light that startled me. It happened to be Mark with a newly discovered flashlight.

"Shine it up there," I said, while Peter was busy inspecting the contents of an old grocery bag he'd found and brought along with him.

The illuminating flashlight confirmed that the dark and rickety stairway, indeed, went from the floor to the ceiling of the cellar. And there it stopped, for no apparent reason. Mark continued to move the light around the area above the staircase, as if he suspected something.

"It looks like a doorway," we both said at the same time. By now Peter, who overheard our conversation, had gotten a closer look for himself by creeping up behind us, apparently still concerned that I might find some rabid bats. And it was about that time that I decided to make something happen.

I stepped on the second or third stair and pushed up with my back against the ceiling. Without much effort on my part, the whole section above the staircase rose up out of the ceiling, emitting a blinding light from somewhere above.

I cautiously climbed the stairs, one at a time, all the way to the top, while holding the door open for the others. I took the final step, and then found myself standing on the covered back porch just off the kitchen, where we had started our descent into the cellar.

Peter and Mark were right behind me, and after they cleared the top stairs, I closed the door. It seemed to disappear into the floor of the porch.

"This is some kind of a secret doorway," I said. "But you can only get out of the basement. There's no way to open the door from out here and go back in." There wasn't a knob or handle of any kind to allow entry from the porch.

We all stood there on the back porch, staring at the floor that contained the escape hatch, and wondered why someone would have that in their home, and what sort of uses it might have had, back when other families had lived there for generations.

"Yankee soldiers came through here," Pete said. "It may have been a way to escape from them." It was the best and only explanation of this curious architectural design.

"Maybe to hide slaves, too," he added.

After several minutes of sharing other theories surrounding the mysterious door, we soon left our discovery behind, only to return several more times that summer. And with each visit, we became more and more comfortable with the creepy cellar, the disappearing stairway, and the mysterious escape hatch from the floor at the rear of the house. Our lack of research skills prevented us from making a definitive explanation of our discovery, only serving to add more mystery as time passed.

The mansion was demolished by year's end. And with it went the answers to many questions we developed that year about the Todd family, their heritage, the significance of the log cabin room, and the escape hatch from a cold, dark cellar.

Has Anybody Seen My Tractor? Fall 1968

"Like a true nature's child
We were born, born to be wild
We can climb so high
I never wanna die
Born to be wild
Born to be wild"[22]

I was just getting started on the assembly of a new model car, a 1964 Chevrolet Chevelle Malibu convertible, when I heard the phone upstairs.

After what seemed like several rings, my mom answered it, opened the basement door and said, "Ricky, it's for you."

I put the stopper back in the glue tube, slightly annoyed at the disturbance, and then ran up the stairs to pick up the phone.

"Can you come over?" Peter said, with a hint of desperation in his voice.

"I guess so. What're you up to?" I asked.

"The Bowies are here. And so is Pat."

I knew what that meant, so I briefly paused before I asked, "What do you need me for?" I was fairly certain of the answer.

"Pat's such an asshole and I don't want to be stuck entertaining him by myself," Peter said before adding, "Hank's at work and neither of my sisters want anything to do with him."

"I'll be there in half an hour," I said, and then hung up the phone.

Pat Bowie *was* an asshole. And he was arrogant, a bully, had a big mouth, and he was bigger AND older than Peter or me.

The last time he visited, he broke one of the neighbor's windows with a rock. Of course, he denied it, although the neighbor swore he saw him do it.

I think Pete's dad paid for damages to prevent a ruckus and keep harmony in the neighborhood.

I'd reached the end of my driveway on the way to Pete's house, when I saw him and Pat coming down the street.

"What do you hicks do for fun around here?" Pat asked me as he

---

22   Born To Be Wild, Mars Bonfire, 1968

approached.

Entertain assholes like you, was my first thought.

"Let's go up to Todd's barn and dive into the hay off the balcony," Peter said.

Pat was a city boy. Exactly what city, I was never able to discern, but he was street-wise and daring. And when Peter and I gave him some details about the barn and a couple of tractors that were parked near it, he was eager for us to take him there to investigate.

During most summers of our youth, we had all day to ourselves with limited to no adult supervision. So, to get to the tractor location, Peter led the three of us on a circuitous route, stopping at Todd's Pond along the way. It was a very small, but isolated pool of mostly stagnant water, fed by a spring from somewhere underneath—and every visit typically resulted in one, or all of us walking too close to the edge of the pond, and getting our feet wet from falling in. Roger had been tossed into the stagnant quagmire just a few years ago, after he'd exhibited typical Roger behavior.

That day at the pond was much like the others—and during the course of our now routine efforts of trying to catch frogs and tadpoles, I slid down an embankment and landed in ankle-deep water and mud.

Peter and Pat had a good laugh at my expense, until they soon suffered the same fate, while trying to cross the pond overflow, unable to perform a standing broad jump the width of the spillway. After scraping and stomping as much as we could of the foul-smelling pond ooze off our shoes, the three of us regrouped and headed up the hill toward the abandoned mansion and idle tractors.

Much to our surprise that summer, the Days left their hay cutting and thrashing machinery out in the open, on top of a hill that sharply dropped off toward Wolf Trap Creek below.

Every year, two tractors belonging to local farmer Fremont Day would show up, mow, collect, and bale the eighty or so acres of grassland within Todd's farm. We usually didn't pay much attention to all this activity, as it gave us a free mowing job of the overgrown outfield grass on our self-made baseball field.

But after the Todds moved out during the summer of 1968, we took an intense and sudden interest in all activity involving the property. After all, a new one hundred fifty home subdivision was going to be constructed, and that life, as we knew it, was about to change. And not necessarily for the better. The gigantic Todd Estate had been our playground for years; the field, the pond, Wolf Trap Creek, the spring house, barn, and eventually the mansion, all provided the perfect blend of adventure and mischief. Those days would soon be over. And whether all of the less-than-angelic behavior we displayed was our reaction to that… who knows?

But, in spite of the impending housing development, the tractors arrived on time, just as they had for years. After the Days baled all of the hay, they stored it in the barn, located within two football fields' length from the main Todd house. From the barn, they soon took it all to feed their cattle, a few miles down the road. We spent many hours jumping out of the hay loft and safely into the loose hay below.

The Days also stored their tractors on the Todd property close to the hay barn, during their two-week operation to mow and bale all of the hay.

"I wonder why they didn't park this stuff inside the barn," I asked, without expecting an answer.

"Why should they, stupid? They're just tractors," Pat replied in a way that seemed to keep his mouth engaged without involving his brain. He apparently did a lot of that.

"I'm first," he then stated, as he climbed up the side of the biggest tractor and then sat in its seat. He then proceeded to push all of the pedals, crank the levers, and otherwise do everything possible without the motor running. He exhausted all efforts to locate the ignition keys.

"Let's go, Pat," Peter said. "You don't know how to drive a tractor anyhow," he then added.

"Shut up and give me a push," he demanded, after he figured out where *neutral* was on the transmission shifter.

"Well, come on. Push!" Pat said once again, but louder this time.

I reluctantly grabbed one of the knobs on one side of the huge tractor tire, while Pete did the same on the other. And we pushed.

"Push harder, pussies," Pat yelled out, as Pete and I dug in our feet, readjusted our grip on the tires, and gave an all-out, semi-synchronized push. Suddenly, the tractor started to move. Very slowly, it crawled along at first, and then it rolled a little faster, as it approached a slight decline.

Pat started whooping and yelling, like he was having the time of his life. Peter and I stood on the ground behind him, watching the tractor begin to roll faster and faster away from us and toward the back side of the hill to the creek. It then seemed to be moving *very* fast.

"Hit the brake, Pat!" I yelled, as the tractor rolled farther away from me.

But Pat was suddenly faced with several options: stay on-board and take his chances on a *really* wild ride, apply the brakes and put the tractor in gear while steering it uphill to stop the now accelerating movement, or jump off.

Just as the tractor began its final descent for the creek, Pat dramatically leaped off, sending the tractor rumbling down a very steep slope. Peter and I gave chase far enough to catch up to Pat, who had landed on his feet and rolled a couple of times without injury. We all stood there, helplessly watching, as it was aimed straight for a giant oak tree at the edge of some thick woods.

By now, Pete and I were genuinely scared, knowing that whatever the outcome, it wasn't going to be good.

"Why did you jump off, Pat?" Peter asked, as we bolted in the opposite direction of the Doomsday Tractor, while watching its certain demolition unfold behind us.

"Cuz I felt like it," Pat said, in an arrogant tone I was already sick of hearing. I would be glad when he went home, hopefully never to return.

We temporarily stopped fleeing the scene long enough to note that the tractor was going even faster, and getting ever closer to a grove of trees at the bottom of the hill. The woods seemed like one solid mass of undergrowth and large trees, capable of swallowing anything it wanted. Suddenly, the tractor started to veer off to the right ever so slightly, missing the giant oak tree by inches, until it finally crushed some saplings in its path, which eventually slowed it down to a stop. We could now barely see it through the thick undergrowth.

The forest had eaten the tractor.

After that, we hauled ass out of there, and didn't quit running until we reached Trap Road, about half of a mile away. At that point, we were too scared and out of breath to talk. Even loud mouth Pat was speechless, but that didn't last very long.

"Shiiit, did you see that damned tractor rolling down that hill? I thought it was going to smash into bits on that tree! That was so cool!" Pat yelled, jumping up and down, while Peter and I struggled to join in his excitement.

"We better get our stories straight about what happened," I suggested, without having a story to share.

"We were never here," Pat replied. Pete nodded his head in agreement, and then we walked home with the satisfaction that nobody would be the wiser.

Monday morning, the Days wanted their tractor. They called the police when they didn't locate it where it was last parked on Friday afternoon, nor see any trace of its disappearance.

The cops couldn't find it, either.

Word got around fast, and soon our parents interrogated us about the missing farm equipment, after the Fairfax County "Mounties" went door-to-door. And, of course, we denied any knowledge of any tractor.

We were never there.

By Tuesday, and after Big Mouth Pat went home to the big city, Peter and I went on a scouting mission, to figure out why farmers and cops alike couldn't find the missing tractor.

We pretended like we were hiking to Wolf Trap Creek, just as we had so many times before, while casually strolling by where we last saw the tractor disappear into the woods. It was barely visible from twenty yards out, but the trail of destruction it left on its way toward its final resting point was quite visible.

"I can't believe those dumb asses can't find that thing," I said to Peter, just to initiate a discussion.

"But you can't see it without standing right next to it. How did it miss that tree?" Peter asked, as we walked by in disbelief at how close it was to a cataclysm.

It took a puzzling and agonizing week for the Days to find their tractor. We were never caught, but I think our parents suspected us having some involvement with the crime.

Pat never returned to Hicks Drive. I think he went to reform school shortly after the tractor heist. I wasn't surprised.

Rick Speight seems to have outgrown everything except his lack of dignity for this photo. 1969 The Trails. Picture taken by Nanci Wood.

Rush Hour Mayhem, Spring 1969

"You're just like crosstown traffic
So hard to get through to you
Crosstown traffic
I don't need to run over you
Crosstown traffic
All you do is slow me down
And I'm trying to get on the other side of town"[23]

    We usually don't recognize the significance of an event until many years have passed that allow us to put it into perspective. But we never fail to immediately appreciate the exceptions—those special moments when time ceases to exist, and we instantly know we're creating something exceptional.

    Like the prank we pulled on the innocent and unsuspecting Kellaghers in 1969.

    Just as we had on so many other warm spring evenings, Peter, Mark, and I started walking down Hicks Drive and toward Wolf Trap Creek in search of solitude and adventure. But, before we crossed at the Trap Road intersection, we stopped to allow an oncoming car to pass by, veering from the left. And, in that moment of hesitation, I saw several traffic cones a short distance away, that weren't there when we'd previously traveled that route. They were strategically arranged to alert the driver of road work in the immediate area, safely guiding them to their destination.

    As soon as we reached the construction area, I picked up one of the cones and held the flat end at my crotch while turning to face Peter.

    "I was just thinking about Marilyn Monroe and look what happened," I shouted, as Mark grabbed a third cone and tried to place it on his chest as a giant uni-tit.

    Peter picked up a couple of rocks and started tossing them at the cones, easy at first, then with more velocity. Soon, we were mercilessly pelting the defenseless, plastic objects. Just as quickly, our aim improved to consistently knock them over, making loud *thud* sounds with each direct hit.

    "Hey, you guys. Wouldn't it be cool to rearrange these things and

---

23   "Crosstown Traffic", Jimi Hendrix, 1968

confuse the hell out of people?" I wondered aloud, while grabbing a cone in each hand, dragging them over by the Kellaghers' driveway, which had two entrances onto Trap Road.

Despite our new discovery, the road construction was not a surprise.

By mid-1968, my Utopia on The Hill, aka Hicks Drive, began a dramatic and very abrupt change. The Todd property, where I had spent endless hours hiking in the creek, fooling around at the pond, or playing ball in the field, had been sold to The Lerner Companies, a local developer, which also had built Tysons Corner Mall. Within weeks of the sale, after the surveyors left their telltale orange flags everywhere, giant earth movers appeared in the middle of the night to begin their tireless pursuit of the perfect road, the multitude of house foundations, miles and miles of trenches and ditches, and the total destruction of my childhood activities.

Bulldozers, road graders, and various other pieces of yellow, heavy equipment had already begun carving road beds and curbs for *The Trails*: the new subdivision of nearly two hundred homes. And, to accommodate all of the anticipated traffic into and throughout the area, Trap Road had to be destroyed and rebuilt into a wider commuter transportation route. The new version would be paved with more and better asphalt, highlighted by brilliantly colored lines painted on its surface to make the lanes more visible and safer. It would have sidewalks along the edge for baby strollers and jogging.

The old version of Trap Road, the only one that all of us knew, had already come to an end; one and a half lanes wide, barely enough for two cars to pass each other, where oak canopies draped invitingly over the entryway, the faithful old road that offered mystery and adventure to everywhere and nowhere in particular.

Trap Road would no longer provide a scenic Sunday drive in the country.

But evening commuters would soon be provided scenery, which they hadn't previously anticipated on their way to work, earlier in the day.

Peter laughed as he initially watched me, then he grabbed two additional traffic cones. "Let's block the road and send all the traffic up to Kellagher's house," he said, referring to Kevin Kellagher, the oldest son, friend, and classmate of ours.

As Trap Road was being transformed, a farmhouse built around 1900, and located directly across the street from the Todd property, was doing its best to live in the past. And, much to the misfortune of the Kellaghers, the home was close enough to the road that they were forced to experience much of the new construction in ways most of us weren't.

The Kellaghers' home was a beautiful old, two story, wooden house, with a partial wrap around porch, and a portico that sat near the edge of a three-acre section of farm and pasture land. High ceilings provided an outlet for hot air to escape the rooms of those yet to know central air conditioning.

Tall windows illuminated the interior, displaying fragile, wavy panes of glass, suspended by ropes and pulleys hidden within the framework.

The property was a true mini-farm with horses, ducks, and a couple of goats grazing an unspoiled, but fenced-in area. And, between the house and pasture was a long, semi-circular dirt and gravel driveway, which began on one side of the property and traversed the entire width, allowing entrance off of Trap Road from two directions.

"You get this side. Mark and I will run over the hill and do the other end. Then every car coming along will get a nice view of Mr. and Mrs. Kellagher doing whatever it is they do," I said, before breaking into a sprint up Trap Road and to the other end of the driveway.

"Don't block the road here before we get to the other side," Mark shouted to Peter, as he followed behind me up the small incline.

By the time Mark and I reached the other side of the hill, we were out of breath from running, but even more excited when we saw about a dozen extra traffic cones placed along the road bed. Several more cars were coming up that side of Kellaghers' hill, signifying that rush hour traffic was beginning to increase, and we had to act fast if we were going to pull off that prank.

Mark and I had blocked Trap Road after the last car had cleared, effectively detouring all future traffic into the Kellaghers' driveway, and through their property.

The scenic route, so to speak.

I yelled "Go ahead, Pete," before realizing I probably shouted much louder than required, and could have easily alerted the Kellaghers to our mischief.

And, before I could stop worrying about that, we heard a car coming up behind us from around the curve in Trap Road. I frantically began looking for a place to hide.

Next to and running alongside the driveway were some decorative bushes of some sort, planted at increments, but large enough individually to provide a hasty hiding place for Mark and I.

"Quick. Get behind these bushes," I demanded, as we simultaneously dove head-first, directly up, over, and behind the vegetation, as the car made the turn on Trap Road. It seemed to accelerate directly toward us as it came up the hill. Mark and I hadn't hidden ourselves exactly like we would have wanted when we saw three more vehicles right behind the first one.

Suddenly, and without warning, the initial car slammed on the brakes and seemed to almost stop in the middle of the road. The driver must have realized, just as we had, that these traffic cones weren't there yesterday. Or even that morning.

I was ready to run if the car had come to a complete stop, but then I saw the right turn signal flashing to enter the Kellagher driveway. The trailing vehicles quickly fell in line after they, too, nearly fully-stopped to make the sharp right turn.

"Dumb ass used his turn signal," I said in a whisper, bubbling with refrained laughter. Mark's face slowly transformed from fear to relief. And then neither of us could stifle the outburst of laughter.

We watched the caravan, ever so slowly, make its way along the Kellaghers' driveway. Soon it started moving over and onto the grass that was part of the yard. The cars had to make room for an old Chevy truck that was coming from the opposite direction—the old truck was followed closely, almost tailgated, by a line of cars, some with their headlights on, others using their flashers, as if trying to illuminate some sense out of the unusual roadway.

We must have had twenty or more hapless cars slowly cutting across the Kellaghers' property, while mom, dad, and kids peered out the window, watching as the progression nearly came into their living room.

When there appeared to be a break in the traffic flow, Mark and I emerged from our hiding place and ran back over the hill to rejoin Pete. He was well hidden when we arrived, but I soon heard him laughing behind some other bushes. Mark and I immediately ran over to where he was, to safely watch our drama unfold.

Cars suddenly came from every direction, with nearly all of them diverting their paths onto the adjacent lawn to avoid the oncoming traffic of the driveway-turned-highway. Many of the drivers vented their frustration making a cacophony of horns.

Suddenly, I heard a voice coming from the direction of the Kellaghers' house. I held my breath. Peter and Mark became statues, frozen with apprehension.

"What's going on, here?" growled a manly voice that I recognized as that of Mr. Kellagher. None of us moved until we heard the sound of footsteps on gravel, loud enough to be heard over the traffic pandemonium. All three of us broke into a full sprint, more or less in the same direction.

"You come back here, right now," again shouted Mr. Kellagher, but much louder than his initial command.

We ran and hid behind the large cedar trees at the bottom of Hicks Drive. From there, I knew we could safely watch for Mr. Kellagher from a safe distance, and still have plenty of time for another escape, if he decided to pursue us.

But we couldn't wait to relive the excitement of what we'd just created.

"Do you think he knew it was us?" I whispered, while trying to catch my breath. Although the sun had gone down and it was getting dark, I was still concerned he might catch a glimpse and recognize us if we ran away. But he stood in the middle of the road for a moment, turned around, and walked back to his house. Suddenly he grabbed one of the traffic cones and tossed it aside, while kicking the one next to it, into the ditch. He removed them from the street, so they were no longer diverting traffic into his yard.

"I doubt it. He woulda chased us farther if he knew who we were," Peter said. Then he asked, "Did you see all those cars going up the driveway?"

"I bet the Kellaghers thought somebody dumped the Beltway traffic on their front lawn," I said, as we headed up The Drive.

Mark suddenly burst out laughing, while making wild hand gestures that mimicked cars approaching each other, then veering off to the side at the last second.

Then all three of had to stop in the middle of the road because we were laughing too hard to walk.

The next day, I was in my room, sitting on the bed, while putting my shoes on to mow our overgrown lawn, when I heard somebody knocking on the front door.

When I opened it, I saw that it was Kevin Kellagher. Luckily, my sister and I were the only ones at home, or my parents would have suspected something was up. Kevin didn't come over very often.

I quickly slipped outside and met Kevin on the steps. An almost imperceptible grin started at the corner of his mouth, but he'd also brought with him, a facial expression that indicated something might be serious.

I didn't want to take any chances that my nosey, tattletale sister would overhear any of the conversation. I grabbed him by the arm and aggressively pulled him along with me.

"Let's go to Pete's," I said, while leading him out to the street before I let go.

But, while Kevin and I walked away for a clandestine discussion, a rapid succession of thoughts filled my head: *What did he want? What was I going to say? How much should I tell him? Was I already in trouble and he'd come to gloat?*

When we were on the pavement, Kevin asked in a very low voice, "Did you guys put those traffic cones around our driveway last night?" He paused, and then smiled.

I couldn't suppress my grin, from the sudden realization that my earlier concerns were likely unfounded, and the unexpected amount of pride that I felt in response to his inquiry.

"We sure as hell did," I said, after taking a moment to let it all come into focus.

I couldn't wait to hear Kevin's perspective of the entire event. He'd made a special trip to my house just to talk about the rush hour mayhem we'd brought down on his family. However, I'd concluded his intentions were still important, though probably not threatening.

"We were in the middle of dinner, out on the porch when the first car came by," began Kevin, with some hesitation at trying to recall the details. "I thought somebody had just made a wrong turn. And I mean, it happens all the time, especially with the road torn up in front of our house.

But then there was another car, and then more from the other end of the driveway."

Kevin's eyes suddenly got larger, and his voice louder and higher pitched. He was really excited.

"Suddenly, my dad got up from the table, shouting, 'what the hell?' as he ran out the door and into the yard." Kevin made a sweeping motion with his hand across his body, indicating his dad vacating the premises rather briskly.

We both laughed at our own images of his dad, in a panic, trying to figure out just what had happened to his dinner.

"*That's* when I knew it was you guys," Kevin said, "so I just sat at the table and kept my mouth shut." He then lowered his voice and returned to his serious tone.

"Then my mom started freaking out, cuz' my dad was yelling at her to take the kids inside, as he's headin' out the door as fast as he could.

But I think my sister, Mary Pat, also figured out it was you, cuz' she got up from the table real slow and started carrying the food back inside, real nonchalant-like. She'd kept a straight face the whole time she cleared the table."

I had to pinch myself to keep from cracking up, but Kevin then spoke excitedly.

"Before he ran out the door, I thought my dad was gonna have a stroke. That big vein in his neck stuck out, like it was gonna burst," Kevin added, while holding his index finger on his neck to dramatize his dad's predicament.

Both of us started laughing at the mental picture Kevin had portrayed at his dad's expense.

Once we'd calmed down, it appeared that Kevin had hit the main debriefing points, so I asked, "Your dad came after us. He seemed kinda pissed. Did *he* know who it was?"

"I don't think so. Well, sorta. The only thing he said before running across the yard after you was *those damned Hicks Drive boys.*"

"Please don't tell him it was me," I said. "Say it was probably Dinky Gray."

"Okay. I will. After he came back from chasing after you, and throwin' those traffic cones into the ditch, he and my mom had another martini and laughed about it. I don't think he called the cops. Nobody came by to investigate, if he did."

Kevin seemed satisfied he'd identified the perpetrators, while giving me a heads-up. Now, I wasn't worried about getting in trouble, because Kevin was a good guy and wouldn't rat us out.

He then turned around and walked home.

By mid-summer, the first of the new families had moved into the development—a final punctuation, symbolizing the end of one chapter, but

the beginning of another.
Life would never be the same on Hicks Drive.

Dale Hall (l) and Ricky Speight. Photos from Montpelier 1970.

Kehoes Under Attack, 1969

> *"I see a bad moon a-rising*
> *I see trouble on the way*
> *I see earthquakes and lightnin'*
> *I see bad times today"*[24]

Detouring traffic through the Kellaghers' yard was a tough act to follow. The adrenaline rush that I got, watching all those cars detour through our neighbor's yard, a scene that *we* had created, was becoming something that I needed on a regular basis. It appeared that was true for the other guys, as well.

But pushing the limits of the law, or increasing the amount of self-imposed danger, in and of itself, wasn't enough if my lifetime friends weren't there to share it.

By the summer of 1969, creating adventurous entertainment that brought the boys from Hicks Drive together had slowly, but progressively, become a habit, with no obvious signs of reaching a limit.

In preparation for the Independence Day celebration, I'd purchased some black market bottle rockets from the neighborhood pyromaniac, who always seemed to have access to them. But I hadn't decided what destruction and mayhem (i.e., fun) I would instigate with my new incendiary devices.

Mark, Dale, Peter, and I had launched several of them one evening in one of the construction areas, where the new homes were being built at the end of Hicks Drive. We were immediately impressed by how far the rockets would travel before bursting into a zillion sparks and then a loud bang.

I had at least thirty remaining after the test phase was completed.

As we were returning home, Peter suggested launching rockets at a neighbor's house at night— to take full advantage of our fireworks show under the cover of darkness.

It didn't require any convincing by Peter to get the rest of us on board with the plan.

The Kehoes would be our victims. The dad, Bob Kehoe, was a very affable, but nervous guy who spoke in rapid fire sentences like they were emitted from a machine gun. It was almost like a stutter—hilarious to insensitive teenage boys who could sniff out a nervous tick or an unusual speech pattern, like a shark would of blood in a swimming pool.

---

24   "Bad Moon Rising", John C. Fogerty, 1968

I discussed the plan of attack with Mark late one weekday morning, and he told me his dad had a megaphone he sometimes used on his construction job sites that could be very useful for our adventure.

"Can you borrow it?" I said.

"Probably for a night. I don't think he'll miss it."

"Let's meet up at the top of Hicks Drive in front of the Kehoes' and we'll figure out where to launch the rockets," I suggested.

I met Peter, Mark, and Dale at the designated spot just when the lightning bugs were emitting their own florescent flashes of fireworks. We all wore dark clothing for camouflage. We looked like ninja rejects of the worst kind.

Peter found some charcoal in his backyard and haphazardly smeared it all over his face. He looked like a corpse. Mark applied axle grease in a very neat, bilaterally symmetrical fashion to each side of his face, but it covered only about twenty five percent of his skin, making the remainder seem to glow in the dark. Dale and I had ski masks—hot as hell and smelling of moth balls.

I brought about a dozen or so bottle rockets and a big box of matches that ignite on practically any surface. We were as ready as we were going to be.

We split up into two teams, with Mark and me going to the backyard, while Dale and Pete stayed in the front. We split the bottle rockets between us. Mark and I had his father's megaphone.

Once Mark and I were convinced we were invisible behind some bushes, a short distance from the Kehoes' house, I flipped the *on* switch to the megaphone. It was all I could do to stifle the giggles, made worse by Mark farting.

"ALL RIGHT, BOB. THIS IS THE FBI. COME OUT WITH YOUR HANDS UP. YOUR HOUSE IS SURROUNDED," I said into the amplification device, with as close to a low, manly voice as I was capable of delivering. I knew I had to sound *official* to effectively pull off this stunt, but I was having trouble focusing.

Nothing was happening, so I put my mouth up to the megaphone again, and with an attempt at an even lower voice, I said "THIS IS YOUR LAST CHANCE, BOB. COME OUT WITH YOUR HANDS IN THE AIR."

About ten seconds later I saw a light come on inside the house.

"COME OUT, BOB. SURRENDER NOW AND NOBODY GETS HURT." I then lit the first bottle rocket and aimed it high over the house. As soon as it exploded in a shower of sparkles, Dale and Peter sent their first rocket skyward.

Mark and I were laughing so hard, my ski mask became saturated with spit around the mouth hole. I looked over at Mark with his war painted face, and I put my hand over my mouth in an attempt to keep myself quiet.

The back pressure I created from that only made my ears pop. I then lit another bottle rocket aiming directly for the lighted window in the house. It arced into the air and exploded within ten feet of my target. Perfect shot!

After we had clearly demonstrated our superior firepower by launching about four or five rockets over and directly upon the Kehoes' house, a bedroom window went up in the back.

"Okay, boys. It's time to go home," Mr. Kehoe shouted in his classic machine gun style from the second story. And, although he probably didn't know who we were, he clearly knew we were not the FBI. So I grabbed the megaphone again. "THIS IS YOUR LAST CHANCE, BOB. COME OUT WITH YOUR HANDS IN THE AIR." This time I couldn't keep from giggling between words.

"If you don't go home, I'm going to call your parents," he replied.

We'd been had. I couldn't take another week of being grounded with my sister all day, so I grabbed Mark by the arm and we ran off in the direction of his house. Running toward one of our homes probably wasn't the smartest thing we could have done to escape being identified.

We made the circuitous route through the woods behind the Kehoes' neighbor, and then met up with Dale and Peter in the cul-de-sac at the top of Hicks Drive, where we had earlier convened.

Peter was sweating profusely, causing the charcoal to run all over his face. Dale lost his ski mask somewhere in the process, and was too afraid to go back and look for it out of fear of getting caught by Mr. Kehoe.

We started walking down the street, reliving every single detail of our night raid. The longer we talked, the better the story became, as each of us swore we saw Mrs. Kehoe frantically running through the house while her home was under attack.

We gathered around the Gossip Fence, and soon our discussion drifted away from the night's rocket attack and toward planning our next adventure.

Wine Making and Poison Ivy One Week Before Freshman Year of High School, 1969

"Poison ivy, poison ivy
Late at night while you're sleepin'
Poison ivy comes a-creepin' around"[25]

Grapes have often been called *Nature's Candy*. And after you've navigated around the seeds, contorting facial muscles, and rapidly flicking your tongue to separate the grape flesh, their high sugar content qualifies them as a tasty snack in almost anybody's lunch box.

A few years before the summer of 1969, we'd discovered the nearly seventy five yards of grapevines growing in the Corboys' side yard. But there was a lot of work picking from the vine, washing off the bird poop, and staying away from the bees who liked grapes as much as we did. So, the attention these delicious goodies received from The Boys had been intermittent, at best.

Until I read an article in *The Washington Post* about making wine.

The process seemed simple enough: pick the grapes, mash them up, put the juice in a sealed bottle, add yeast, and wait a couple of months for Nature to take its course.

What could go wrong?

I would start my high school curriculum and social life in about a week. What better way to prepare for that, than having a large supply of fermented grape juice that I could bring along with me on a date? Alcoholic beverages were extremely difficult to procure, so having my own stash would be the ultimatum cool thing. I was really into *cool*.

A big part of being cool was going out on dates, and I was eagerly anticipating the Friday night football variety, particularly since a neighbor of mine had a car, and we'd already double-dated a few times that summer.

It took nearly two hours of picking in the hot, August sun to gather a full Giant Food grocery bag of the Corboys' grapes. Yellow jackets were <u>swarming everywhere</u>, like they typically did at the end of summer, preparing

[25] Poison Ivy, Written by Jerry Leiber and Mike Stoller, 1959

for the next generation of swarming pests. Yellow jackets *really* liked grapes and were hesitant to surrender them without at least a fly-over, somewhere near the head of their competition.

The vines were a mixture of white grapes at one end, red at the other. But I didn't discriminate, thinking wine was wine. Who would care once they were all mashed together into one delectable and fermented concoction?

With the grocery bag finally filled to the top, I walked home, hoping on a beautiful, but warm Sunday afternoon, that nobody would notice a gangly kid strolling up Hicks Drive, toting a grocery bag full of grapes. That wouldn't have been cool.

When I got to the house, I placed my stash near the basement door so I could enter through the kitchen in the back, go directly downstairs, surreptitiously retrieve the bag and then start making wine.

But once I was home, I saw that my mom was watching some silly animal show without a plot she'd have to follow, my sister was on the floor of the living room playing with a couple of dolls, and my dad was in the basement doing something on the drill-press.

Making *Chateau de Ricky* would have to wait.

Monday arrived slowly. I was already impatient, thinking I'd lost a critical day of fermentation time, but both parents would be away at work. If I could figure out a clever method to keep my sister, Robin, away for an hour or so, then I'd be on my way to finishing this project.

I woke up earlier than usual, thinking that the storage location of my vintage would be critical, and there was no way I could do that at home. So, why not bury it somewhere safe, somewhere private, where nobody would steal it? Somewhere dark?

I skipped breakfast and went straight down into the basement to start squashing grapes. But, before I descended the stairs, I grabbed the colander, a huge plastic biscuit-making bowl, and three large, glass, soda bottles that were long forgotten, having been stuffed under the sink. Fortunately, the caps of the latter had been screwed back on and were relatively clean.

With my equipment in hand, I looked around the messy basement, stacked with junk my dad couldn't part with. I found a table near the wall: the same surface I'd used to assemble model cars and airplanes in the recent past. I placed my armload of material on the table, and then went outside to fetch my stash of grapes. They were right where I'd left them, hidden under a bush near the basement door. I grabbed them and went back inside.

I filled the makeshift washing bowl with grapes and held them under the laundry room faucet for a minute or so. As almost an afterthought, I rinsed out the glass bottles, as well. One can't be too fussy when making wine.

Within minutes, I was mashing and straining, before pouring a mixture of sweet white and red grape squeezins into the glass "wine bottles".

It was so easy I wondered why I hadn't done it before. I filled one

Pepsi bottle, then the next, and then finally topped off my third and final one.

After I'd added an unmeasured quantity of yeast, I made sure the caps were on as tight as I could safely secure them without stripping the threads, and then stashed them under some old clothes tossed beneath the stairway leading up to the kitchen. But I knew I couldn't keep them there very long. Upon finding new "valuables", Dad would poke around every possible storage spots, leaving no hiding place ever safe in the long term.

But, if there was one person I could trust with my secret, and help me find a suitable storage location for my wine cellar, it was Rick Duncan.

Rick always seemed to have a solution for every problem. And, relevant to my situation, he had access to privacy, since he was the sole occupant of his basement, and we could operate virtually undetected. His parents had volumes of research books in the house if we needed them— and most critically, he didn't like wine.

For several years, the Duncans and a few of the other residents on Hicks Drive, had milk delivered to their door about three times a week. The milkman would leave the bottles in a semi-insulated box that sat on their customers' front porches. Sort of like temporary refrigerators.

But, tragically, by the late sixties, home milk delivery was declining, as grocery stores became more convenient and cost effective, being a one-stop-shop for all grocery items. But, when deliveries ceased, the customers often kept the insulated boxes. At least the Duncans did. And Rick and I found theirs hidden under the basement stairs.

"Look what I found!" Rick shouted, as he began to dig out the Thompson's Honor Dairy milk box. A suitable container for my stash.

"Wine could be kept in that thing, forever!" I said, in a squeakily pubescent voice.

Rick tugged and pulled at the milk box until it was free from the pile, before placing it on the ironing board. Inside of it was a cardboard cap off an old chocolate milk container, a single thumbtack, and two dead, desiccated spiders.

"This'll hold those wine bottles perfectly," I said. "I'll bury this box somewhere, and soon I'll have some wine, Rick," I said, with a wide grin.

"I don't think anybody will notice it's gone," Rick said. "We quit getting milk delivered ever since you and I started intercepting chocolate milk before my mom could get it off the porch." We laughed about the recent memory. Stealing just-delivered chocolate milk from the boxes tasted even better than plucking it from the fridge.

As I was carrying my prize down Hicks Drive, I briefly considered burying it in my backyard, but I knew my dad would notice every molecule of displaced dirt from the hole I'd dig. Rick had said his yard wouldn't work, either.

Just as I'd reached home, I came up with a great idea. I'd bury the wine box in a poison ivy patch, somewhere not on Hicks Drive—go home and wash off the blister-causing poison, and then return when grape juice had turned into wine. Nobody would dare search for treasure in a poison ivy patch. And if they did, they would pay a heavy and uncomfortable price.

I knew a perfect spot I'd found and ridden my bike past a hundred times—a poison ivy patch so overgrown that nobody would even see it from the path, one accessible only via bicycle or on foot. It was right next to Cochrans' house on the bridle path that cut through the woods from Beulah Road to Brookside Lane.

Since I couldn't drive, it would require two trips to bury the wine. The first trip, with shovel in hand, I would walk nearly a mile and dig the hole. Then I would return home, carry the wine-laden box to the hole in the middle of the poison ivy, drop it in, and kick dirt in to fill the hole. Go home, take a shower, done.

But I had to wait until Saturday to do the work. My mom had promised my free lawn mowing services to a friend she used to work with, so two whole days were spent pushing around a lawn mower and raking leaves for somebody I didn't know, and for money I'd never receive. I suspected my mom pocketed the dough, but she would never admit it.

Saturday finally arrived. And every step of this plan went without a hitch. I carried the shovel a mile, dug a hole, went home, retrieved the box and carried to my secret hiding place, buried it, and then headed for home.

I walked home slower than I usually did. I was tired from carrying the heavy wine container, lackadaisically thinking about its contents, and anxious for everything to fall into place as I had planned.

As soon as I'd gotten comfortable in my bedroom, I heard the phone ring.

It was Rick Duncan and he wanted me to come over to his house and listen to the recording he'd made on his new cassette tape recorder. I was at his place in five minutes.

When I returned home later in the evening, I began to notice I was scratching more than normal. It started with a couple places on my legs, and then it was my arms.

By Monday morning, I was covered head-to-toe in poison ivy. I had that stuff in places on my body I didn't know existed until that day.

I probably should have gone to the hospital for a severe allergic reaction, but my parents thought Calamine lotion would cure any skin rash. So, the treatment began in earnest, because the first day of high school started in less than twenty-four hours.

I was solid Calamine pink, from top to bottom, when I entered the front door of James Madison on the first day of school.

New penny loafers, matching shirt and pants for the first time since June, and a fresh haircut couldn't hide the stigma of a pink freshman.

The first day of school we had to report to Home Room at 7:45, to receive our class schedules and take care of other, mostly administrative, tasks.

My assigned seat placed me directly across from Frances, a pretty girl who talked a lot and seemed to get a lot of attention from the other students. But I was so self-conscious about my new skin condition, I was afraid to even strike up a conversation.

I imagined other students clearing a path when I walked down the halls, afraid of contracting a near fatal case of poison ivy, or whatever else they thought I had. Truthfully, I'd only hoped it was fatal.

I was reluctant to initiate a conversation with *any* of the girls in my classes, for fear of them noticing my severe skin rash, and then me being ostracized for eternity.

As the agonizing hours passed, the temperature in the un-air-conditioned school increased.

I soon learned that when Calamine lotion gets warmer, it begins to stink. So, by two o'clock, I was not only an extremely uncomfortable and sweaty, rosy-colored freshman, I smelled like Grandma's medicine cabinet.

The self-inflicted torture lasted for two more days until the blisters from the poison ivy began to dry up and wither away. Calamine stayed on for an extra day to make sure the rash didn't return.

Even today, the smell of that stuff makes me extremely nauseous. And, when I see poison ivy, I quickly grab the closest herbicide, for its certain eradication.

But, despite this totally unexpected turn of events, wine was waiting for me in the woods, football season was winding down toward the final game, and it was against our bitter rival, the Statesmen from George C Marshall.

And I *finally* had a date, again.

There was only one kid in our neighborhood who'd never contracted poison ivy, a real freak of nature. He could not only forget to bathe after exposure to it, he could bathe *in* it and not break out in that dreadful rash.

So, I promised Mike Corboy, that if he would retrieve my stash, I'd give him an entire bottle as reward for his efforts. A quart of free wine for digging a hole seemed like a reasonable offer. And, besides, the grapes came from his own yard, so it was the least I could do.

Mike agreed, and I was soon left with two bottles of cloudy liquid that I was determined to try. And if my date, Carol Beatson, was adventurous enough, she could have some, too.

She wasn't.

As soon as I opened the glass container of my stash, liquid began to spew out of the top and onto the floorboard in the backseat of my friend, Steve's car. And it smelled like rotten grapes.

Fortunately, Carol's clothes were completely spared from the effervescent eruption, and Madison beat a very well-coached team in Marshall, by a score of thirteen to twelve.

But the evening was a bust.

No better way to ward off the romance than the stench of rotten fruit.

I gave the last bottle of *Chateau de Ricky* to Peter, who reported a mild case of diarrhea after trying a large sample.

Real, honest to goodness wine consumption for me, would have to wait another year, when I received a fake ID from a classmate who provided Xerox copies of his brother's draft card.

But, at least *Boone's Farm Strawberry Hill* smelled better than *Chateau de Ricky*. And it didn't itch.

Part III

Girls, Girls, Girls

Lee Ann about 1972.
Photo provided by Lee Ann Andronico.

First Girlfriend, Make it Count, 1970

"It's the time of the season
When love runs high
And this time, give it to me easy
And let me try with pleasured hands"[26]

In Vienna, Virginia the inaugural Earth Day on April 22, 1970 was a combination work detail and pep rally for the volunteers congregating at the Vienna Community Center. The high school students at James Madison were released early that day to beautify our little piece of the Earth, and establish a new way of looking at how we were taking care of our home.

A large crowd gathered for live music, proper instructions for picking up trash, and a few words of inspiration from town leaders, before we were released to perform our civic duty.

It must have worked.

I was an awkward freshman, just trying to fit in somewhere, and enjoy the company of two friends, Steve Carter and Karen Ferguson, who were dating each other at that time. We were comfortably stretched out on a blanket, close enough to the stage to hear what was going on, but far enough away for us to have a conversation without shouting.

Suddenly, I saw this tall, beautiful brunette purposefully walking in our direction, like she knew exactly where she was going. She had the longest legs I had ever seen.

Steve glanced up and quickly got to his feet, as this lovely girl abruptly stopped in front of him.

"Ricky, this is Lee Ann, the girl I told you about in my Western Civ class," he said very graciously.

I stood up and couldn't decide whether to shake her hand or not. I nodded, mumbled *hi*, and motioned for her to join us, by pointing at the ground. *Yeah, that could've been a little smoother*, I thought, but it was too late to fix it.

Fortunately for me, she didn't run away as fast as she could.

---

26   "Time of the Season", Rod Argent, 1968

We remained at the Community Center for nearly an hour—listening to motivating words from local politicians, music, and litter protocol. The four of us sat on our blanket, taking it all in, while we got acquainted.

Lee Ann wanted to know all about me: family, favorite sports teams, pizza toppings that I preferred, and when I'd get my driver's license. I told her that I needed to wait another year, but she informed me that she'd be sixteen and would get *her* driver's license in six months.

When she spoke, she looked inquisitively into my eyes, and held the gaze until I responded to her, as if she was sincerely interested in what I was saying.

Within a week, Lee Ann and I were talking to each other every day via telephone, which quickly led to a real date. Steve had a driver's license and a car, so he, Karen, Lee Ann, and I frequently went to the Lee Highway Drive-In Theater in Merrifield, before grabbing a pizza at the one and only Pizza Fair—or we just hung out at Karen's house listening to *In-a-gadda-da-vida* or The Beatles' *White Album*.

Lee Ann and I had somehow become a couple, and the more time I spent with her, the more confidence I gained in myself from the experience. I was proud to be with her, and to be seen in her company, strolling down the halls at school between classes, at Tyson's Corner Mall, or the Vienna Theatre. Arm-in-arm with Lee Ann just put a little bounce in my step.

Until Lee Ann got her license, and we able to get a ride, we used whatever transportation we could find in order to see each other as frequently as we could—bicycle, borrow a neighbor's motorbike, or walk.

"Let's go swimming," Lee Ann said, not so much as a suggestion, but more of a directive. We'd just spent several hours at my non-air-conditioned house, trying to stay cool, while sharing details to each other we previously hadn't divulged: strange family members, emotional wants and needs, and what we wanted to be when we grew up.

We actually accomplished more than we should have, because my annoying-and-always-in-the-way little sister loudly and often knocked on my closed bedroom door, breaking whatever momentum Lee Ann and I may have generated.

"Yeah, we should," I responded. "Robin's never going to leave us alone, and going for a swim will get us out of here." My voice filled with frustration of the moment, and relief that there was an alternative.

We decided to head to Cardinal Hill Swim Club, a nearly new facility close to Lee Ann's home. My parents were still at work and unavailable as taxis for teens, so we decided to walk to Lee Ann's house, where she would change into her bathing suit, and we'd proceed to the pool from there. She lived less than two miles from me.

Before we'd made it halfway to Lee Ann's house, we were tired from walking in the heat, and I was ready for Plan B.

When a car came by on Old Court House Road, I stuck out my

thumb. The driver made extra effort to maintain his speed and, as he drove away, he did his very best to pretend I didn't exist. Then I put my thumb out again for the next approaching car, while trying to display a little more salesmanship body language: chest out, good posture, eye contact. Same result. And again. And then, about three more times.

"Can I try it?" Lee Ann asked, while flashing her big, brown eyes in a playful, yet determined expression. I certainly couldn't let my girlfriend do something I should be doing for her. Hitch-hiking was not for girls. It was a man's game.

"Let me do it one more time," I replied, trying not to sound defensive or patronizing.

"Okay, but it's hot as hell out here, and I told my mom I'd be home by four, and I'd call her when I got to the house."

Unfortunately for hitch hikers like us, there was never an abundance of traffic on Old Courthouse Road in the early seventies. Sometimes ten minutes might pass without a single car. But soon after I had bought some time with Lee Ann to solve this dilemma by promising a final attempt, I heard another car rapidly approaching. I looked up and saw that it was a middle-aged lady driving a white convertible.

As she approached, I impulsively pulled the pants leg of my swim suit up as far as I could without ripping a seam, and stuck out my newly exposed leg. The lady slowed down, turned to look at me; her eyes initially fixed on mine, but then to my bare leg. She suddenly started laughing.

When she'd slowed the car to a near-stop, adjacent to where Lee Ann and I were standing, I saw she was wearing a flowing dress and scarf that seemed to match her car. Once she'd stopped laughing, she continued to smile at us with such a friendly expression that I knew right away we'd found our ride.

Before I approached the car, I glanced over my shoulder and saw that Lee Ann was flashing that beautiful smile.

"Need a ride, I guess?" The lady laughed again. "Get in," she said, while giving both of us the once-over to determine if we were Bonnie and Clyde.

"I can't believe you did that," Lee Ann whispered in my ear, as I opened the passenger side door to let her in. I climbed into the back seat with her.

"Where to?" the lady asked, while finally trying to quell her laughter. Lee Ann told her Fairway Drive was our destination. So, immediately after I closed the door, our new friend stepped on the gas, pushing us back into our seats just enough to make it exciting.

"That was the funniest thing I have seen in a long time. Very creative." The lady slightly turned her head to address us directly behind her.

"I probably wouldn't have stopped without the leg show," she continued, as she slowed the car through the S-turn at Wolf Trap Creek.

"Nobody would stop and pick us up, so I tried something else," was all I could say.

We made our way along Old Courthouse with the wind in our hair and not a care in the world. And in a few short minutes, we turned onto Creek Crossing Road and reached our destination at Fairway Drive. The car pulled over to the side of the road in front of Lee Ann's house and then stopped, I pushed the front seat forward, opened the passenger side door and we got out.

"You two take care," the lady said, and then, when the car door was closed, she stepped on the accelerator and sped off like she was in a hurry.

We briefly watched the lady speed away, before Lee Ann took my hand and led me up her driveway. Soon after we got inside the carport door, she released my hand and immediately headed to her bedroom to change, while I waited for her in the den. This was the room where we usually hung out when I visited. It had a stereo, television, and much more privacy than was offered at my house.

Before I could get comfortable on the sofa, I caught a glimpse of Lee Ann's feet, out of the corner of my eye, just as she'd reached the landing of the split-level home. With just three steps down the stairs, she came into full view, wearing only a white bikini and a smile. She now had my full attention.

I got up off the couch and began walking in her direction. I guess we couldn't resist finally being all alone and undisturbed, so we starting making out while standing in the middle of the room.

Suddenly, she paused and looked into my eyes, before she softly whispered, "Why don't we stay here and get some sun in the backyard, instead of walking all the way to the pool?"

She didn't have to ask twice.

Lee Ann's invitation to remain at home, alone with me, sent my mind spinning with hopes and dreams, about where our cozy get together would lead. We'd matured considerably since we'd first met, both physically and emotionally, but I still had some of those nagging teenaged doubts about what others thought of me.

All doubts temporarily disappeared, as I intently watched Lee Ann walk away. I eagerly followed right behind her, as we ascended the short flight of stairs into the kitchen, where we fixed some ice-water to take with us. We then went outside, found some chairs on the patio, and made ourselves comfortable.

In the short time we'd sun-bathed, we managed to solve all of the world's problems: pollution, Vietnam, Civil Rights, men on the moon, and acne. And, while we discussed those weighty topics, I didn't miss any opportunity to admire my lovely girlfriend, who seemed to get prettier the longer we talked.

When it was time to get out of the sun for a while and go inside, Lee Ann stood up and asked me for a piggy-back ride, complaining that her foot was bothering her from the long walk we'd made from my house. A subtle pang of guilt unexpectedly hit me about her injury, because we'd walked so far before I'd flagged us a ride.

I think Lee Ann was well aware of that, perhaps using it to her advantage.

I walked over to where she was standing, turned around with my back toward her, slightly bent my knees, and she climbed aboard.

The skin-to-skin contact was warm, but exhilarating.

Then she started tickling me.

I nearly dropped her, as I reached for the door-knob. She continued to dig her fingers into my side, but I finally managed to open the door.

But, the mood had suddenly shifted from wishful anticipation to childhood playfulness.

Once I'd closed the door behind us, I didn't want to release my beautiful rider from her impromptu saddle, so I started running for the stairs and back into the den. I started prancing around the house, horsey style in my bathing suit, with a barely dressed girl on my back who was trying to hold on while laughing hysterically.

Lee Ann wanted to play. I was more than willing to be her playmate.

We must have been quite a sight—one teenager riding on the back of another, both stripped down to the barest of essentials.

I practically sprinted from one end of the room to the other, as Lee Ann continued to jab me in the ribs to make me laugh, or run faster. I wasn't sure which one. Then I started hopping up and down like a bucking bronco. Lee Ann started screaming, as we continued this strange, adolescent courtship in the comfort and privacy of her den.

Then her Dad walked through the door.

He stopped, slowly placed his briefcase on the floor next to his feet, defiantly put both hands on his hips, and stared at us.

It seemed to take about half a second for him to process the image of his nearly naked daughter on the back of a boy he barely knew, who was wearing not much more clothing than her. The cognitive delay was immediately followed by disturbing recognition, as his eyebrows lowered into a frown, lips tightly pursed. Then he folded his arms, very slowly—like he was restraining himself from doing something he'd regret.

I distinctly heard Lee Ann suck all the air out of the room and into her lungs, and then held it there for the longest time.

About half of my life flashed before my eyes under the gaze of her dad, as he repeatedly turned his eyes from Lee Ann to me, then back again. He took another step forward, and looked straight into his daughter's eyes. "Lee Ann, go to your room," he firmly said.

I slowly, but immediately lowered Lee Ann to the ground while looking around the den for my lost clothing. I'd never wanted to leave somewhere more than that moment.

In her embarrassment, Lee Ann couldn't make eye contact with her father, nor me, so she just sprinted up to her bedroom on the second level. I deliberately did my best not to watch her, as she departed.

Suddenly, I found myself alone with the dad, his eyes fixed on his daughter's retreat, without as much as a glance in my direction.

Adrenaline was still coursing from the horse-play with Lee Ann, but now it was solely used for the purpose of getting the hell out of there.

Mere moments later, though, I breathed a long sigh of relief, as her dad graciously left the room for me to get out. I picked up my shirt and shoes off the floor and sat on the couch just long enough to put them on. I somehow restrained myself from sprinting out the door, thinking that might do more damage than good.

I didn't return for about a month, naively thinking everything would be forgotten. Eventually, and with each successive visit, it got a little less awkward. And, perhaps best of all, her dad never told her mom, which cut our anxiety in half.

Lee Ann and I dated for nearly two years—almost a lifetime, really, by high school standards. And, during that time, we matured into the young adults neither of us had been before we'd met. We spent as much time together as we could, leaving more of our childhood behind with each moment.

Toward the end of our second year in high school, we gradually began to go our separate ways. We never had a fight, or even a loud disagreement. We hadn't pushed each other aside, because we'd found someone better; we just drifted apart, like teenagers are supposed to do, I guess.

But there was no doubt that the close relationship we experienced as a young couple gave me the confidence and self-esteem I'd need for adulthood.

Last Stop in *Cans for Christmas Drive*, 1969. Park Terrace Apartments. Behind the old Drug Fair in Vienna.

The Girl From Ipanema

"Tall and tan and young and lovely
The girl from Ipanema goes walking and
When she passes, each one she passes goes"[27]

I approached the last apartment building of the night, feeling extremely confident and full of Christmas joy, knowing that our *Cans for Christmas* food drive had been a tremendous success. It was the final night of the competition, with everything on the line, and I'd been red hot the entire evening. I'd already collected more donated food than my teammates, and by the end of the evening, we'd convinced ourselves we would win the competition in a landslide.

Our last stop was Park Terrace Apartments, located just behind Drug Fair in Vienna. I'd made a routine of starting on the third floor of each building, so I wouldn't have to lug my donations up the steps, but rather, gently tote them down when I landed a big score.

When I'd reached the top floor of the final building, I knocked on the door of the first residence—but there was no answer. I had much better success at the next, where an older lady handed me six or seven cans of various items. I placed them in my large canvas carrying bag. I proceeded down to the second floor with the same initial result—no answer at Door Number One. But when I knocked on the second door, I was immediately greeted with a very pleasant surprise.

A young girl, probably a year or so younger than I was, answered on the third knock. She opened the door wide enough that I could clearly see that she and her family had been enjoying a late dinner. The aroma from the food wasn't something I'd recognized, but was very appealing, nevertheless. It reminded me of something the Canciglia's might've prepared—a delicious combination of Sicilian and Greek cuisine, perhaps.

Despite the dinner interruption, I stood there, beginning my spiel, as the girl smiled a perfect row of shiny white teeth.

She didn't say a word, but before I'd finished speaking, took a half step back, then made a rapid *come on in* motion with her hand. When I'd crossed the threshold, she reached past me and shut the door.

---

27   "Girl From Ipanema", Antônio Carlos Jobim & Vinicius de Moraes; Norman Gimbel (English lyrics), 1964

This was the first time I'd been invited inside a potential donor's home, so I took a moment to glance around the room, before resuming my presentation.

I finished while in their foyer, and then asked for a donation. The expression on her face indicated she understood some, but, perhaps, not everything that I'd said.

I hadn't been in such a joyous Christmas spirit since the time I saw my first bike under our tinsel decorated tree, soon after we moved to Hicks Drive in the early sixties.

I'd started high school in 1969, just a few months before volunteering for the Christmas benefit. I was immediately impressed, sometimes overwhelmed, by the enormity of about two thousand students, all in the same building at the same time. We had an outstanding football team that year, and it was easy to get caught up in all of the emotions of that. There were screaming pep rallies before every game, and one or two Division I college prospects, who were clearly the best players on the field every Friday night. It was a great time to be a Warhawk from James Madison.

My friend Steve, who lived across the street from me, was a junior that year. And soon after school started, he joined the Madison Club, an after-school, mostly philanthropic group that performed various charity events throughout the year.

Just before the Christmas break, the Madison Club launched a *Cans for Christmas* food drive to provide for needy families in the community. Their food gathering mission was astutely turned into a competition to see who could collect the most canned goods the week leading up to the holiday. Steve asked me to help him win the prize, and I was excited to do so. Newly discovered school pride, a light dusting of snow the previous week to put us all in the Christmas spirit, and a friendly competition among my high school friends, was all that was needed to get me motivated for charity work.

So, instead of studying that week, I spent several evenings and nights canvassing the neighborhoods in search of canned food. Our presentation was quite simple. We would knock on somebody's door, introduce ourselves as students from Madison High School and give our sales pitch for them to fork over as many cans as possible. Most were all too eager to get rid of things like meat paste or *Veg-All Mixed Vegetables*, which someone in their family had mistakenly purchased with good intent. Add *Cream of Broccoli Soup,* and the possibilities for donations were practically endless. Where appropriate, we would divulge the part about it being a competition among the students for some unspecified prize. There was something about competitive games that stirred the blood of even the most slothful couch potato. The marketing geniuses at the *National Football League* learned that lesson a long time ago.

For five consecutive nights, our hunt for cans was a success. Our group, consisting of Steve, his younger brother Greg, and I, would fill the trunk of Steve's Ford Falcon with everything from green beans to Spam, donated by generous families throughout Vienna. And, regardless of the outcome, everyone greeted us with a smile when we arrived and a "Merry Christmas" when we left their front porch stoop.

The girl continued to look at me, her expression suggesting that it was *I* who should make the next move, since it was *she* who'd invited me into her home.

"Would you *please* make a donation of food for our Cans for Christmas Drive?" I asked her again. A wave of thoughtful understanding suddenly swept across her face. Perhaps it was the emphasis on *please*.

Suddenly the woman seated at the dinner table, presumably the young girl's mother, turned and said something to her daughter that sounded like it was spoken in Spanish. Then the man, perhaps her father, said something, also in Spanish. The next thing I knew, everybody except me, was rapidly chattering back and forth in Spanish with a steady increase in volume of their conversation.

After their initial exchange, I didn't know if I should stay, or gracefully bow out and thank them for their time.

They continued talking, glanced back at me, and then talked some more, but louder.

I had no idea if they were buying into what I was saying, or trying to figure out a way to get rid of me.

On the other hand, I'd never been in a non-English speaking home, so I was really in no hurry to leave. Rather than being intimidated by all of the shouting and bantering, I was more interested in seeing how it would play itself out.

Then all of a sudden, the girl turned and briskly walked to the kitchen. She stopped and reached into a cabinet above the stove and then grabbed a bag of something, turned on her toes like she was a ballet dancer, and pranced across the room, back to where I was standing.

I just stood there taking it all in—the girl, her Spanish chattering parents, the aromatic dinner waiting on the table, and a black and white TV, playing softly in the background.

There was that smile again, as the girl looked me straight in the eyes and proudly handed me the bag she had gathered from the kitchen. I reached out my hand and gently received it, while never removing my gaze from her face. Once I had a grip on the donated item, I looked down to see what it was that I'd been holding.

It was a bag of chocolate cookies.

I quickly thanked her and her family for their generosity, but then tried to explain, by making odd-looking hand gestures, that what I really needed was canned food.

I reached down and carefully placed the bag at my feet—so as to not break any cookies; I needed both hands for what I was about to attempt. The best hand-delivered communication for canned food that I could muster was to spread apart the fingers of each hand and oppose them in such a way that it might look like a… can. But it appeared more like I was trying to grab hold of something invisible between them. That clumsy attempt didn't work, at all. So, I tried to talk louder, reasoning that volume could somehow compensate for clarity.

The dad, who momentarily had looked away from the television to check me out, then returned to his meal.

The mom focused her attention back to the dining room table, as well, signaling my time was up.

"Thank you for coming," the girl said, in perfect English, but with a slight accent.

Her words were a poetic end to the evening.

I thanked the girl and her family once again for their generosity, while I'd reached down for the bag I had placed on the floor by my feet.

I was all smiles as I repeatedly bowed to them graciously—thinking that was the appropriate response.

Throughout it all, I couldn't take my eyes off of the attractive young girl with the long brown hair, her beautiful smile, and those graceful ballerina moves.

She looked like an angel.

Almost reluctantly, I left the apartment with chocolate cookies in hand, and headed to the car, without knocking on the two remaining doors of the apartment building.

Those nice people, probably recent arrivals in my country, had graciously invited a total stranger into their home. They'd trusted me enough to do so, in the presence of their young daughter.

Then, they gave me a Christmas present.

All I had to do was figure out a way to ask for it.

Merry Christmas from the Pretty Girl Who Moved Into the Neighborhood, Karen Ferguson.

A Pretty Girl Moves Into The Neighborhood, 1970

"I ought to say no, no, no sir (Mind if move in closer?)
At least I'm gonna say that I tried (What's the sense of hurtin' my pride?)
I really can't stay (Baby don't hold out)
Baby it's cold outside"[28]

Even in the rural countryside of Hicks Drive, we witnessed first-hand the explosive growth of Fairfax County throughout the sixties. And while none of the guys in the neighborhood were happy with the new development of The Trails, which took away our baseball field at the end of the street, we found ways to remain optimistic. One was the Trap Road traffic diversion through the Kellagher's yard during their dinnertime.

The other positive thing that came from the demolition of life as we knew it in Todd's field, was the arrival of a very pretty girl, Karen, and her really hip family: the Fergusons.

Karen had brown hair, a friendly smile, gorgeous brown eyes, and a fun-loving personality that made her an instant hit. She was our age, liked the same music, and generally seemed like a good fit in the neighborhood. But, while she was certainly adventurous, she was not borderline juvenile delinquent, like the rest of us.

Even her little brother, Jimmy, was cool.

But unlike the other parents on Hicks Drive, the Fergusons liked to party. They went out to dinner at Westwood Country Club and the finer restaurants in Washington. They went to the Kennedy Center to see the latest play or catch the trendiest musicals. They stayed out late and came home happy, nearly every weekend.

And, for those outings, they often left the children at home.

New Year's Eve 1970 began with extreme anticipation. The parental Fergusons were going to a party, while Karen and Jimmy were staying home. But the left-at-home children were planning their own party, and several kids in the neighborhood were invited.

I couldn't wait. I'm almost certain that I showered, might have even applied some Brut cologne for what promised to be an eventful evening.

---

28   Baby It's Cold Outside, Frank Loesser, 1944

And the weather was perfect—low thirties with a slight dusting of snow to provide additional holiday scenery to an already festive landscape.

About twelve to fifteen kids showed up for their party that night. Most were in their mid-to-late teens, like the boys from Hicks Drive. Two or three may have been older: two attractive girls and a boy, from Karen's private school in McLean. But the girl who attracted the most attention of everyone at the party was the host, Karen. She wore an eye-catching Christmas dress, and her hair was arranged with just enough alluring curl to highlight her gorgeous face.

For most of the party's duration, I'd wanted to direct the focus of my conversation toward this interesting girl, who intrigued our neighborhood so much. And I found myself liking her more and more as the evening progressed. When we spoke, she made me feel like I was the only person in the room, and I was most attentive when she talked about how much she enjoyed her new home and neighbors.

Most of the kids brought their own alcohol to the party, typically no more than a six-pack to be divided two or three ways. But everybody at one point or another had a drink in their youthful clutches. Nobody happened to get drunk. I guess those days arrived soon enough after a bit more practice.

It was a socially well-adapted group of kids, so everyone seemed to enjoy each other's company, and could do so without excess liquid courage.

Against the front wall of the rec room, where most of the partiers had congregated, the Fergusons had one of those large, furniture-like stereos with the radio/record player console in the center, and a speaker built into the cabinet on each end. Woodstock had happened just a year before, so we enjoyed reminiscing about the Greatest Rock Event Ever—which we didn't actually attend—by listening to Hendrix, The Who, Janis, and the rest, on a variety of records.

The hours passed too quickly, and soon all of us gathered around the television to watch the ball drop at Times Square. The stereo was now off, with only the sound of Guy Lombardo's band doing their annual presentation. When the final seconds approached, Karen, who was sitting next to me on the sofa, turned and gave me a lengthy kiss. I was surprised at first, but recovered without an awkward delay.

"We should do that again, soon," Karen suggested, as the clock struck midnight, immediately followed by Lombardo's rendition of *Auld Lang Sein*. I smiled, nodded in quick agreement, and immediately contemplated where and when that would happen. *Did she want me to make a move now, like two of the other couples already had?*

I just sat there, paralyzed.

One of the girls from Karen's school and her date, were having no hesitations about getting to know each other a little better. And the other couple had gotten out of their seats and left the room holding hands, going who-knows-where.

I just sat there, on the couch, next to lovely Karen, with my confidence going in the wrong direction.

By 12:30, the party-goers began gathering coats and gloves in preparation for their journeys back to reality. I didn't want to leave, yet. I had just gotten acquainted with a girl I was now very attracted to, and all I could think about was Karen's suggestion about going a bit farther.

But the opportunity was lost, the party officially over.

Yeah, I walked home along with Roger, Peter, Dale, and Mark. And we slowly but surely made our way up the street, stopping only to pick up some fresh snow, pack it into a ball, and throw it somewhere. Everywhere, really.

But Karen was the only thing on my mind, as I was strolling up the street. I wanted to go back. I messed up, and I knew it.

When I reached home, I continued walking around the corner of our house and through the side gate toward the back door. I knew the interrogation would commence once I was inside, before I could lock the door behind me. So, I was planning my responses while I walked.

I slid the key into the lock, turned the handle, and opened the door. Actually, nobody was there to greet me.

Miraculously, my parents had gone to bed before I got home. That had happened only one other time, when the whole family, except me, had the Hong Kong Flu. I arrived home one day about eight in the evening, and everyone had gone to bed with fever and the chills.

I crept into my room as quietly as I could.

I lay in my bed and just stared at the wall for a bit, again having that itch. I didn't want the night to end like that.

So, I then planned how I was going to silently open my bedroom window, climb out of it and down the tree next to the house. And then I considered how I would get back home again without being caught.

After twenty minutes of listening to my mom snore like a drunken truck driver, I climbed out of bed. The hardwood floors under my feet creaked with every step, so I crawled on my hands and knees over to my bedroom window and waited. So far, so good.

I then quietly stood up, unlocked the window, opened it as wide as I could and climbed out, reaching with my lead foot to find the branch of the tree that would allow me to keep going.

After much probing around in the dark, I finally located a foothold. After that, I knew it was easy work, so I closed the window and descended.

Once on the ground, I started walking rapidly, then built up speed until I was running down the street, anticipating seeing Karen again.

Within minutes, I was standing in the Fergusons' front yard, but excitement immediately changed to disappointment when I saw the parents' car in the driveway.

However, the front porch light was off, and Karen's window was directly over the front door.

The Fergusons' house was made of brick, with alternating layers protruding out to make a sort of three-dimensional visual effect. But that same 3D structure also offered a built-in ladder at the corners, and one of those corners was only five feet away from Karen's bedroom window.

All I had to do was straddle the corner of the house while ascending the step-like bricks that stuck out no more than an inch. Then, when I got to window-level on the corner, I'd reach out to the ledge, grab the window and pull myself inside.

I walked over to the corner of the house and looked up to see how far I needed to reach with my arms, while simultaneously stepping on my initial foothold.

Climbing the corner was, actually, easier than I anticipated. But once I'd reached the proper elevation of nearly ten feet, I learned that letting go of a nice safe place, only to reach out toward danger, made it very difficult. Falling was not an option, at least not where the only thing to catch me was a concrete sidewalk below.

But, under the influence of the powerful New Year's Eve cocktail of regret and testosterone, I found the courage to grab onto the window ledge while releasing my hand from the corner. Suddenly, I was standing on top of the front door frame and holding on to the ledge of the window.

I tapped on the glass.

Once again, but louder.

Then I banged on the glass really loud. The window suddenly jolted open.

"What the hell are you doing?" Karen looked on in astonishment at this lower primate hanging onto her window sill for dear life.

"Hi," I said. "Can I come in?"

I didn't wait for an answer. And, luckily, she didn't try to stop me, as I climbed into her bedroom as quietly as I could, when my immediate goal was *terra firma*.

"My parents are right down the hall and they just got home, so they're still awake," she sharply whispered at me, to make sure I understood the severity of her situation.

But, as she was making her case that I would soon be on my way, I couldn't help but notice again how radiant she was, and how infatuated with her I had become. These distractions quickly made me ignore everything she was saying.

So, what I heard was more like "I'm so glad you're here, and I can't wait to get started."

Even in the near total darkness of her bedroom, Karen could see I was gazing at her, so she instinctively grabbed her bathrobe that was lying on her bed and pulled it tightly around her.

Then, she surprised me with a passionate kiss on the lips, an even better one than the previous at midnight, holding my face with both of her delicate and warm hands.

I could have died right then without any complaints.

I had successfully snuck out of my home, walked down the street to the house I'd left an hour earlier, literally Spider-manned up the wall to enter this gorgeous girl's bedroom window. And right then she was kissing me.

"You need to go," she said.

It felt like someone had hit me in the head with a hammer.

"But… uh… uh," was all that emerged from my slackened jaw.

I couldn't even intelligently or coherently reply to what had become my goodnight kiss. And, when I tried for another smooch, I received only the side of her face after she turned her head. Not a *no*, but definitely not a *yes*.

"Well, I better go out the front door. I don't think I can do all that backwards," I whined, as I pointed to the window from whence I came.

"Okay, but if you get caught, you're on your own, Big Boy."

We sat on the edge of Karen's bed and talked ever so quietly for about fifteen minutes. And, after her third attempt to see if her parents' bedroom light was off, it finally was, engulfing the upstairs hallway in darkness.

So, I gave Karen a reluctant goodbye hug, and then slowly slithered down the hall to the top of the stairs: my only escape route.

It took me longer to get out of the house using the stairs, than it did to climb into the house up the wall. I didn't want to be discovered by her parents as the burglar, which I certainly was, so I went church-mouse quiet all the way to the front porch.

Once I was outside, I looked up at the wall I'd scaled barely an hour ago, and wondered how I had done it. My eyes then followed my previous trail to Karen's window, and I saw the curtains had parted ever so slightly with her standing there watching me.

She raised her hand, about chest high, and then gave me a very slow, but deliberate wave.

I smiled, waved back, turned around and headed for home.

And while the evening didn't end exactly as I'd hoped, I was more than a little relieved that I had no regrets.

"Get out of here, you tramps!"
1971

"I took her home to my place
Watching every move on her face
She said look, what's your game baby
Are you tryin' to put me in shame
I said slow don't go so fast
Don't you think that love can last
She said love, Lord above
Now you're tryin' to trick me in love"[29]

    With the confidence I'd obtained from dating Lee Ann, and soon after our break up, I began to ask out a lot of girls. And my personal favorite courtship activity, popular with the other guys in my high school, was taking our dates into Washington, DC. It was an easy, thirty minute drive into The Big City, where we could find first-run movies, be served alcohol without EVER being carded, or stop at one of the scenic overlooks on the George Washington Parkway to watch the submarine races.

    By this time in our lives, my best buddy Dale and I were double-dating quite frequently. We liked to do many of the same things and had numerous friends in common, so getting a foursome together was easy and entertaining.

    And, Dale had a car.

    One evening in late winter, when there was a chill in the air, but signs were beginning to indicate the approach of spring, Dale asked a girl out that he'd known for a while, Barbara Something. When she agreed, he asked me if I would like to bring a date and join them for the evening. At that time, I knew a girl named Frances, who I'd been planning to ask out. She and I had a couple of classes together, and I was already attracted to her.

    Frances was very alluring, always impeccably dressed, with long, light brown hair, which she seemed to curl in all the right places. Frances was also extremely outgoing, so I knew in advance that an evening with her would be very enjoyable. As soon as she agreed to go out with me, Frances explained that she and Barbara had actually been friends since elementary school. Once

---

29   "All Right Now", Andy Fraser and Paul Rodgers, 1970

plans were finalized, I was confident that a night out with all of us together would be very lively and engaging.

Dale and I decided we would take our girls to one of our favorite restaurants in DC, Giusti's, where we had an alcoholic beverage or two, and a delicious meal of Italy's finest cuisine. The evening went perfectly: good food downtown, gorgeous girls, camaraderie, and alcohol.

After dinner, we drove to the nearby Lincoln Memorial and parked in a convenient spot where we could stroll along the Reflecting Pool, without too much discomfort to our dates in high heels and dresses. Soon, we returned to the car and drove back to Virginia, along the George Washington Parkway.

Before we reached the Theodore Roosevelt Bridge, Barbara had snuggled next to Dale as he drove, while I scooted closer to Frances in the back seat. She was radiant with her hair all fixed up, adorable dimples in her cheeks, great legs, and a voluptuous body that was the envy of most of the girls in my class. And she smelled good, too. I was more than hopeful that night would end well.

Dale must have been doing some wishful thinking, too, as we exited the Parkway and headed to one of the overlook parking areas for some serious making out with our girls. The first one we stopped at was packed with teenagers in their parents' cars doing the same thing we were trying to do. But we wanted a little privacy, so we drove to the next one: More cars filled with lusty teens. Dale, always the innovator, then drove us to a secluded neighborhood somewhere in McLean. How he knew where to go was a mystery. Within minutes, he'd found an out of the way cul-de-sac without street lights, making it very dark and private for amorous teenagers looking for some action. This was the perfect spot, so Dale pulled the car to the side of the road, turned off the engine, and lit up the radio dial to one of the local FM rock stations.

With the chill in the air outside, and the body heat generated from four panting adolescents on the inside, it didn't take long to completely fog up the windows. We couldn't see out and nobody could see in.

Frances and I were in our own little world, kissing and hugging with a healthy dose of heavy breathing. Soon, I was quickly approaching the moment that can define a teenage boy for life; how do I take this to the next level, and will she let me? So, I went for it. Frances and I were staring into each other's eyes like we were the only humans inhabiting the earth.

I slid even closer to Frances, and leaned in for another kiss, when I heard a noise coming from somewhere outside the car. But I quickly dismissed it, thinking it must only be the neighbors. After all, we *were* in a neighborhood.

My real attention, though, never left Frances' eyes and the pleasures that were right in front of me. Then, suddenly, I heard it again. But this time it sounded like pounding, somewhere near my head.

Almost instantly, passion was overcome by confusion. The only thing that I'd *wanted* to happen was replaced by a genuine, but uninvited distraction.

Once my brain had sufficiently recovered to process the noise, I realized it was coming from the driver's side window, like someone was trying to break the glass with their fist.

The fist pounding percussion was disorienting, resonating incessantly throughout the car. I released Frances so quickly, that she would have hit the floor had we been standing up. Dale and Barbara, previously hidden somewhere behind the seat in front of me, bolted up like a couple of scared cats, their eyes opened wide in fear.

Dale glanced at me, and then we both looked toward the window, and cautiously slid closer to it to have a look. Slowly at first, I began to rub a spot through the condensation on the glass to see who was standing next to the car, and interrupting our glandular exercises. I then attempted to wipe off the entire window—because I couldn't believe what I initially thought that I saw, and I wanted a better view.

There was a very large woman in curlers, wearing a muumuu, one of those gigantic cover-all circus tent/nightgowns, her face pressed against the driver's side window. She made frantic motions with her arms, like she was drowning or hailing a cab.

"What the...?" I stammered, as Dale rolled down the window just enough to get a better look.

"You tramps! You get the hell out of here, before I call the police!" Lady Muumuu yelled, within inches of Dale's face peering just above the crack of the window.

With that threat firmly established, Lady Muumuu began waving her gargantuan arms in a *this-is-the-way-out* motion, like a spastic traffic cop in a busy intersection.

Frances seemed to have determined the severity of our predicament before I did. She'd already gotten as far away from the angry woman as she could by pressing herself into the corner of the seat on the other side of the car.

She didn't speak, but the frightened expression on her face pleaded with me to do something to get her out of there.

Suddenly, truly terrified, Dale fumbled with the keys in the ignition, tried to button his pants, and quickly rolled back up the window, all at the same time.

But Lady Muumuu was not going to be denied.

Before the engine had a chance to crank over, the woman had grabbed the door handle and tried opening the door!

"Just go, Dale. Just go!" Barbara screamed.

Dale finally got the car started and put the gear shift into *Drive*, but the woman had managed to partially open the door, just enough to raise the anxiety to yet another level. Muumuu screamed even louder than Barbara, literally trying to pry us out of the car.

"You tramps, coming into our neighborhood and parking. I'll show you!" she yelled, as Dale tried to drive away. She held onto the door handle, while the door opened ever wider, in a tug-of-war that we were in danger of losing.

I felt uncomfortably helpless. I was in the backseat, couldn't reach the door handle without impeding Dale's effort to drive away, while Frances was scared out of her wits and I couldn't comfort her.

Muumuu ran alongside of us, her enormous body bouncing and jiggling, as she tried to keep up with the accelerating car, hanging on like her life depended on it. She was tugging the door open, as Dale desperately and unsuccessfully, tried to close it, while trying to get away from this gigantic woman from hell.

"Go, go, go!" Frances and I yelled out.

The only thing that made Lady Muumuu release the door was our driving away with it still attached to the car. Dale's trusty Plymouth Valiant spun its wheels in the gravel during our escape, and nobody spoke until we'd reached a safe distance out of the neighborhood.

"Oh, my God," whispered Frances, as she slowly exhaled in relief.

I turned and looked out the back window, wondering what would have happened had Muumuu pulled Dale out of the car. Or worse, if she'd actually managed to force her way in with us.

I saw her standing in the middle of the road, defiant and triumphant, with hands on her hips.

Needless to say, that ended any chance of romance for the rest of the evening. And we sure as hell never went back to *that* neighborhood. May Lady Muumuu rest in peace with the knowledge and comfort that she cleansed her street of passionate teenagers that chilly March night.

Deja Vu, Summer 1971

"Wake up Maggie I think I got something to say to you
It's late September and I really should be back at school
I know I keep you amused but I feel I'm being used
Oh Maggie I couldn't have tried any more
You led me away from home just to save you from being alone
You stole my heart and that's what really hurt"[30]

For two years, I had known Arlene, a girl who lived nearby on Beulah Road. She was a very pleasant, easy to talk to person who often created, then immersed herself, in drama. In doing so, she had the well-deserved reputation as the neighborhood busybody—and by extension, a well-intentioned matchmaker—always getting absorbed into a variety of others' relationships.

That sometimes involved introducing this boy to that girl, allowing Nature to take its course. And if Nature needed a little help, Arlene was more than capable of providing her assistance. Perhaps, for those reasons, rather than in spite of them, she was well liked by everyone, including me. She genuinely seemed to care about those in her circle of friends, and would often go out of her way to make everyone happy.

She was a good friend.

Arlene loved to talk. And you could be sure that if her mouth wasn't moving, she was probably dead. She particularly loved to talk on the telephone. And when you answered her call, you knew you would be on the receiving end of a lengthy conversation, most of it originating from her.

One Saturday afternoon, Arlene called to tell me she had a friend, Alicia, who had come over to her house for the day. Before I could respond to this rather random announcement, she further offered to bring Alicia to Hicks Drive and introduce us to each other. I quickly agreed, but added that I had to close the Orange Bowl at Tysons Corner Mall and wouldn't be home until about 9:30.

The Orange Bowl was a short-order, counter-service restaurant that sold slices of pizza, hotdogs, and soft drinks. For a slice of pizza and a Coke, "that'll be one dollar and four cents, please." It was my first real job.

Since I didn't own a car, until I could save enough money to buy one—about four more months— my dad picked me up from work that

---

30 "Maggie Mae", Rod Stewart and Martin Quittenton, 1971

evening, like he typically did. When we got to the bottom of Hicks Drive, I saw Arlene and Alicia cross the street in the high beam of the car headlights, about two hundred yards ahead. It looked like they had just perfectly arrived in the neighborhood about the time I got home.

As we pulled into the driveway, I nearly cramped a muscle in my neck, trying to get a peek at Arlene's new hottie friend. When I got out of the car, I saw the two girls slowly approaching me, highlighted against the backdrop of an almost darkened summer sky.

"Rick, this is Alicia. Alicia, Rick," was all Arlene said. Before me, stood a very attractive girl, probably younger than me, and about five and a half feet tall. She had very long dark hair and a gorgeous smile that looked just a bit familiar. Her face was radiant, softly reflecting off of the front porch lights illuminating in the distance.

Alicia and I said *hi* to each other at exactly the same time, before giggling like the nervous kids we were.

The three of us proceeded to the split-rail fence a few feet away from where we were standing. We sat on the top rail, making small talk for more than an hour. It was a popular gathering place for me and my friends for many years, and to think, that night I invited a gorgeous guest to our favorite spot.

That evening, I learned that Alicia had moved to the United States two years prior, from some South American country I'd never heard of, and couldn't properly pronounce after a couple of attempts. Her parents had gotten divorced in her native country, and she and her mom left home before immigrating to the United States. Soon after, her mom remarried, and the three of them lived in Vienna. The day after Labor Day, she would be entering the ninth grade at my high school, James Madison.

When it was my turn to share, I revealed that I'd lived in the Vienna suburbs all my life, the same house for ten years. My parents had been married long enough to get on each other's nerves, and would probably remain so indefinitely. I'd never been more than a few hundred miles away from home; my parents never went anywhere with no plans to change that status in the foreseeable future.

Alicia and I were truly worlds apart.

She told me she learned how to speak English before arriving in the US, but still struggled when suddenly immersed in the classroom. Her slight Spanish accent was almost musical. Soon I found myself asking her questions just to hear her deliver the answers. If I had a C&P telephone book nearby, I would have asked her to read me a few pages.

The longer the evening went, the more interested I became in seeing this beauty again. After a while, Arlene suggested that she and Alicia head home before her dad came looking for them both. We exchanged our goodbyes and departed.

I probably hadn't been in the house for more than thirty minutes before the phone rang. I grabbed it before the second ring to forego my parents having a cow about getting a call so late at night.

It was Arlene.

"Can you come over next Saturday? Alicia will be here all day, since her parents are going out of town for the night. And I'm taking care of the house next door while they're away on vacation. I know where they keep their liquor," she said, before I could say a word.

Me, a beautiful girl, liquor, and an empty house. I couldn't wait to say yes.

I hung up the phone to see my dad standing next to me with that authoritative look on his face to point out some egregious offense I may have committed.

"You tell whoever that was, not to call so late. It's almost eleven o'clock and some of us have to get up in the morning," he said.

"It's Saturday night, dad," I said, demonstrating my extensive calendar knowledge.

"What does that have to do with what I just said?"

It was useless to argue, so I mumbled an incomprehensible *okay,* before heading to my room.

I spent the rest of the week thinking about nothing else but Saturday and seeing Alicia again. But it had been several months since I had just ended a serious and committed relationship, and I wasn't sure if I was ready for that so soon. I quickly put all of that out of my mind and decided to make the most of a very promising evening. Even if there would be three of us.

When Saturday came, I ran, not walked, from my house to Arlene's to see Alicia. We seemed to pick up the conversation right where we'd left off the previous week, and soon we were talking like old friends. I was beginning to really like her—a lot. And I was soon after, phoning her most every night, and finding ways to get together for official dates.

It was about to get serious.

After school started for the fall semester, it wasn't long before I was invited to meet the parents. I must have passed the First Impression Test, because quickly thereafter, I was invited to Alicia's fifteenth birthday party. I didn't realize it until later, but in many Latin American countries, a girl's fifteenth is similar to turning Sweet Sixteen in the United States, but bigger. Much bigger. This special day is sometimes called *Quinceanera,* and marks the transition of a young girl from childhood to womanhood.

I hadn't been to a birthday party in years. My mom had not given one for me or my sister in *many* years, and child-featured celebrations on Hicks Drive were few and far between.

It was sad, actually. Birthday parties were usually fun. But this one, the Quinceanera for my new *Bonita Latina* girlfriend, was huge. Her attractive mom, Elsa, and stepdad, Horatio, invited several of their co-workers, all who spoke Spanish and very little English. Their adult female guests were stunningly beautiful. Her mom's sister and Alicia's aunt, Blanca, was there as well. She, too, was a native of their home country.

Did they bring the whole family? I wondered.

Soon I felt right at home, in someone else's home. But I kept having this strange feeling I had been to this apartment before. It all looked so familiar—the parking lot out front, the steps into the building, the layout of the room. And then, all of a sudden, it hit me; it was The Chocolate Cookie People from Christmas past. This was the nice, chattering in Spanish family, who'd donated the chocolate cookies to my Cans for Christmas Drive two years earlier.

I glanced over at Alicia, who seemed to be having an in-depth conversation with her aunt. That beautiful young lady in front of me was a stranger, just a little girl when I'd first seen her, in that apartment. And there we were, two years later, in the same apartment again, and I was attending the official ceremony and celebration of her becoming a woman. But at this time, I was her boyfriend.

The party lasted well into the night. The food was unlike anything I had ever seen or tasted—caviar on dainty little crackers that were most definitely not Premium Saltines, a delicious sweet potato concoction with a pie-like consistency that was sliced into thin pieces and eaten with a wedge of a soft cheese. And, just when I had gotten comfortable with all the delicacies spread out like a banquet, Horatio proudly entered the dining room carrying a whole roasted piglet on a platter, complete with the obligatory apple-in-mouth!

And, of course, we just *had* to toast the Birthday Lady of the Evening with a glass of champagne—something else I had never enjoyed until that night. The entire evening was the best time I'd ever had around adults. Everyone treated me like a guest of honor, and seemed genuinely pleased that I was there. If permitted to do so, I never would have left. And, given my subsequent re-visits, I actually didn't leave for about two years.

The Quinceanera deeply immersed me into Alicia's family. Her mother and I developed a very close relationship, one that influenced me well into adulthood. And it wasn't much longer after the party that I was able to communicate with Alicia's stepfather using an often unstructured mix of English, Spanish, and impromptu hand gestures.

The two adults took us everywhere from fine dining and Latin clubs in DC, to the Washington monument, and a brief sneak-in at the Kennedy Center.

And, as for the teenagers, Alicia and I remained a couple until the early months of 1973, when divergent interests sent our lives in different directions.

But having a girlfriend from another culture and being part of that family, if only for a couple of years, made me a better person in ways too numerous to count. And I will always be appreciative of those memories, the moments we spent together, and certainly Arlene, who made it possible.

Take a Picture… It'll Last Longer, Spring 1972

"Hey man, ah leave me alone you know
Hey man, well Henry, get off the phone, I gotta
Hey man, I gotta straighten my face
This mellow thighed chick just put my spine out of place"[31]

Dale's father passed away when he was about eleven years old while his older brother and sister were young adults, living somewhere on their own. And when the siblings moved out, Dale and his mom had all to themselves, the entire two-story brick rambler, with a finished basement and a screened-in porch. Since Dale's mom had extreme difficulty climbing stairs in a home with a bedroom and bath downstairs, it made for a perfect teenage boy crash pad, requiring Dale to be a cellar dweller. And he was.

Living in one's basement has many advantages, especially knowing the only supervising adult in the home won't drop in uninvited—complete and continuous privacy, unlimited access to "sneaking out" after curfew, and the Crown Jewel of Teenaged Living: the ability to have girls over whenever you wanted.

It was a bachelor pad for teenagers!

Many times I would spend the night at Dale's and we'd plan a late night adventure of drinking beer at strip clubs in DC until the wee hours of the morning, or invite a couple of girls to have a nightcap with us after we'd had dinner at a nice restaurant.

I was home alone, getting ready for a date, one Friday afternoon, when the phone rang.

It was Dale.

"When can you come up and see my new camera?" he asked, and then in almost a whisper, he said, "I'm going to take pictures of Andrea."

"I'll be there in half an hour. I'm gonna jump into the shower first. I'm taking my honey to the Kennedy Center," I said, sharing details about an upcoming date, while wondering what the always adventurous Dale was up to now.

After I'd gotten dressed, I didn't have much time before picking up

---

31 "Suffragette City", David Bowie, 1972

my girlfriend, but I wanted to hear about Dale's plans before I left. I drove up the street, got out of the car, and then knocked on his door.

"What are you going to do with that camera, Dale?" I inquired as soon as he opened the front door.

"I'll show you," he said, then turned and walked toward the basement and to his bedroom.

When we got to his room, he reached under the bed and withdrew a box clearly labelled *Polaroid Land Camera*.

"Gonna take some pictures of Andrea nekkid," Dale said, sitting on the bed while he opened the box.

"Where you gonna do that?" I asked.

"Right damn here," Dale instantly replied, as he waived his free hand around the bedroom studio, holding the box in the other.

I pushed the subject, "You're gonna get nekkid with Andrea, and take her picture right here in your basement?"

"I won't be nekkid. She will!" He pried the camera out of the box, and handed it to me for my inspection.

"When?" I was hoping it was sooner rather than later. I held the camera up to the light and examined it from several angles.

"Tomorrow, while my mom is at work," Dale said, as he eagerly looked at me for a reaction.

"Have you asked her, yet?" I asked, handing the device back to Dale.

"Who? My *mom*?" Dale asked, with a frown.

"No, man! Andrea!" The temporary, and ridiculous, misunderstanding caused both of us to laugh at each other.

"Sorta'. She knows I have this camera, and she's already posed for a few sexy pictures. Here, take a look."

Dale had discovered, actually created, the ultimate perk of private, basement living by inviting his girlfriend, Andrea, to spend the day with him and his new Polaroid camera. And they were planning to do it again!

These marvelous photographic devices had been around for more than twenty years, required no development of film, and were relatively inexpensive by the early seventies. To make the possibilities even more interesting, Andrea was a very good-looking girl, with a voluptuous body, and long, blond hair. And she wasn't shy. At all.

Dale reached behind the dehumidifier in his room and pulled out a stack of about ten photographs, before dropping them onto my lap. The expression on his face was a combination of pride and anticipation of approval.

"Nice," I offered at the first one of Andrea sexily displaying her legs in short shorts.

"This one's even better," I suggested, while staring at the fourth or fifth picture, which showed Andrea in a provocative pose with leg and cleavage.

I glanced over at Dale, and saw a mischievous grin that said it all.

"I think she's ready for The Super Bowl, boy!" yelled Dale, at the top of his lungs.

I matched his enthusiasm with, "Can't wait for those," as I handed the pictures over to Dale.

He quickly reviewed them one last time before standing up and returning them to the dehumidifier.

About two weeks had already passed, so I kind of forgot about the Polaroid Party that Dale and Andrea had planned. But, upon heading outside to get my mail, I saw his Plymouth Valiant speeding up the street and immediately remembered. I wanted to hear about everything.

When Dale saw me, he accelerated, sending a puff of blue smoke from the tailpipe, arriving in front of my house with screeching tires.

I nearly dropped the mail in my eagerness to hear the Polaroid update.

"Get in," was all he said through the partially opened window, as he reached across the seat and unlocked the passenger side door.

Before I entered, I turned around and crammed the mail back into the box.

"You won't believe the pictures I've got of Andrea. You just won't believe it!" A slight trace of spit had accumulated in the corner of his mouth. He was drooling about it all.

Before the passenger door was fully closed, Dale floored the accelerator on his Valiant, sped the short distance to his house, and turned into his driveway in mere seconds.

"You won't believe it!" he repeated, in case I forgot.

We opened both car doors, before the Valiant's six-banger had come to a complete rest, and then jumped out and nearly ran to the front door of his house.

I followed Dale through his living room, dining room, then the kitchen to get to the basement door.

The two of us banging down the enclosed steps in unison must have sounded like a small herd of buffalo, and when we reached the final two, we both jumped off the steps and onto the basement floor. From there, we must have looked like Wile E. Coyote, running in place without advancing.

Dale was still in the lead, reaching his bedroom door and then the dehumidifier, as I entered the room.

Emerging from the darkness of Dale's secret cabinet was a stack of nearly twenty pictures. Maybe twenty-five.

"You can't tell anybody," he said. "I'm dead meat if Andrea knows I showed you these," Dale said, with a serious expression that told me he'd already considered the downside of his adventure.

"I won't tell anybody. Lemme see," I nearly begged in anticipation of what I'd hoped was in his hand.

When I saw the first one, I nearly dropped the rest of them.

But they weren't what I'd expected.

Sprawled out, on full display, was the lovely Andrea wearing a tiny, revealing bikini and a smile.

"Wow," was all I could think to say, as I slowly placed the first picture on the back of the stack to get to the second.

"Keep going. There's more," Dale almost yelled, impatient with my slow progress.

"A lot more," I mumbled while placing the second, then third picture on the back of the pile.

I looked up at Dale, who began rapidly rolling his hands in a circle, telling me to hurry the hell up.

Then there was one of Andrea, provocatively posed, out on the patio.

"She went *outside*?" I asked with my voice cracking as I tried in vain to swallow at the same time I was speaking. It sounded more like gurgling.

"Never hesitated," replied Dale with a slight, but confident tilt of his head.

"But, I thought you were gonna do nekkid," I asked, while trying not to sound *too* disappointed.

The remaining pictures were variations of the first two—different poses, some slightly more explicit, but all first-rate basement photography.

"She wouldn't take off her bikini," Dale said with a noticeable tone of disappointment in his voice, before adding, "But they're still pretty hot, dontcha think?"

I went through the stack a second time without answering his question. Then, quickly, a third.

When I was done, I set the pictures aside, stood up from the sitting position on the bed, and applauded, a one-man standing ovation.

"Dale. These are primo. No doubt about it," I said.

Dale quickly grabbed the stack I left on the bed, thumbing through them again. The changing expressions on his face from each photograph clearly conveyed his preference of one from another.

"Look at this!" he proudly announced, while displaying one of the outdoor photographs.

"I thought Choo-Choo Charlie might come out and have a heart attack. But he didn't," Dale said, referring to his next door neighbor, with a hint of relief that interruption never happened.

Dale went through the rest of the photos, never allowing the perpetual grin to slip from his face.

A few weeks later, I learned that Dale had shared his now worn-out photo collection with everybody on the street. So much for secrecy. The story behind them kept getting better every time it was told. Soon enough, Andrea was the centerfold, the girl next door, and the object of our rapt attention, all rolled into one.

But Dale's big mistake was not sharing his girlfriend's photogenic features with tens if not hundreds of hormone oozing boys, but in his aversion to housekeeping.

Despite her ill health and inability to leap tall stairs with a single bound, Dale's mom must have eventually followed the stench of a teenage boy's bedroom directly to the door of Dale's domain. And once she got that far, the vacuum cleaner and Spic-and-Span were not far behind. Soon, she transformed herself into a self-perpetuating, cleaning mom-machine, with nothing to stop her but a complete room rehabilitation.

Evidence later suggested that she'd gathered all of the dirty clothes lying about the floor, dresser, and unmade bed, and flung them into the hallway. Some probably stuck to the wall.

Then she started to vacuum the floor, reaching under the bed and nightstand.

She must have pulled the dehumidifier away from the wall and realized it was unplugged. She'd have thought that was unusual since dampness in a basement is very common, and she remembered it was operational the last time she visited Dale's bedroom.

But, as she slid the dehumidifier to the side, she would have seen something in the tray, normally used for water collection.

She tugged on the tray, removed it from the back of the unit, and pulled out a few of what she must have thought were documents. No doubt she was already concluding they were purposefully hidden from view.

At that moment in time, I was nearly a half mile away when I heard thunder in the distance, that rumbling sound that seems to predict an onslaught of a major storm.

It began slowly, building into a gradual crescendo in volume and frequency.

Dale later told me he was upstairs making himself a sandwich when he first heard the roar from below, like Hell had opened its door.

When he saw his mom, her head had already begun to split down the middle, with fire shooting out of the top all the way to the ceiling—or so that's what I had imagined.

The scream she let out was more horrifying than any human being could possibly make.

"DALE!!!" was all she needed to say.

Her eyes likely popped out of the sockets as she looked at those sexy photos.

Dale must have been dumbstruck as she raised her hand in the air, still clutching the pictures.

The top of her skull, by then would have begun mending back together, her eyes returned to their sockets, just in time to create a laser beam focus on the child she was about to kill.

"Where did you get these? Who is this girl? Why is she lying on my sofa? Is this her in our backyard?"

It would have been impossible for Dale to reply to any one of those machine gun questions before the next round was shot.

Apparently, she wouldn't have even wanted any answers, as she stormed past Dale's slack-jawed temperament, heading out of the room, stomping demonically up the steps loudly on every stair.

Although the photos didn't contain nudity, I doubt if Mrs. Hall recognized the distinction.

Paradise was lost; Dale's collection of pictures, certainly his relationship with Andrea along with his ability to EVER bring her home again, and perhaps, his entire way of life in the basement, as well.

Mrs. Hall never spoke of her discovery, apparently too embarrassed to discuss the nearly nude photographs with anyone. Particularly taken in her own home.

From the day the pictures were discovered and destroyed, Dale had to make extra effort to hide secrets from his mom. He could no longer assume she was incapable of going down the stairs and into his domain.

The hopes and dreams of the impervious teenager bachelor pad had been shattered.

Part IV

But What If I Don't Want To Be A Responsible Adult?

The Strip along 14th Street NW Washington, DC.
Thanks to Fairfax Underground for the photo.

Eddie The Pimp

"And everything looks so complete
When you're walkin' out on the street
And the wind catches your feet
Sends you flyin', cryin'
Ooo-woo-wee, wild night is calling
Ooo-ooh-wee, wild night is calling"[32]

Washington, DC offered an unlimited number of entertainment options for teenagers from Northern Virginia. Several factors contributed to the menu. The legal drinking age in DC was eighteen years old until 1986, Virginia's was twenty one. I had a fake ID, someone else's draft card with no picture, which looked like it was made on the copy machine at the Patrick Henry Library in Vienna. And Washington had total nudity gentleman's clubs, while Virginia's beauties wore tiny panties and pasties. But, perhaps most importantly, DC was a quick fifteen minute car ride from the comfy confines of suburbia.

Dale was a big fan of adult entertainment venues, and introduced many of us on Hicks Drive to those visual delights. Actually, I saw my first adult magazine at Dale's house. He was quite the adventurer. But Dale didn't have to work very hard to convince me to go with him to a couple of our favorite gentlemen's clubs like *Clancy's* (home of the nine-inch sausage pizza) or *Good Guys*. Both were on Wisconsin Avenue, just above the rows and rows of trendy Georgetown mansions and townhouses.

It became a regular event: get off work at The Orange Bowl in Tyson's Mall around 9 pm, Dale picks me up at 9:01, and we're crossing Key Bridge by 9:15.

Oh, the trouble we could get into after working for a dollar sixty an hour.

But on this trip, the driver was a friend of Dale's, Larry Something. And Larry drove a hot two-door, Ford Torino with a 390 cubic inch V8 motor in true seventies muscle car fashion.

We made the usual rounds on this particular Saturday night. Clancy's featured their typical assortment of lovely ladies working two stages on separate floors, while Good Guys offered a couple of large breasted babes

---

32   "Wild Night", Van Morrison, 1972

that kept the money flowing into their little garter belts, and various legal crevasses. But, rather than going home with ample buzz to last well into the next day, and a few dollars still in my pocket, we headed downtown to the 14th Street seedy area at New York Avenue. Hookers, pimps, and drug dealers of all kinds were found on nearly every street corner, eyeing and approaching businessmen in three-piece suits, college and high school students, and everyday Joes just enjoying a night of sin and debauchery in the strip clubs and triple X peep shows.

Like most Saturday nights, the streets were particularly crowded, and parking was difficult without having to walk several blocks. But, after driving around in circles for ten or fifteen minutes, Larry soon found street parking for his machine about six or seven blocks from our last stop. I was past ready to go home, but eager with anticipation of what the evening may have to offer—and I didn't want to miss out on something special.

So, we made the late night rounds, visiting establishments like *Gold Rush*, *Benny's Rebel Room*, and *Butterfly*. The rest of our money soon vanished along with our energy level and enthusiasm for more entertainment. We were done and heading for the car.

But, here's three, young white boys from the suburbs, wearing young white boy suburb clothes, walking past a group of people on the street who were waiting for the light to change so they could cross. Suddenly, out of the crowd, stepped a short and stocky middle-aged man, wearing a hard hat and work clothes, like he just finished his shift, working on the new DC Metro subway system. He made sure to get our attention by stopping directly in our path.

"Hey, ya'll looking for some action?" the stranger said without introduction, and to all three of us at the same time. Hard hat Metro guy got right down to business, and now he was walking along side of us, eagerly anticipating our answer.

His initial attention-demanding sidewalk maneuver certainly caught me by surprise. That instantly changed to anxiety and concern when he stated his intentions.

"Nah, we're just headin' home," I replied, as Dale and Larry started to walk just a bit faster, while giving our uninvited sidewalk companion a quick sideways glance, hopefully without him noticing.

"My name's Eddie. You want to come with me? We can get the best lovin' in town," he persisted, as we continued to walk without breaking stride.

Eddie was much shorter than us, so he had to walk much faster to keep up; faster still to get in front of us in an attempt to slow us down.

"We don't have any money," stated Larry with more disappointment than conviction in his voice.

"Don't need none. We'll beg for it," insisted Eddie, still trying to keep pace while holding his hard hat with one hand to prevent it from falling off his head.

It was crystal clear, even to our alcohol-clouded brains that this guy was not going to quit. He had plans for us, and it didn't involve "the best lovin' in town." Begging for it was not how it was done.

We knew we had to ditch him, and do it fast, or face serious consequences.

But, Eddie had no way of knowing that our getaway car was now within sight, half a block away. Quickly, but without drawing attention to himself, Larry gave me a thumbs up and casually veered away from us, before going more directly to his car. Dale and I kept walking, to distract our determined adversary.

"So, Eddie. You live around here?" I asked, as I looked directly at him for the first time. I didn't want him to even catch a whiff of our plans to escape.

"I stay right up the street, where the old church used to be," Eddie replied. I had no idea where that was, didn't care. He likely made it all up, anyway.

From behind us, I heard Larry crank up the Torino, so I began thinking exactly how we were going to run away. Then, within a few moments, I saw Larry out of the corner of my eye, driving ever so slowly and coming up the street behind us.

"Where'd that other dude go?" asked Eddie, when he finally figured out there was one less mark.

"He had to use the restroom," Dale interjected, before old Eddie could finish his sentence.

I glanced over at Eddie and saw that the expression on his face indicated he didn't believe a word of that excuse. He then made a quick visual sweep of the area in search of Larry as we walked, with frustration becoming more evident as he did so. I suddenly became concerned that this would-be-mugger was onto us.

Suddenly, Larry and the Torino stopped in the middle of the road and right beside us, and Larry yelled "get in" after Dale and I had already taken two steps in his direction.

I reached the partially opened passenger side door first, and dove over the seatback without flipping it forward. And in my frightened haste, I banged my left knee on the narrow window opening in the back. Dale was right behind me and jumped into the passenger seat.

But Eddie instantly began chasing Dale, knowing his opportunity for some quick cash was about to slip away from him. Immediately after Dale got in the car, but before he could close the door behind him, Eddie had grabbed onto the door handle as Larry was driving down the street at near idle speed.

I started to panic, as we approached an intersection and the light had just changed from green to yellow. There was no way we could stop the car and still make our getaway from this aggressive pursuer.

Dale saw the light change, too, and screamed "Step on it, Larry!" while trying to keep the car door between us and that bastard, by hanging onto the handle with both hands.

Larry laid down about five thousand miles of rubber from his Torino's tires, as Eddie finally let go of the door handle, to keep from doing a face plant onto 14th Street.

We shot through the intersection just as the traffic light turned red.

I turned around in my seat and saw Eddie standing in the road, with his hands on his hips in resignation.

"What the hell was that?" Dale yelled, completely out of breath from the sprint to freedom and the ensuing tug-of-war over the car door.

"I think that pimp, or whatever the hell he was, was gonna roll us somewhere," offered Larry, stating the obvious truth.

My adrenaline was still furiously pumping, as we hit one red light after another, slowing down our retreat from DC at every intersection. I nervously kept looking out the rear window, just to make sure Eddie didn't figure out some way to follow us. That guy was highly motivated.

When we'd reached the Teddy Roosevelt Bridge, and with Virginia now in sight, on the other side of the Potomac River, we all started nervously laughing, as Larry pushed the accelerator down and we quickly built up speed. Dale found a tape on the floor by his feet, picked it up and popped it into the eight-track dashboard player: The Allman Brothers, first album. Perfect.

Peter's guard dog, Shultz, 1971.

Bourbon, Spring 1972

"After midnight
We gonna let it all hang down
After midnight
We gonna chugalug and shout
Gonna stimulate some action
We gonna get some satisfaction
We gonna find out what it is all about
After midnight
We gonna let it all hang down"[33]

Most of us on Hicks Drive discovered the mild altering effects of alcohol in middle school. It started innocently enough, when we would sneak a little from the adults' liquor cabinet from time to time—and then would add an equal measure of water to the bottle.

With the exception of Roger, none of us during our high school years showed any signs of developing alcohol dependency later in life. But, all of us definitely revealed our individual presentation of how too much booze could make us do stupid things.

Rick Duncan and I asked two girls, who had known each other for several years, to join us for a double-date on a warm spring night in 1972. We went to one of the favorite places of nearly all high schoolers from across the DC metro area: *Luigi's*—located between K and L Street on 19th Northwest. It was popular because it served the best pizza in the city, was in a safe part of DC, where sometimes you could order beer, and most importantly, it was The Cool Place To Go.

So, a large pizza and a pitcher of cold beer for the four of us, with the cost split between Duncan and I, was a homerun in any ballpark—and that night was no exception.

Plus, my date and I had the backseat on the way home, so we could get reacquainted after a busy week of school, work, and play.

As the night was coming to an end and we were driving back across Key Bridge, Duncan and I began the inevitable but responsible process of delivering the girls safely to their parents. Rick's date lived in Falls Church, which was on the way to our homes in Vienna, so we dropped her off first at

---

33   "After Midnight", J. J. Cale and Robert Neuwirth, 1972

about eleven o'clock. My girl was next, so we escorted her back to Vienna, and then Rick and I headed for home.

As Duncan's stodgy, but extremely reliable '66 Dodge Dart was slowing down on Trap Road to make the turn into Hicks Drive, we saw a familiar dog lying on the side of the road—though he was upright so as to see everything going on around him.

It was Schultz, Pete's psychotic German Shepherd.

Upon recognizing the dog, my first thoughts were: *What is Schultz doing at the side of the road, and why is he doing it in the middle of the night?*

Duncan completed the turn onto Hicks Drive, and then pulled over to the side before parking. I quickly opened the passenger side door, and then jumped out to see what was going on.

I'd only taken a few steps before noticing a body lying next to Schultz. It was Peter.

"What the hell are you doing, Pete, taking a nap?" I asked, before I could determine if he was hurt or not. He responded with an unintelligible groan, so I got a little closer. Apparently too close for Schultz, because he reacted by emitting a very subtle, but definitely audible growl, as if to say, "don't even think about it."

By this time, Duncan had gotten out of the car and approached the scene, stopping at about the same distance as I was away from our fallen friend. Schultz didn't like that too much either, and exhibited the nervousness that over-protective dogs all too readily display.

"Peter, what happened?" I asked again, without getting any closer.

"Too mush fuggin' bourbon," Peter finally slurred, merely seconds before throwing up, while his face was buried down in the weeds. The size of the barf puddle around his mouth suggested that it wasn't his first hurl of the night.

He dry-heaved a few more times, before finally passing out again.

"Now, what do we do?" Duncan asked, with the serious kind of concern that I hadn't yet displayed.

"We can't leave him *here*," I answered, ruling out one of our options.

"I don't think Schultz is going to let you get any closer," observed Rick, as he took two steps away to emphasize his point—or perhaps to just put a little safer distance between he and Peter's protector.

Suddenly, I remembered we'd left a potential doggie treat in the backseat, leftovers from a previous stop for snacks—something I'd hoped that Schultz would like.

"Wait!" I shouted, while running around to the passenger side of the car. The Dart was a two- door coupe, so after I opened the door, I flipped the front seat forward and reached under it from the back. I found what I was looking for on the first try.

"Let's see if Schultz likes Oreos," I announced while looking at the dog, but seeking approval from Rick by glancing in his direction.

"He'll eat that in half a second," countered Duncan, letting a little of the air out of my euphoric balloon.

"Well, then let's lure him into your car, and then lock him in there when he goes for the cookie. Then we can get Pete home," I said, without a *real* plan as to how we'd do it. "How about, if I get on one side with the food, lure him in, and then you close the other door behind him?" I asked.

This was a good plan, if Duncan didn't mind locking up a vicious dog in his car, that is.

Duncan crossed his arms in thought, his facial expressions changed from skepticism to enthusiasm, as he must have considered this dilemma from several angles. And, although I was the one with Schultz' treat, it was Duncan who made the first move.

Apprehensively at first, Duncan turned his attention to Schultz... "Come here, Schultz, good dog, we have a treat for you," he said, before adding, this time with much more conviction and confidence, "Come here, Schultz. Good boy."

I ran back to the passenger side door, Oreo in hand, and then opened my door, as Rick opened his. In doing so, he saw that the window was rolled down, so he quickly cranked it back up.

By then, Schultz was licking his lips, so he must have gotten a whiff of the sweet treat I had for him. Then he got up for the first time since we had arrived. And, most important of all, he wasn't growling.

Duncan ever so slowly stepped behind the driver's side door to allow Schultz a comfortable path to satiate his hunger, straight into the trap we had laid for him. The dog cautiously approached the open door, keeping his eyes fixed on what I had in my hand.

He was clearly hungry. He was a dog. He was always hungry.

"Come on, Schultz, come and get it," I pleaded, while extending my Oreo-clutching-hand closer to the drooling mouth of this now docile beast.

Finally, Schultz couldn't take it any more so he hopped into the front seat, as I dropped the bait onto the floor, and then slammed the door shut, all in one motion.

Once the dog's hind legs were cleared, Duncan closed the driver's side door.

"Got him!" we shouted at the same time.

It took Schultz about one millionth of a second to inhale the cookie, and then once it was gone, he started ferociously barking. But that didn't matter now, because he was temporarily rendered harmless; we could get Pete home and deal with the dog later.

I closely approached Pete for the first time. The smell was practically overwhelming: bourbon, puke, and whatever else he had for dinner. It looked like pizza. The whole mixture formed a large, chunky puddle around his face, which was right in the middle of it. Not an attractive sight, at all.

"Let's get him up and hopefully the two of us can walk him home,"

Duncan suggested, as I pulled on Peter's arm.

Pete started to wake up a little, and was able to somewhat get to his feet with our help. Soon, Duncan and I had him between us, so we started walking. It was less than a quarter of a mile up the street to Pete's house, so I was more concerned about getting covered in vomit than the physical exertion. I knew I could carry him by myself if I had to, but the risk of him barfing on me was too great of a cost.

I was still wearing my fancy date clothes.

Schultz' barking became frantic, as we walked by the car with his master, of whom he no longer guarded. Soon, we would return to let him out, and he would go home.

We approached my own car, parked on the street in front of my house, signifying we were about halfway to Pete's, and that everything was looking better than it had a few short moments ago.

Fortunately, the kitchen door to the Canciglias was unlocked, so we guided him into the home, confident that he could locate his own bedroom.

It took a few days to get the full story from Pete. He and Mike Corboy, a kid that lived at the end of Hicks Drive, but on Trap Road, had gotten their hands on a bottle of bourbon; a whole-entire-bottle of bourbon, which they drank in about ten minutes.

After about an hour, once the full force of the alcohol had kicked in, Corboy passed out in his barn, and Pete slowly but surely headed for home toward Trap Road. He got as far as the end of Corboy's driveway, where he fell down in the middle of the road.

Somehow, he had the wherewithal to crawl into the ditch on the side of Trap Road to avoid getting run over by the next car. He said that when he got to the ditch, two people who were driving by had stopped and asked if he was okay. Apparently, Pete was able to muster together enough words to convince the Good Samaritans that he was still alive. If barely.

He crawled on his hands and knees, along the ditch, over a hundred yards to the bottom of Hicks Drive.

Let me repeat that: he crawled one hundred yards, the length of a football field, on his hands and knees, in a clear state of alcohol poisoning—a journey that took about an hour, delayed by his repeated hurling and episodes of unconsciousness. And then that's where Rick Duncan and I'd found him.

Pete easily could have died that night in any one of several ways: alcohol poisoning, aspiration on his own vomit, or under the wheels of a passing car. But he didn't. Perhaps tricking Schultz into the car and getting him home improved his odds of survival just a little, but it was a long time before Pete formed another friendship with the liquid gold of Kentucky.

Grave Digging, Halloween 1972

"The scene was rockin', all were digging the sounds
Igor on chains, backed by his baying hounds
The coffin-bangers were about to arrive
With their vocal group, 'The Crypt-Kicker Five'"[34]

"How'd you learn about this place?" I asked Rob, as he slowed the van in preparation for turning into the graveyard. It was a little late into our Halloween adventure to be asking *that*.

"My mom sometimes does grocery shopping at the Giant on the way home from my uncle's place in Burke. I saw the sign for the graveyard a few weeks ago, while I was sitting in the car waiting for her. So, I checked it out."

It was already dark, with Trick or Treaters of all sizes and shapes everywhere—walking along the sidewalks and crossing the busy streets in front of us, as we approached the cemetery from a residential neighborhood.

We pulled into a partially paved entry way, which seemed to almost disappear into the middle of the burial grounds. The entire property was surrounded by a thick growth of trees and underbrush, which gave it a sense of seclusion. But, not only was it in the middle of Fairfax City—which was like Grand Central Station to prowling law enforcement, it was between two major thoroughfares, with lots of traffic passing directly by it on a continuous basis.

I couldn't help myself from having second thoughts. But, we already had a van-load of helpers with picks and shovels, ready to go. I, sure as hell, wasn't going to be the first one to back out. And besides that, we were seniors. We had an obligation to do something memorable, on our last high school Halloween.

We carefully followed the driveway, deeper into the cemetery, while I tried to recall who'd devised the idiotic plan to dig up a grave, in the first place. But as soon as word got out amongst my more adventurous friends, we didn't seem to have any difficulty getting people to help us.

And word definitely got out—fast and furious. October 31, 1972 was on a Tuesday. In the hallways at school that day, kids I didn't know very well came up to me and asked if I was really going "grave digging" that night.

---

[34] "Monster Mash", Bobby Pickett, 1962

A few underclass girls, some still in braces, asked if they could tag along. And once I counted how many people knew about The Grave Digging Plan, and how many more of them wanted in, the easier it was to say *no*. It was crowded enough, with the demented people we'd already committed to bring with us.

In all likelihood, my close high school friend, Rob Lappin, and I were the instigators.

In what seemed to be the center of the cemetery, the belly of the beast so to speak, we unloaded the van of all the hardware and occupants. Rob then cautiously drove out of the complex with his lights off until he reached Route 50, and then headed somewhere to leave the vehicle while we worked.

When he returned to the group a few minutes later, he told me he'd left the van in the Giant Food parking lot.

"I parked underneath one of those big light poles, so it wouldn't look like an abandoned vehicle sitting in the dark," Rob said, as I nodded in agreement with what sounded reasonable.

At least if trouble came, we wouldn't be hemmed-in at the cemetery with no way out, I'd tried to reassure myself.

Another classmate of ours, Billy Watkins, was wise enough to bring some beer to the party, so about twenty minutes into the operation, we all had a good buzz going and we hadn't so much as removed a square inch of dirt. We eventually took turns with the shovels and picks, the rest standing around not doing much of anything. Kind of like a city road project, where there's only one guy down in the hole working and four white-shirted supervisors looking over the edge. Regardless, we soon could see that we'd made some progress.

"So, how long is this going to take?" whined another high school prankster friend, Fat Pat.

"Not as long as it takes for you to find your pecker," countered Rob.

"Here," he handed Fat Pat the shovel. "It's your turn."

We had removed a relatively small portion of dirt, no more than two feet deep, in about an hour. And, if there was any truth to the "six feet under" adage, we were going to be there all night.

Suddenly, everyone froze at the sound of someone, a girl's voice, squealing very close to our location. Within minutes, a large group of girls, along with Billy, who was grinning ear-to-ear, had joined us for our graveyard party.

"Look what I found walking by," Billy said, as a general introduction to about four or five local high school girls.

"We're gonna need more beer," I predicted out loud, so as to get the rest of the guys to check their pockets for refreshment money.

I already had a gorgeous and steady girlfriend, so I wasn't too interested in some slightly intoxicated, but very immature, young girls—but there was one in particular who caught my eye.

She was dressed in a pirate's costume: short skirt and an eye patch, but luckily no parrot. Her blouse was slightly unbuttoned with enough push from below to offer a glimpse of cleavage. She was the only girl who wasn't incessantly giggling.

She and I were just getting acquainted with the usual chitchat about school, where we'd planned to go to college, and what we were going to major in, when I saw a light out of the corner of my eye, moving back and forth in a search-like mode. It happened to be heading straight for us.

The occasional sound of sticks snapping on the forest floor from the intruders' determined foot-steps, caused all of us to stop and look in that direction.

And then I saw another moving light, like a flashlight, right behind the first. That's when I saw the reflection off of the medal, pinned to the approaching individual's chest.

"Cops!" I yelled, while making a quick scan around me for a path out of harm's way.

At that instant, everything changed.

What began as an un-official senior prank, barely eight months before graduation, had suddenly become inundated with law enforcement personnel, placing me, all of us, in serious danger of being arrested.

"Everybody freeze! This is the Fairfax City Police Department! Don't even think about running!"

There must have been at least four cops now trying to fight their way through the underbrush and surround our position.

Most of us were too fast and too nimble to be caught by some thirtysomething, over-weight and out of shape cops, so we all scattered.

There was no way I was going to raise my arms in the air and give up.

But, I instantly forgot all about Pirate Girl, and somehow found a running lane under a canopy of low hanging tree limbs, right between the now rapidly approaching glare of the cops' flashlights coming at us from multiple directions. I knew I had to run fast or I'd certainly be caught.

After a frantic sprint toward freedom, I no longer could see or hear anyone else, until I'd reached the clearing on the far side of the graveyard. Rob had been obliviously right behind me the whole way.

"This way," Rob motioned, as we found an alley behind the grocery store that took us farther away from our potential captor's pursuit.

Though we had stopped running, from fatigue and to attract less attention to ourselves, blue lights were flashing everywhere. And we still had to safely retrieve the van to get home.

We continued to briskly walk toward Mister Donut, about half a mile away, in hopes we'd find someone willing to fetch our means of escaping.

When we reached the restaurant, Rob and I cautiously opened the front door and then stepped inside. Fortunately, because the cops were out looking for the now-fleeing grave robbers, they weren't at Mister Donut having their early evening snack. But once we stood closer to the counter service area, we could see a group of kids, sitting in the corner having the usual café fare.

"Man, we need a favor," Rob asked the oldest guy, who looked about twenty, accompanied by two under-aged girls.

"Sure, man," the guy said, without us even saying what we wanted, yet.

"Can you walk over to Giant and get our van for us," Rob asked. "Cops are looking for a bunch of guys, not someone with two girls."

He looked us over, and then said, "Okay. Ten bucks."

Rob handed him two fives and the keys to the van without negotiating, and then our three new best friends walked out the door.

"I hope he comes back," was all I could add.

It seemed like an eternity before we saw them reach the van, still brightly illuminated under the glare of the parking lot lights. But this time, it looked like our getaway vehicle was no longer secret. I was already feeling anxious about getting caught, so the longer I looked at the beacon that was now our means of escape, the more I recognized we should have parked it somewhere else.

I watched intently, as they all climbed in and closed the doors, before starting the engine and slowly pulling onto the highway, back toward our temporary refuge.

Within minutes, they pulled up in front of us, got out and then handed the keys back to Rob, before returning to the same corner they'd occupied.

No cops in sight, no sirens in the distance. Maybe we'd escaped, after all. Maybe the cops never considered that the van under the spot light was the perpetrator's getaway vehicle, I hoped more than I believed.

"Thanks," was the only word offered by Rob, as he and I climbed back into the van, with a cautious, but definite sigh of relief.

I couldn't believe we'd pulled it off—surrounded by cops and running for our freedom one minute, then driving away from the crime scene, the next!

I pushed an eight-track tape into the dashboard player, reached into the floor space of the backseat, and grabbed the paper sack with the leftover beer. I pulled one out and handed it to Rob, before pulling another off the plastic ring for myself. This was time for a celebration!

But, we no sooner had started high-fiving our way down Route 50 heading for home, when I saw a police cruiser approaching from the opposite direction we were driving.

Instinctively, we held our breath and intently watched as it drove by. I grabbed Rob's beer out of his hand and shoved it, along with mine, under the seat. Mere seconds went by before the cop hit the flashing lights, then the siren, and then made an abrupt U-turn in the middle of the street.

The Great Grave Digging Event of 1972 was over.

The cops hauled us down to City Hall, where several had gathered around the prankster wannabes. And all of them were curious about our plans, when they weren't laughing their asses off about it all.

"So, what were you Bozos planning to do with the body?"

"How'd you come up with such a stupid idea?"

"Did your mamas drop you on your heads when you were little?"

But the laughing soon stopped when our parents arrived to bail us out at the building adjacent to the jail. I guess, had I been a year older, I would have been charged with something as an adult, and been waiting in the pokey for pickup, rather than that casual police semi-rec room.

Unknown to Rob and I until later, but the rest of our crew had already been rounded up, brought to City Hall, and were scattered about the precinct in several rooms, questioned individually about their plans, and their sanity.

We were still juveniles and nobody was hurt, so we got off with a scolding and a promise to never again try to dig up a grave in Fairfax City.

And, since we were not adults, we were *detained*, and not *arrested*. At least that's what the precinct captain told us. But it did sure feel like getting arrested. I was surrounded by police, had made a temporary getaway, only to be pursued by multiple vehicles with flashing blue lights and sirens blaring into the night, before finding myself in the back of a police cruiser.

But, I was *detained*.

On the way home from City Hall, the only words my dad could offer in his obvious embarrassment and disgust was, "Where's my shovel?"

High School Graduation Celebration in the Wolf Trap parking lot-June 12, 1973.

Roger Gets Another Lesson, Spring 1973

"Oh, won't you
Gimme three steps, gimme three steps, mister
Gimme three steps toward the door?
Gimme three steps, gimme three steps, mister
And you'll never see me no more
For, sure"[35]

Springtime in Washington, DC makes many promises; cherry and dogwood blossoms offer the promise of beauty and warmer weather, our elected officials promise that everything will be better in their new term, young ladies who shed their winter clothing for skirts and short shorts promise a visual treasure.

And Roger's frequently difficult personality and surly disposition promise to get him his annual beating.

One very warm evening in late April, he and I stopped at our favorite 7-11, the one located on the north end of Maple Avenue in Vienna. Actually it was only *Roger's* favorite, since most of the clerks knew him by name and the brand of his favorite beer. Rick Duncan and I would be graduating from high school in two months. The day after the ceremony at Wolf Trap National Park for the Performing Arts, he and his family were moving to California and marking with their departure, the end of another of life's chapters.

Rick and I'd been buddies since childhood—about twelve years of having fun, getting into and out of trouble, solving the world's problems with youthful naiveté, and sometimes just palling around. We had dated some of the same girls, a couple of them more than once. We never had a fight, not even a serious disagreement. He was someone I trusted without reservation. He was my friend and an integral part of our group on Hicks Drive. He would certainly be missed.

Duncan had a job at one of the restaurants in Tyson's Corner Mall, and typically didn't get off work until nine pm, at the earliest. That's when the mall closed and everybody started heading for home. Or not, as was our

---

[35] "Gimme three Steps", Ronnie Van Zant and Allen Collins, 1973

plan that evening.

That night, Roger and I would pick him up from work, cold beer on-hand, and drive along the George Washington Parkway into Washington to hit a few nightclubs. But we would go only to those where we didn't have to worry about a cover charge, or being the legal drinking age of eighteen. I was seventeen.

We arrived at Tyson's a few minutes early, just as the mall was closing for the day. As usual, Roger had a few too many sixteen-ounce Budweisers and it was only 8:55 pm. We left Hicks Drive about seven o'clock, and he'd been complaining for two solid hours about some work-related issues I couldn't relate to and about life in general. Like friends are allowed to do, I supposed he was just venting.

While in those moods, Roger would sound a lot like I imaged his parents did. One of his favorite targets was an individual's decision about college, especially mine, to attend Old Dominion University later in the fall.

"You're gonna be one of those uppity college boys, ain't ya?" Roger asked, but with a slightly exaggerated up-from-the-country accent usually reserved for humor. He was serious.

"I don't really know what I want to do, so I'm staying in school, Roger," I said, trying to diffuse some of his increasing hostility, but actually sharing the truth.

Then, he complained about living with Mommy and Daddy, though it was by choice. He yelled at every driver on the road that he thought was in his way (all of them), and was convinced everyone else's lives were so much easier than his.

His mom *had,* in fact, told him, he'd never succeed in college—that he ought to get a trade, as he described it. But his mom had also told him *I'd* never be college material, either. And here I was, off to school in the fall. That contradiction must have been difficult for him to accept.

After he'd flipped off a couple of other drivers, and cut-off another who'd had the nerve to change lanes in front of him, we eventually made it to Tyson's. Roger then parked farther away from the mall entrance than most people, so that he could finish his beer without being seen by any rent-a-cops cruising with their yellow flashing lights atop white Ford Pintos. After the last gulp and subsequent burp, we got out of the car and walked through the front door of the mall, heading the short distance to the place where Duncan worked.

The pulldown steel- reinforced gate at the restaurant was partially closed, indicating that business was concluded for the day. Roger and I casually walked under it, bending slightly to accommodate the structure from overhead. We were immediately greeted by a very well-dressed, business-like, but friendly manager.

"Can I help you?"

"We're here to pick up Rick when he gets off," I said, while trying to look over the shoulder of the manager to get a glimpse of our friend.

"He should be about fifteen more minutes. He's cleaning up in the back."

"He's supposed to be off at *nine*," snorted Roger, without hesitation.

"Well, he can't leave until he's done. About *fifteen* minutes," the manager repeated.

"Oh yeah, who put you in charge?" demanded Roger, who suddenly seemed more than willing to pee on this guy's leg for no apparent reason.

The manager's tone changed instantly.

"Why don't you get the hell out of here, so we can close, Smart Ass?"

"Why don't you make me, Shit for Brains?" Roger asked. "Wanna step outside?"

"I'll meet you in the parking lot in twenty minutes," was all the manager had to say to forewarn me of what was about to happen. The whole scene had just gone from *zero* to *out of control* in about forty five seconds.

I turned to quietly walk away with Roger, but as Roger ducked slightly under the gate, he spoke over his shoulder, "I'm gonna kick your ass, you little turd."

"Roger, what the hell's the matter with you?" I asked, though I already knew the answer.

"No little SomeBitch college boy is gonna tell me what to do."

"How do you know he's a college boy?"

"Can't you tell by his attitude?" Roger said in that I-know-everything, you-know-nothing tone of his.

It was no use arguing. Roger was much bigger and drunker than I was. He'd bullied me around for more than ten years and counting, and I was not about to intervene in something I didn't initiate. Or even understand.

I didn't have a dog in this fight.

We went out to the car and waited, leaning against the front side panel, while Roger lit one Kool cigarette after another, sipping on a freshly opened can of Bud. Fifteen minutes passed, then twenty, then it was almost half an hour before Duncan and the manager emerged together from the side door.

As they approached, Duncan gave me that *what's Roger done, now?* look of exasperation, but he was going to get his answer very soon, without me saying a word.

"You wanna piece of me, asshole?" the manager asked, as he pulled a twelve-inch butcher knife out of his back pocket and then waved it in front of Roger's face.

Instinctively, I took a couple of steps away from the well-armed manager, fearful of being injured during the imminent street fight. I glanced over at Rick, who seemed to have the same concern, as he, too, backed away.

"Whoa, I thought we were just gonna fist fight!" Roger said, his voice and nerve beginning to crack. "I don't want any part of knives," he added with fear now clearly in his voice.

"You should have thought of that before you called me out here, Dickhead."

Before the manager could finish his sentence, Roger turned and ran toward the back of the car. The manager gave chase with the first step.

Duncan and I watched helplessly as the manager, butcher knife in hand, chased Roger around the car.

On the second revolution, the manager grabbed the radio antenna on Roger's car to help him cut the corner faster. But in the process, the antenna broke off in his hand. Now, he was armed with two weapons: a twelve-inch, razor sharp butcher knife and a three-foot-long, thin, metal whip.

Roger was now squealing like a little girl with the manager hot on his tail. The pursuer started whipping the antenna in the air, slashing back and forth like Zorro, while chasing Roger around the car at the same time. The whistling sound it made while slicing through the night air promised pain for whoever it struck.

Seconds later, the manager got close enough to take a swipe at Roger with the antenna and it caught him on his right side. Then he struck him again with the backstroke. Then again, and again the sword-like antenna hit its mark, whipping Roger with precision. This was brutal and likely to get worse. I could only imagine what would happen if he got close enough with the knife to stick it into Roger's guts.

Roger started yelling like I hadn't heard since we were children, as the manager repeatedly whipped him with the antenna. Roger then made a sudden right turn from the car and headed toward the mall, hoping to escape and be rescued from someone he clearly should not have taunted. He was at full speed in two strides, screaming the whole time. I stood there gawking at the spectacle before me, watching my clearly overmatched friend, flee the scene of yet another beat down.

The restaurant manager took a few more steps before he stopped, out of breath. He'd clearly made his point, with Roger on the run with his tail between his legs.

Duncan profusely apologized to the guy who had the power to fire him on the spot.

"Don't let that prick in the store again. Ever."

"I won't. Sorry," said Duncan, with all sincerity.

When the manager started walking to his car, I turned to Duncan and said, "Why does he do this every year?"

"Hell, I don't know. But I hope I don't get fired for it. My dad will kill me," was all he said.

Roger had stopped running when he no longer heard the antenna whipping through the air behind him, then he turned around to calculate his next move. He saw that the manager was getting into his car to go home, so Roger slowly started walking back toward us. Suddenly, he stopped to make sure his tormenter was leaving the area, and continued when he saw the tail lights of his car go over the hill. He reached around and rubbed where the antenna got him in the side and shoulder.

As he approached, he quickly wiped a tear that had formed in the corner of his right eye.

"I could have beaten him if we'd just used our fists," Roger said.

Rick and I remained silent.

We all got into Roger's car and headed for DC. Nobody spoke for a full twenty minutes, as Roger tried to adjust to the lingering sting of the antenna body blows. He was lucky he wasn't killed.

"Hand me a beer, Duncan, will ya?" Roger said, as we approached Key Bridge from Rosslyn, with Dixie Liquor coming up on the horizon. "I think I'm gonna get drunk tonight."

Roger's constant need to physically assert dominance any time he felt threatened or rejected, was something that all of us on Hicks Drive had witnessed many times. But as we got older, as we left the protections of childhood and into the uncertainties of becoming adults, Roger seemed to focus most of his hostility toward professional, educated people.

And, it continued, unabated.

When I'd tried, repeatedly, to determine the origin of it, to get an understanding of why he felt that way, all he'd give me was vague answers about *their* attitude, *their* upbringing, or nameless opportunities *they* got, but denied to *him*.

But, over the years, as Roger shared with me more of the comments his mother had made to him about *his* limited career paths and, especially *my* inability to ever go to college, the more Roger's attitude made sense.

Perhaps, Roger had finally realized that his mother had been at least half wrong, all along.

Or, maybe he'd wished he'd at least tried to go to college—only to be reminded by Mommy that it was hopeless.

And alcohol only made it worse.

Sadly, I never learned the truth.

A true Vienna institution. Picture from Facebook Group "Vienna Kids".

The Grim Reaper Let Us Get Away, August 1974

*"Lord, I was dancing, dancing, dancing so free
And dancing, dancing, dancing so free
And dancing, Lord, keep your hand off me
And dancing with Mr. D., with Mr. D., with Mr. D"*[36]

We pulled into the 7-11 on the north end of town that Friday night, about the same way we had on so many other Friday nights. I had been riding shotgun in Roger's *Blue Streak*, a powerful Dodge Challenger, with a four-speed transmission and plenty of horsepower under the hood. It was *fast*. Pete was in the back, talking a mile a minute. Which is why we'd always put him in the back seat.

"Think you'll flunk out *this* year?" Roger asked, directing the question to me, but making sure that Pete heard it, as well.

"You didn't think I'd pass freshman year, did ya'?" I said. "One down, three to go," I continued, with as much enthusiasm as I could, just to antagonize Roger.

He parked his car and got out, mumbled something else about college that I couldn't understand, and went inside the store, to get some beer. We'd intended to pick up Rob in half an hour. What we would do after that was up for discussion.

Then it started raining.

Roger was gone longer than a typical convenience store stop-over, so Pete and I went through his selection of tapes lying about the car. I found one we liked, just as Roger returned and climbed back into the car.

"Some damned foreigner behind the counter," Roger said, with no effort to hide his contempt, while putting the key into the ignition. "That's why it took so damn long."

He squealed the tires on the wet pavement, backing out of the parking space, and then lit a cigarette, still fuming about the guy behind the counter who'd taken so long.

Then he turned his frustration toward me, again.

"What the hell you gonna do *if* you finish school?" Roger asked, but

---

[36] "Dancing With Mr. D", Keith Richards and Mick Jagger, 1973

not really wanting an answer, because he then quickly added, "Mommy says ain't nobody hiring."

I'd already heard enough about what Mommy said about this, or what she thought of that, so I didn't answer. I'd planned to have a good time, since I had to go back to school in a couple of weeks.

We'd polished off four of the beers, taking the scenic route to Rob's, before pulling into his driveway. Roger, as usual after two beers, had to take a leak, so he quickly got out of the car and ran behind the nearest bush, just as Rob walked out of his front door.

"Roger, what the hell are you doing? We have two bathrooms inside, ya' know?" Rob yelled. Upon noticing a silhouette of Roger peeing from the streetlight, I laid into the car horn. Roger pissed on his own leg trying to do a quick zip-up.

"Quit it, dumb ass," Roger demanded, as he headed out from behind the bush, toward the Blue Streak. And, while the stain on his leg made the rest of us laugh even harder, Roger's frustration and aggression seemed to be increasing.

Rob climbed into the back seat with Peter, and then the four of us began the process of planning our evening. Why we never seemed to do that before we got into the car, I'll never know.

"Wanna' go to Clancy's?" I asked, thinking about the topless club on DC's Wisconsin Avenue.

"I don't have enough money for that," Rob said.

"We could swing by Pizza Fair," offered Pete with the best local idea on a short list.

"What're we gonna do at Pizza Fair?" I asked. "There's always a bunch of cars driving around in circles."

"There are always a lot of people hanging out there. And besides, it doesn't cost anything" Pete said.

And then, before we could discuss it any further, Roger fired up the Blue Streak and backed out of the driveway. He then revved up the engine and laid rubber for a good three seconds, before squealing the tires in second and third gear. It was going to be one of those nights.

"Remember what Clouser said to you the last time he pulled you over, Roger?" I casually asked, as the speedometer indicated sixty five miles per hour in a twenty five zone. Clouser was a Vienna cop, the nemesis of every kid with a hot car who lived in, or passed through town.

"Yeah, I remember that somebitch. He'll never catch me in the Blue Streak, these are my roads."

That was Roger's answer anytime he was questioned, cautioned, or advised about driving faster than he should.

We made the two mile drive to Pizza Fair in record time. And Roger finally had slowed down a little after further posturing that he would never get caught by the likes of Officer Clouser.

Despite the steady rainfall, the parking lot was full. Again. The Pizza Fair lot had been a gathering spot for Vienna kids since the beginning of time. And tonight, just before many of us would go back to college for the fall semester, was an event.

We'd made a few passes around the perimeter, when I caught a glimpse of Fat Pat's truck parked near Maple Avenue. Roger pulled up behind it and we all saw the big boy himself talking to two girls sitting in an adjacent car.

"Hey Pat! Layin' the heavy rap?" I yelled, interrupting his conversation with some local honey I recognized, but didn't know. A distant rumble of thunder in the distance was loud enough to cause Pat to look up, rather than at me to answer my question.

"What are ya'll up to tonight?" Pat then asked, as he walked over to our car.

"We got cold beer, and thinking about Georgetown later," said Rob from the back. Actually, we hadn't mentioned Georgetown, but it sounded okay to me.

"I've got some, too," Pat said. "You mind if one of these babes joins us?" Pat sounded more hopeful than realistic about the prospect of separating one of the girls from her herd.

"Come on. We got room," Roger said, apparently excited at the idea of some female companionship.

This was *all* Roger needed—he was already half lit, complaining all evening about everything not going his way and endlessly badgering me about college. Suddenly, he's given the opportunity to strut around like a rooster, trying to attract some girl he didn't even know.

Fat Pat and his gal pal climbed into the backseat, while Peter jumped in the front and rode on the stick between the two seats. With six of us, we had about two people too many for the car.

A bolt of lightning then lit up the sky, with the ensuing crash of thunder right behind it.

The storm was closing in.

"This is Debbie," Pat said. "She lives across the street from me."

I knew the girl from school. She was very attractive with long blonde hair and bright blue eyes. That night she was sportin' a halter top and short cut-offs to reveal about two miles of long, tanned legs.

Before she nestled her way into the crowded backseat, Roger intently stared at her in his rear-view mirror while revving his engine. He then reached over and turned on the radio to one of the local FM stations, cranking out *Born to Be Wild* as he peeled out of the parking lot.

We'd barely gotten onto Maple Avenue, when it started to rain even harder. One of those typical late August-in-DC-thunderstorms had formed directly over our heads, dumping rain like it was the end of the world.

Completely undeterred by it all, Roger drove north on Route 123, maybe ten or fifteen miles over the speed limit. We approached the edge of town, and Roger dropped it into second gear before stepping on the gas, pinning all of us to the back of our seats.

Roger had total control of all of us, and he knew it.

Sixty-five miles per hour and we were barely out of town. He shifted back into third gear and then floored it, ejecting the ashtray from the dashboard with the acceleration. Eighty, ninety miles per hour on a rain-drenched stretch for slow poke commuters.

"Roger, slow down! It's raining like hell out here! Are you crazy?" Pete pleaded from his perch between the two front seats.

But Roger didn't slow down.

"What's the matter? Don't ya' trust me," Roger said, as we accelerated until the speedometer showed one hundred ten miles per hour.

I was *really* scared, but stubbornly refused to give Roger the satisfaction of knowing he had the upper hand.

I just stared straight ahead, hopeless to do anything, just like the other passengers.

Off in the distance, I saw the red tail lights of a car barely creeping onto the highway. Fortunately, Roger saw it, too, and released his foot from the gas pedal. I instinctively glanced at the speedometer and saw that we were still exceeding a hundred miles per hour. And, the unsuspecting driver of the slow car certainly hadn't anticipated that the vehicle approaching from behind in their lane was traveling that fast.

I felt Roger tap the brake pedal, but then his car started to fishtail down the highway. I thought it was the end.

Stunned silence overcame the passengers, with the roar of the engine and tires slashing through the downpour, the only sounds I could hear. Even the radio mysteriously went dead.

As that Debbie girl screamed out, all I could do was grip the arm rest on the door as tightly as I could. I had buckled my seat belt after Pete had wedged himself next to me, but almost instinctively, I reached down to confirm it was indeed securely holding me.

Then the car started weaving, nearly out of control, as it rapidly closed in on the car ahead of us.

The Blue Streak then bumped the curb in the left lane, bumped it again, jerking our heads from side-to- side.

The slow car stayed on the right. In an instant, we blew right past it, with Roger continuing to tap on the brake pedal. Our car finally stopped fishtailing, as we slowed down to a manageable speed.

My right hand was aching, cramping from clutching the door. Peter, having shifted in his seat away from Roger and toward me, was nearly unrecognizable, having pulled his knees to his chest to brace for impact. I glanced in the backseat, where I saw Debbie in the fetal position, between Rob and Fat Pat.

"See. I told you these were my roads," Roger said.

The next day, news of our escape from death was all over town. Roger was the self-proclaimed hero, because of his superior driving skills.

And rather than serve as a warning, our near catastrophe merely provided affirmation to Roger for skills and abilities he didn't possess. What it also did, was demonstrate to the passengers that ol' Roger was becoming more than a know-it-all.

He was dangerous.

The Bridge, Spring Break 1975

"Take it back
Take it back
Oh no, you can't say that
All of my friends
Are not dead or in jail
Through rock and through stone
The black wind still moans
Sweet revenge
Sweet revenge
Without fail"[37]

On December 1st, 1974 TWA flight 514 crashed into Mt. Weather, the soon to be famous presidential bomb shelter. I was driving on I-95, to go back to school in Norfolk, after a few days off for Thanksgiving, when I heard the news on the radio.

Like most catastrophes involving multiple deaths, the details were difficult to comprehend at first. Two other students from school, who were riding back with me, just stared out the window, as the news commentator talked about the tragedy that'd happened just a few miles from where we were.

I knew that area. I also knew that mountain, since I'd driven past it several times on the way to Winchester on one side, and Bluemont on the other.

About four months later, I decided to visit the crash site, since I had the time during my Spring Break. So, one Saturday afternoon, Pete, Roger and I met Chili Dog, one of Roger's friends in Sterling, and off we went to the first range of the Blue Ridge Mountains. We would reach Mt. Weather in barely over an hour.

It was cold that day. But not so much so, after the tequila started to kick in. Soon, we were all leaning back, listening to the cassette player, and enjoying the ride like we had nothing else to do. Perhaps we didn't.

Mount Weather is a labyrinth of tunnels built to house up to two thousand people from the Federal Government including Congress, Cabinet, Supreme Court, and President of the United States, in case of nuclear war—

---

[37] "Sweet Revenge", John Prine, 1973

or worse. It is made of solid rock, or more to the point, a solid mountain of rock. Security is as tight as one could expect of The White House, though certainly not located at 1600 Pennsylvania Avenue. Driving past the entrance gate on Route 601 is about as close as most of us will ever get to the really cool stuff at the ultra-secure fortress. Just by cruising too slowly past the main gate, would cause the shoot-to-kill, fully-armed soldiers to get a little nervous.

But on that cold spring day, we didn't make the drive into the mountains to see the presidential bomb shelter—we went to see a plane crash site.

When we'd reached the town of Round Hill, we stopped to use the restroom at a convenience store. Roger was first-in, first-out and lit a cigarette while he leaned on the car to wait for the others. When I walked by him on the way to the car, he stuck his foot out to trip me. I saw it just in time to avoid falling, but I intentionally stepped on it to make a point.

"Watch where you're going!" he said, as he gave me a shove.

"Oh, didn't see ya, Roger," I said, to avoid escalating the tension further.

Roger then tried to give me another shove, but missed and lost his balance. He was drunker than the rest of us, and his energy level had significantly declined since we'd left Sterling, or he'd have tried again.

As we neared the crest of the mountain, about eighteen hundred feet in elevation, the temperature quickly declined about ten degrees. The windows began to fog up as we approached the low-lying clouds, engulfing us in the mist.

We didn't precisely know where the site was located, so Chili Dog slowed the car to almost an idle. I reached over and turned off the cassette deck, and all of us intently gazed out the windows. The conversations in the car livened-up, as we anticipated something none of us had ever seen. Suddenly, the combination of tequila and the excitement of the event revealed itself, causing everyone to speak louder.

Chili Dog's car slowly rolled around an outcrop of rock and we all knew exactly what it was: the point of impact of the plane. We all looked on, breathless. Chili Dog slowly pulled the car off the side of the road, put it in *Park,* and then got out. I slowly opened the passenger side door and very, very slowly put my foot on the ground.

I stood up and all I could do was gaze at the destruction that surrounded us. I then found myself joined by my traveling companions without having heard any of them approach.

I turned and looked northwestward, before noticing that the top half of all of the trees in a one hundred foot wide path had been sawed off. Like a giant chain saw at work. But it was an airplane that did it—filled with nearly one hundred people.

The aircraft had approached from the northwest, sawed off the trees as it approached the mountain peak, hit that rock which I was then touching, and then tumbled up the hill in flames.

I started to feel a little nauseous, but I wasn't about to hurl in front of my buddies. So, I slowly climbed up and around the point of impact, and then started walking up the hill. Pieces of luggage and bits of personal items were everywhere: suitcase handles, doll heads, belt buckles, and part of a child's shoe. Burnt trees were all that was left of this part of the forest. All of the underbrush was incinerated.

We all wandered in silence, each of us perhaps trying to comprehend the massive destruction of human life that occurred that day. Many of the passengers were returning home from the Thanksgiving dinner that they had three days prior, before they died. And the cruel irony stacked upon tragedy was that the plane was supposed to land at National Airport, about seventy miles to the east, on the banks of the Potomac River. This flight had been diverted to Dulles International because of bad weather at the scheduled location. They shouldn't even have been there that day.

As I turned and walked back to the car, I saw something shining amid the charred underbrush and burial grounds of the passengers and crew. I reached down and picked it up, a piece of the plane, a tiny corner of a window attached to a three-inch sliver of fuselage. I stuck it in my pocket.

My parents had dragged me to see deceased relatives in cemeteries on countless occasions, but I had never been to a gravesite like this.

I'd read in the newspapers that the investigators from the National Transportation Safety Board had thoroughly combed through the wreckage in search of answers. But it seemed that much debris still remained.

We slowly walked back to the car, individually, rather than the group that had made their way up the mountain. I, too, was looking for answers. All of us scoured the ground while we walked, occasionally kicking at an object, or bending to examine something a little closer.

When we'd all gotten in the car, I didn't feel like turning the cassette deck back on, but I took the aircraft part out of my pocket and passed it to Peter. Eventually, everyone in the car examined it without speaking.

I opened the bottle of tequila, took a swig and then passed *it* around, as well.

Soon after that, though, the radio was turned up loud, and the tequila took its effect.

We drove down the south end of the mountain much faster than we had gone up the north side, and were soon cruising down US 50, back toward Vienna.

We still had plenty of daylight left, but the tequila was running dry, so we pulled over and stopped at a 7-11 for some cold beer to finish the trip.

Chili Dog suggested we take the scenic route, so we turned off the four-lane and onto a little side road in the country. The gently rolling hills of Loudoun County were simply beautiful. This was horse country—the kind that gave us Genuine Risk, only the second filly to ever win the Kentucky

Derby. It was the kind of horse country that attracted the Washington D.C. icon and former Redskins owner, Jack Kent Cooke. Senator John Warner and his wife, Elizabeth Taylor, lived in nearby Middleburg. Averell Harriman, nationally known politician, diplomat, and businessman was a brief resident. Television and radio personality, Arthur Godfrey, often broadcasted from his Beacon Hill Estate.

But conversations kept drifting back to the crash, and as they did, Roger began turning back to the jerk that he all-too-often became when he drank too much. For some reason, he seemed to be focusing much of this surly behavior in my direction.

"What do *you* know about airplanes, Rick, you ever flown one?" he asked. Earlier, I had shared with the group my conclusion about the aircraft's final approach as it clipped the tree tops and hit the rock. It was quite obvious what had happened.

"What do *you* think happened, Roger?" I replied.

"I think it hit that rock from the other direction and burst into flames."

"Then how did all that stuff get scattered backwards?"

The others started laughing and apparently Roger didn't appreciate that. He turned slightly and hit me in the shoulder.

Then, he slurred something about me being a know-it-all-college-boy.

Although I was finally bigger and stronger than Roger, I was still a bit intimidated by him—the years of bullying he put me through. I had about as much as I was going to take from him that day, but, soon, as was often the case, all was forgotten, and we changed the conversation to the Redskin's prospects for the 1975-76 campaign the following year—how we wished they were as good as the '72 team that went to the Super Bowl.

Just then, the car began to fishtail, as we sped down the now dirt road we'd found ourselves traveling.

We had a flat tire.

As Chili Dog let off on the gas, a bridge about three hundred yards ahead, conveniently came into view.

"If you can make it to that bridge, we'll have a flat spot to the change the tire. Better than this gravel road, huh?" I tried to persuade him, since it was his car and he would probably do all the work. I just wanted to get away from Roger and out of the backseat of the car.

It easily got to the bridge and we all got out. We hadn't passed another vehicle in the twenty minutes we had been on that road. Nor would any car pass while changing the tire.

It was a relatively new bridge over the historic and pristine Goose Creek. Since it wouldn't require four healthy young men to change a tire, I reached into the trunk and retrieved a football, while Pete and Chili Dog got to work.

Roger and I put about thirty yards between us and started to pass the ball back and forth.

He must have gotten bored or tired because soon he was intentionally making difficult and off-line throws, requiring extra effort to catch. And it kept getting worse. He threw one completely over my head by ten feet.

I was just starting to get a little aggravated, when he intentionally threw the ball near the edge of the steep road embankment. I had no chance to catch that one, so I carefully climbed down to retrieve the ball.

As I was climbing back up, ball in hand, nearing the top of the embankment, I saw Roger standing where I wanted to climb. There I stood up and Roger, in an awkward, yet aggressive way, tried to push me back down the embankment.

I didn't say anything, but maneuvered around him, and then I guess the game was over. Roger seemed to have trouble focusing his eyes, becoming more belligerent by the moment.

The tire was done, as well. So, Pete rolled the flat around to the back of the car and tossed it into the trunk. Chili Dog put the jack next to it.

As I reached into the trunk of the car to place the football behind the flattened tire, Roger walked up, stood close, and then hit my shoulder with his fist. That time, I didn't see it coming, so I lost my balance, hitting my head on the trunk lid. It really hurt.

Roger opened his mouth to laugh, but before he emitted a sound, my fist landed between his eyes, shattering his glasses in all directions, opened a wound on the bridge of his nose, sending Roger stumbling backwards.

I knew that as soon as he regained his senses, he would kill me. So, I hit him in the face again, then once more. I had backed him into the guardrail with three punches.

"Now I'm going to throw you off this damn bridge," I yelled, before grabbing his shirt in the front with one hand, and his belt buckle with the other. I lifted him off the ground like he was made of feathers and tossed him over the side of the bridge into the icy water below.

I'll never forget the expression of total surprise on his face as he looked up while falling down. He hit the water flat on his back with an enormous splash. The creek was only about three feet deep, so Roger quickly struggled to his feet, looked up at me and slurred these immortal words: "I'm gonna kill you…" just before he passed out, falling backwards onto the shoreline of the water.

In a panic, I raced to the end of the bridge, but Peter and Chili Dog had already reached the edge of the creek near Roger. In a sudden moment of bravado, Chili Dog stood in my path and said, "Don't hit him anymore."

As Roger lay motionless on the creek bank, Pete carefully lifted his feet out of the water. As he did so, Roger slowly regained consciousness.

It was ten years of frustration and humiliation built up in that rage.

I had actually *tried* to kill him.

By the time Roger was on his feet, assisted by Peter and Chili Dog, I had made it down to the water's edge, as well. So, I followed the wobbly trio as they climbed up to the bridge.

Once we had reached the car, I got in front of Roger and saw a steady stream of blood running down his face, where his glasses were driven into his flesh by my fist. I grabbed a cold beer and told Roger to hold it to his cut to slow the blood flow.

I intently watched Roger, as I tried to sort out the emotions I was feeling: *relief* that I'd finally vanquished the neighborhood bully, *amazement* that it was so violent, *frustration* that I'd waited so long to do it, and *gratitude* that I didn't kill him.

We drove back to Sterling, where we had left my car, and soon departed Chili Dog's house after applying first aid to Roger's face. The cuts had stopped bleeding, but his whole face was swollen like it had stopped a fist or two—or three.

I actually felt sorry for him.

I knew he deserved the thorough beating I'd given him. I also knew that he provoked it, just like he had with so many before me. But, I also knew it would never be the same between us.

Curiously, I wasn't sure if that was good or bad.

This adventure began as an exploration of a crash site, sacred ground to anyone and everyone connected.

Then it suddenly, and without warning, became something completely different.

There was no going back.

Karen's Uncle Ricky, Aunt Fran, and their daughter Kim, 1975.

Jaws and Aunt Fran's Wig, June 1975

The most influential beach movie of all time, *Jaws*, premiered in June of 1975. Prior to that mind-numbing event, most of us had never considered or cared about what might lurk below the surface of the green, silty, usually smelly, Atlantic Ocean we'd visit in the summer, a mere three hour ride from Vienna.

The beaches of choice were typically the Jersey shore, Virginia Beach, Ocean City, and Rehoboth, not necessarily in that order.

But *Jaws* changed that nonchalant, carefree attitude for everyone. And the change was not subtle—at all. This movie was horrifying, brought to life through the directorial genius of Steven Spielberg, by an awkward, but nevertheless frightening mechanical shark. Add an Oscar-worthy performance by Robert Shaw, believable characters played by Richard Dreyfus and Roy Scheider, and a soundtrack we all know by heart, and this movie would prove to be a classic of epic proportion.

However, during the summer of 1975, my mind was not pre-occupied by man (and woman) eating sharks. Nor was I necessarily interested in going to the beach. I had spent two years away at a college that was less than thirty minutes from the Atlantic Ocean, so I already had enough of that.

I had a new girlfriend, at the time.

Karen Adams and I had been regularly dating for two years, so by 1975 our relationship was developing into something serious—something special. And as we spent more and more time together, it was inevitable that those times would also include family.

My parents didn't typically invite more than one person to our house at any given time, so large dinner parties and celebrations were never a holiday option for me. But for Karen, it was.

Thanksgiving, Christmas, and Redskins games filled the homes of whomever hosted the event with fifteen or twenty family members, including children of all ages. Since I was untrained in the art of family gatherings, it took me a while to get used to all the activity, and Redskins/Cowboy games required further mental preparation. They were always high intensity contests, with decibel levels of excitement to match.

It seemed to me that a small handful of Karen's relatives attended more functions than other family members did. And among the former were her Aunt Fran, who was married to Karen's uncle and her father's younger brother, Ricky. Fran was an only child from somewhere in Florida, and one of the nicest people I'd had ever met.

But what made Fran interesting, was that she was different, maybe a bit quirky. I didn't pay much attention to how people dressed back then, so I guess Fran's attire was classic seventies tacky-funky. These outfits were entertaining enough to begin with, but Fran also had this unusual habit of wearing a plethora of wigs in an attempt to match her current ensemble, often with mixed results; some of her hair augmentations looked like they were still alive. I could have sworn that I saw a furry tail swishing out the back of one of them, as it comfortably sat upon her head.

But Fran proudly wore every single wig. Loud bell bottom disco pants, an oversized and horizontally striped top, platform shoes, and her wig—Fran was good to go.

And go she did, along with Ricky, to the Tyson's Cinema premiere of *Jaws*.

Tyson's Cinema was a gigantic theater on Route Seven with over one thousand seats. Add the latest theater sound technology, with low-end base speakers that vibrated the seats, and Tyson's was a cinematic treat.

Fran and Ricky waited in line for tickets for about two hours. Tyson's was one of only five DC locations to premiere this soon-to-be-blockbuster movie, and everybody for miles around wanted to experience the terror.

With tickets finally in-hand, Ricky and Fran made their way inside the mega-theater, stopped for sodas and a tub of artificially buttered popcorn, before taking their seats about midway to the screen; certainly close enough to feel the man-eating sharks, especially with those seat-vibrating speakers.

The theater ushers and tech crew helped to perpetuate the drama by refusing to start the projector until everyone was seated. They threatened, and actually did, lock the doors once the movie had started, and kept them locked until the end of the first scene. So, too bad for you, if you were stuck in traffic, ensnared in the popcorn line, or incapacitated by the bathroom wait.

But, as we all now know, Spielberg didn't need any help from well-intending, but overly- controlling ticket takers.

That evening, the eyes of Fran and the other nine hundred ninety nine theatre-goers at Tyson's were glued to the screen in anticipation of the first shark encounter.

Tension in the audience began with the first note of the shark attack, before it crescendoed, as viewers could only watch the innocent skinny-dipping girl, be so totally clueless and helpless in the middle of the ocean.

The still unseen shark approached ever closer with one objective.

The startled audience squirmed in their seats when the shark took its first bite, tugging the swimmer underwater with those unseen gigantic teeth. Then once again, only more violently.

At that moment, Fran couldn't it take anymore, letting out an honest blood curdled scream, while gripping her husband's arm in sheer terror.

But the opening scene of *Jaws* gripped all of us for the rest of our lives and never let go. And from that point forward in the movie, it was a roller coaster ride; terror in one scene, followed by almost a calm anticipation in the next, continuing on for two hours and ten minutes.

Everyone in the theater squealed out with every shark scene. The build up to the next attack was almost overwhelming, facilitated by the most appropriately accurate soundtrack in the history of cinema.

But the dramatic fashion in which *Jaws* held us in its grasp was best illustrated by the scene in which the oceanographer, Matt Hooper (Richard Dreyfus), was in SCUBA gear, checking out the sunken remains of a small boat. He and Sheriff Brody (Roy Scheider) had discovered the wreckage, while looking for a couple of guys who went missing earlier in the day.

Everyone was on the edge of their seats when Dreyfus went into the water, since we all knew the shark was nearby. It was always nearby. Dreyfus circled around the boat and found several of what looked like punctures in the hull. That's right, about the size of a shark's gigantic mouth.

Then, just as we, the viewers, were starting to get really

uncomfortable with a SCUBA-clad nutcase swimming in dangerous waters, suddenly and without warning a head popped out from inside the sunken boat, instantly filling the entire screen, as only Spielberg can do. Everyone, and I *do* mean everyone, screamed like little girls.

And that night, in Tyson's Cinema at the premiere of the scariest movie since *The Exorcist*, Fran screamed the loudest. And with her scream, she leapt out of her seat, instinctively, compulsively, and uncontrollably. She was like a cat awakened by a bullhorn, went into orbit so fast that gravity couldn't contain her; her black wig catapulted from her head, and went right into the lap of the poor guy seated behind her.

Most people don't bring spare underwear to a movie premiere, not even to see *Jaws*. But if that guy in Seat 17, Row L didn't soil himself at that moment, then there will never be another situation in which he would—but he *did* start screaming. He grabbed the wig in one hand, while spilling his drink with the other, and flung the wig about twenty feet behind him. He'd thrown it so violently, with unplanned precision, that it hit some poor old lady in the forehead, before ricocheting and coming to rest in *her* lap.

The second victim of Fran's aerial wig attack had screamed as well, before grabbing it, and throwing the offending pseudo-head onto the floor, before it caused further chaos and pandemonium.

I never knew for sure what happened to either of the wig's victims after that night, but I heard a rumor that both completed their therapy in about five years.

And neither goes swimming in the ocean. Never. Ever.[38]

---

38   Story told by Ricky Adams, circa 1975

Hard at Work, December 1975

"She is like a cat in the dark and then
She is the darkness
She rules her life like a fine skylark and when
The sky is starless"[39]

College students are always broke. I accepted that because I was self-supporting and naively thought everyone else was, too. And self-supporting college students are not supposed to have any money.

Fortunately, my good buddy from high school, Rob, helped me get my first construction site job the summer after my senior year in high school. And with the confidence I had from that experience, I was able to say *goodbye* to low wage retail jobs at Tyson's Corner Mall.

The DC metro area was still booming from the post WWII years until, well, right about now. And in the 1970s, if you were willing to work hard, and didn't mind getting out of bed at six am every summer weekday, you could make $4.00 per hour, more than double the minimum wage; overtime was for the asking, and I asked often.

While working construction was great student money, I was usually tapped out after the spring tuition was paid in November. So, during every Christmas break, I was looking for a temporary job to generate enough money to get me to May, when I could start my full-time construction job again. It was a vicious cycle: make enough money during the summers for college tuition, books, room and board—run out of money by November, work a couple weeks during Christmas to make it until summer recess.

So, with empty checkbooks in hand, my buddy Rob and I hatched a plan to earn some cash after final exams in December 1975. We bought some of those jumbo index cards, the ones that were about twice the size of a normal one, and hand-printed the following:

---

[39] "Rhiannon", Stevie Nicks, 1975

> **WE WILL DO ANYTHING!!**
>
> *Ready, willing, and definitely able college students
> with various home repair, landscaping,
> and general handy-man skills ready for hire.*
>
> *Call Rick at 703-938-2764 or*
>
> *Rob at 703-555-1212 for estimates.*

If the bold text wasn't enough to catch someone's eye, we outlined the edge of each card with one of those bright yellow HI-LITERS everybody used to mark every sentence in each of their brand-new college text books. I still haven't figured out why we marked up those text-books.

After we completed our marketing pieces, we spent a few hours the next morning placing these artistic gems on every cork bulletin board in every Vienna retail establishment that had one—Giant Food, Dart Drug, Magruder's, Safeway, The Vienna Inn, Firestone Tires, Weber Tire in Fairfax, plus several others.

Now all that was left to do was wait for the phone to ring, and when it did, Rob and I would have a job. It would be that simple.

For the remaining few hours left in the day, after we had placed our Glow-In-The-Dark outlined index cards in all the right places, the phone hadn't rung a single time.

But the next day I received a call from a nice elderly lady wanting me to come get her cat out of a tree. She was slightly confused and kept calling me *Rob* after I had already told her three times my name was *Rick*.

"Well, Rob," she said, as she began describing her cat, starting with its name and how long she had it.

"Missy has never climbed that tree before today. I had her de-clawed as a kitten, and she usually stays inside the house, but she escaped."

My first thought was *how did that cat climb a tree with no claws,* but I didn't ask because it really didn't matter anyway.

"I can come over today, ma'am. Where do you live?" I asked, but she abruptly hung up before giving me any further information. The skeletal remains of poor kitty are probably still up in that tree waiting for me.

In the day following kitty lady, Rob and I were getting frustrated with the lack of any response for work, and my mom was starting to get on my nerves with her incessant prodding.

"You got a job lined up, yet?" she would ask me every-freakin' day. She knew that for every dollar I earned was one dollar less that I would try to get from her.

But soon our luck changed. I got a call from a very energetic and enthusiastic guy, who said he lived in Springfield. His first question after exchanging pleasantries was, "So you'll do anything?" He still hadn't introduced himself, but wanted to immediately confirm the bold print in our ad.

That was just a little odd.

"Yes, that's right," I replied.

"Can you come to my house tonight?" he asked with more hope than determination in his voice.

"What do you want us to do?" I innocently asked, with my curiosity starting to rise, and suspicion making its first appearance. I'd already noticed a couple of red flags, but I was determined not to pass-up this potential opportunity. And it was our only lead—not counting kitty lady.

"It's too much detail to get into over the phone," the man said, "and it's kind of private, so if you can be here at seven o'clock, we'd love to have you."

"We?" I asked, a little confused by the addition.

"My *wife* and I would love to have you," he quickly clarified, with emphasis on *wife,* and in a very approachable voice I hadn't yet heard from him. He then gave me his address and some directions how to get there. It was simple enough.

"I'll be there at seven. Thanks for calling," I said. "And what is your name, sir?" But he hung up without answering my question. I was already wondering what the heck I just agreed to do.

Right away, I called Rob and told him of our fortunate turn of events, and that I'd pick him up at 6:15, about three hours from then. That would give us plenty of time to be in Springfield by seven. I told him what I knew about my mystery caller—but what I didn't know was what concerned me.

Somehow, I convinced myself that everything would be okay. Rob and I were college boys, we'd figure it out.

In the interim, I knew I was going to someone's house, but that was about it. For that, I knew that I should, at the very least, shower up and shave the peach fuzz off my face. It was, after all, a job interview. I then found the least wrinkled shirt and a pair of somewhat matching-pants to make myself presentable, and then headed to Rob's house.

During the short drive to Rob's, I wondered if I was unnecessarily paranoid, and that our soon-to-be employer was really just a good guy with a great opportunity. Or were the hairs that stood up on the back of my neck an indication that something wasn't quite right with this guy?

What was the role of his wife, who sounded more like an afterthought?

Rob was on time, as usual, as he ran out of his front door, just when I was pulling into the driveway.

"So, what's this all about?" Rob asked me again, apparently not satisfied with my previous explanation.

"Like I told you, he wouldn't say. Actually, he was kind of evasive, so I guess we'll find out when we get there."

"Well, what if he's a weirdo, or something?" Rob asked me, as I was merging into the heavy, late rush-hour traffic so typical of the DC Metropolitan area. Two tractor trailers were single-file in the lane I needed, so I accelerated past them and went to the front of the procession.

"Well, what if he is? He's married. At least he said he was," I replied.

We both laughed at how stupid the conversation was going, so I turned on the radio to our favorite station, the so-called *alternative,* WHFS out of Maryland.

During the rest of the drive, Rob and I talked about other things we might pursue to make some money before school—just in case this mystery job didn't pan out.

But our minds were still clearly on the opportunity that would present itself in about two minutes, as we arrived at our destination. It was a beautiful and relatively new, two-story home in one of the myriad of neighborhoods that sprang up all over Springfield—and everywhere else around the Capital Beltway, for that matter. It was really nice.

As we got out of the car, I instinctively ran my tongue across my top row of teeth, trying to remember if I'd brushed them before I left home.

Rob and I were standing at the front door before I had time for further anxiety, so I reached over and rang the doorbell.

I heard the distinctive latch of the deadbolt, followed by the sight of a rotating doorknob. Then the door creaked, loudly at first, opening ever so slowly. The entire effort seemed almost deliberate.

Before the door was fully opened, I saw, standing in front of me, The Goddess of Beauty.

Initially my gaze was drawn to her face; high cheek bones seemed to frame her illuminating brown eyes, and an almost devious smile that displayed two rows of perfect, shiny teeth. However, I couldn't maintain eye contact for more than an instant, because I enjoyed the sight of her long black dress, ornamented by a pearl necklace, and matching bracelet—all a perfect ensemble for her tall, thin body. The Goddess' dark, shoulder-length hair accentuated her large breasts, which really didn't even need accentuating.

When she stepped back to let us in, I caught a glimpse of a well-toned and slender thigh peeking out from the slit in her dress.

My earlier concerns instantly disappeared.

"Hi, I'm Rachel. Rachel Smith. Please come in."

"I'm Rick. This is Rob," I clumsily offered, while watching Rachel's every move.

"Would you like some champagne?" she asked in a tone that was almost musical.

"That would be great," Rob quickly interjected.

I suddenly and rather forcefully stepped in front of Rob, as we followed Rachel from the front door into the kitchen. My eyes never left her hips, as they swayed ever so rhythmically. She looked as good from the back as in front.

There was an opened bottle of champagne and two glasses on the counter, so I figured Rachel and her husband must have gotten an early start, while waiting for their young men to appear as instructed.

But the guy with whom I spoke on the phone was nowhere in sight.

"My husband told me you're a student at George Mason, right?" Rachel asked, turning to face me as she spoke.

"That's right. I transferred from Old Dominion this year," I let myself get a little more comfortable, allowing my eyes to go where they wanted.

"Well, I'm confident you're going to like what you see here tonight," responded Rachel, who seemed to be reading my mind.

When Rachel slightly turned to speak to Rob, I saw a grin on his face as he spoke, assuring me that he was thinking the same thing I was. This would be beyond great. And we were getting paid for it.

I kept thinking of all the stories I had heard about older couples hiring young guys to spice up the boudoir boredom. I had it all figured out, and we'd been there about ten minutes.

Raging hormones and a lurid imagination is a dangerous combo for a twenty year old college male.

"This way, please," Rachel said, as she slowly walked down a somewhat dimly lit hallway, champagne glass in her delicate hand.

I once again immediately fell in line behind her so I could watch her walk without obstructions in my view. I no longer had suspicions about this opportunity, and my heightened confidence was now in control. Politely averting my eyes from Rachel never entered my mind.

Suddenly, she paused at a closed door, hesitated for just an instant, then opened it and took a step down. She was definitely not entering the master bedroom. We were going into the basement.

When I got to the door, I saw that the level below was well-lit, almost like a conference room. I had anticipated seeing the flickering shadows from candles or a crackling fire in the fireplace, since we weren't descending into a bedroom.

"Hi again, everybody," Rachel announced to the room. But when my foot landed at the base of the stairs, I saw a lady about fifty years old, two men in their forties wearing mismatched clothing, and a grandpa who had to be at least eighty. They were all sitting in a semi-circle, strategically arranged in front of a pull-down screen for a projector, with presumably Mr. Smith facing the group.

"This is Rick and Rob. They will be joining us, as well."

Instantly, the group turned to face Rob and I, each with a forced grin that revealed they were as perplexed about that evening's event as I was.

I glanced at Rob, who'd developed an expression beyond disappointment, more like resignation.

I no longer anticipated an evening with Rachel.

Mr. Smith had taken control of the room. He placed himself in the precise center of the semi-circle and asked each of us to introduce ourselves.

The fifty year old lady was a school teacher nearing retirement, the two men in their forties arrived together, both unemployed, while grandpa didn't hear the question and just helped himself to the snacks on a nearby table.

After their introductions, Rachel stood beside her husband and began the historical review of a very successful American company that had its start with people like us.

Us?

An almost retired spinster school teacher, two unemployed old farts, a deaf and nearly dead grandpa, plus two tragically poor college students practically begging for employment? That's what she meant by *us*?

Rachel then paused for dramatic effect before taking a half step toward the slide projector. She reached out her delicate arm to the media device. Her husband then puffed out his chest, and proudly announced, as a picture of the company headquarters beamed onto the white screen:

"Welcome to the world of Amway: the most successful small company in America."

I thought I would die.

I intently stared at the screen, then Rachel. Her devious smile that I had practically drooled over just moments ago, had transformed into a megawatt marketing magnet.

The faces of the other victims weren't so easy to read. But their blank stares, mouths opened just enough to gasp for air, let me know they were not prepared for this, either. The unemployed twins nervously opened, and just as quickly, closed the folders they were clutching, as if they somehow contained the answers they sought.

Grandpa and the half century woman had the look of defeat.

I couldn't even look at Rob. I wasn't ready.

Rachel and her husband traded presentation topics reviewing in excruciating detail everything that was Amway. Rob and I sat through their two-hour presentation—too afraid to leave, too apprehensive to ask questions that might prolong the agony, and too polite to tell them exactly what we thought of their trickery. Two hours of our life we would never get back.

Rachel continued to flash her beautiful smile to punctuate every point she would make in her segment, and occasionally offer a tantalizing glimpse of thigh through the slit in her little black dress. Her long, trim arms gently moved about in symphony with her alluring facial expressions. And as she talked, she rhythmically took deep breaths, causing her almost overflowing breasts to take leave of their uplifting constraints.

After what seemed an eternity, the formal presentation ended. I endured by watching Rachel work the room, only averting my eyes when her husband spoke.

As the group gathered their belongings while they rose from their chairs, Mr. and Mrs. Smith recognized this was their only chance to get commitments from their ambushed sales hopefuls. Rachel set the exiting pace by reaching the stairway first, while Mr. Smith continued on a point about reaching sales goals, and bonuses, and commissions.

They were relentless in their pursuit to convince at least one of us to sell products we knew nothing about, and cared even less.

When we got to my car parked on the street, in front of the Smiths' home, I prayed the engine would start up, so we could just leave that place of dread. The 1969 Opal Kadett was notoriously unreliable, but it cranked over like Old Faithful and we were on our way.

The awkward silence that Rob and I brought with us from the Smiths' basement didn't survive for very long. Laughter soon erupted so loud, I had to turn up the volume on the radio just to hear the distinctive guitar work on *Sixty Minute Man* by Billy Ward and his Dominoes.

Though the song was recorded nearly twenty five years before I had ever dreamed of encountering a sexy woman like Rachel, the provocative lyrics provided the perfect irony to an evening that began with mystery, accelerated to naïve anticipation, and culminated with complete disappointment.

> *"Well if your man ain't treatin' you right*
> *Come up and see your Dan*
> *I'll rock 'em, roll 'em all night long*
> *I'm a 60 minute man"*[40]

When the song ended, my mind flashed back to Rachel, when she had initially revealed herself to me from behind the slowly opened front door.

She was the bait. I was the prey. And Amway was the predator.

I never had a chance.

---

40 Sixty Minute Man, Billy Ward and Rose Marks, 1951

Part V

It's Never Too Late

Rick Speight and Karen Adams, 1975.

Karen Adams, September 1977.

Leaving home, friends and family. Goodbye, Vienna 1982.
My son, Matt 1 ½
301 Plum Street, SW.

When I get older losing my hair,
Many years from now
Will you still be sending me a Valentine
Birthday greetings bottle of wine,
If I'd been out till quarter to three
Would you lock the door
Will you still need me, will you still feed me,
When I'm sixty four.

Middles.

You'll be older too,
And if you say the word, I could stay with you

I could be handy, mending a fuse
When your lights have gone.
You can knit a sweater by the fireside
Sunday mornings go for a ride
Doing the garden, digging the weeds
Who could ask for more?
Will you still need me, etc.....

Mid. Every summer we can rent a cottage,
In the Isle of Wight, if it's not too dear.
We shall scrimp and save
... Grandchildren on your knee
Vera, Chuck and Dave

Send me a postcard, drop me a line,
Stating point of view
Indicate precisely what you mean to say
         wasting away in a form
Yours sincerely   me your answer fill in a form
                         mine for ever more...
                                           etc...

"When I'm Sixty Four"
Written by Paul McCartney when he was sixteen years old.
Published June 2, 1967 in the US.

So, What Happened to Everybody?

The boys from Hicks Drive are not young boys anymore. Rather, we're trying to grow old as gracefully as we can, recognizing that the end is much closer than the beginning.

And, that's certainly been a powerful motivator to spend as much time together as we can, while we can.

We owe our parents a sincere *thank you*, because a stable home is one of the qualities that contributed to our relationships—each of us remained on Hicks Drive at least through high school. But, our parents lived there for a combined total of one hundred seventy-seven years.

We moved away, while our homes remained.

Acceptance of each other's quirks and peculiarities is another contribution to our friendships' longevity. We never judged.

We still enjoy each other's company, laughing and acting stupid whenever we meet, just like we always did. Only now, just a little slower, and more deliberate.

Much has happened with all the boys since the dawn of the new millennium. For me, most of it seemed to begin with losing a dear friend and former teacher from Joyce Kilmer Intermediate.

Mr. Richardson died on April 7th, 2000, caused by a lost battle with lung cancer. He never smoked a single cigarette his entire life. He called to say goodbye in January of his final year, and told me he wasn't expected to make it past St. Patrick's Day. I lived in Asheville, NC at the time, a short five-hour drive from where he spent his final days. I immediately should have hung up the phone, packed an overnight bag, and went to see him.

I didn't.

But my inaction after that final conversation taught me a few valuable lessons: If a close friend or relative is experiencing a life-changing event, do not hesitate to reach out to them, talk to them or better still, go visit them. If someone, somehow made a difference in your life, write them a letter, reach out via social media or call them. Life is too short and the clock is ticking, often with lightning speed, to ignore their due recognition any longer.

And, perhaps the biggest lesson of all, don't allow time or distance to separate you from someone who you were close to in the past. Relationships come together for a reason. They won't go away, unless you allow them to do so.

So, here's an update on most of the individuals we've visited in this book—but what's more important, are some examples of how I've tried to follow my own advice.

In the mid-seventies, Dinky Gray climbed over an eight foot chain link fence topped with barbed wire, where he proceeded to set fire to nine police cars parked inside the enclosed area that was owned by Fairfax County. Apparently Dinky did not make a very clean getaway. He was caught trying to escape, while climbing over the fence, flaming police cars directly behind him.

He denied everything.

I heard a rumor that he was still holding the gas can when his feet hit the ground after scaling the fence.

Dinky was driving a car in Front Royal, Virginia on July 13th, 1978, when he collided with a police cruiser from that town. He was placed in the rear of the police car during the investigation of the incident, where he was observed "attempting to stuff a plastic baggy" behind the seat. The contents of the baggy were later determined to be PCP, a controlled substance. Although the case was later remanded on a procedural error and re-tried,[41] Dinky continued his rapid descent.

On May 7th, 1983 Dinky was living at his parents' home in Herndon. He'd messed with the wrong people once again, a pattern that seemed to repeat itself throughout his life. This time, his victims were a deranged group intent on sending a message to anybody who might consider double-crossing them in the future. I was never clear about the details leading up to the end, but the horrific outcome was never in doubt.

One or more individuals broke into the Grays' home, found Dinky asleep on the sofa, soaked him in gasoline, and set him afire. And his death was not instantaneous.

Although all of us from Hicks Drive had moved away by 1983, some scattered throughout the country, word quickly spread about the execution style death of Dinky Gray. All of us had memories of growing up with him; some good, most not so good.

But the consensus was unanimous—Dinky Gray died a horrible death at the youthful age of thirty. And no matter what he did in life, nobody deserved what he got in the end. We'll never know what demons possessed him, guiding him in his pursuit of less than acceptable behavior. Was it genetic? Was it environmental? Or was he just someone who took a wrong turn in life and never found his way back?

Although he wasn't a resident of Hicks Drive, Rob Lappin (Grave Digging Halloween 1972 and Hard at Work 1975) was a very close friend of mine for over ten years. So was his wife, Su. They, along with my future wife, Karen Adams, and I had often gotten together, during and after we completed high school. And we seemed to enjoy each other's company

---

[41] Howard Mason Gray, III versus The Commonwealth of Virginia, 265 S.E.2d 705 (1980)

whenever we did. But life got in the way for more than twenty years, when Rob went to medical school, followed by Karen and me leaving Vienna.

Rob died in 2005. But, thankfully, and a bit ironically, we had already reconnected with his then soon to be ex-wife, Su, as they were going through the early stages of their divorce, about five years before Rob passed away. And since that time, we have communicated with Su on a regular basis; she visited us in North Carolina in 2011. It was like we were never apart. Since she recently retired, we hope to see her more often.

My only sibling, Robin, died suddenly on November 15th, 2014. And in an instant, I was the final surviving member of my childhood family, as my parents were already gone.

Robin and I did not have a close relationship. At times, it was distant to adversarial. But we tried to remedy that after our parents passed away, when suddenly, it was just the two of us. It wasn't too late to try and fix it, so we did. I spoke to her at length a week before she died, and we discussed how and when we would get together again.

It was at her funeral.

Roger Martin lost his job, his career as a skilled electrician, and then he lost his immediate family to alcohol-related decisions and actions, all taking place around 2006. When his friends (Dale, Mark, Peter, and I) from Hicks Drive learned of his conundrum, we reached out and went to see him barely surviving in, an unrecognizable life. And, while that trip to Edenton, North Carolina didn't turn out like we planned, at least we tried. We were there to help, but you can't save people from themselves.

Roger died on June 22nd, 2017, from the same addiction he'd already forfeited so much. And, while his death was not a surprise to anyone who knew him, it still hit us like a ton of bricks, because he was the first of The Boys to reach the end of Hicks Drive's cul-de-sac and not return. Right up until his death, despite his often confrontational and irrational behavior, Roger was one of us—our friend for life.

For more than half of a century we had convinced ourselves we were invincible. Roger's death, more than anything else, reminded us that we were not.

Peter's youngest sister, Mary, passed away in June of 2018 while this book of memories was in the early stages of its creation. In November, she was laid to rest at Arlington National Cemetery, with full military honors.

As a child, adolescent, young adult, and finally senior citizen (she'd strongly object to that word choice), Mary tried her best to maintain a healthier lifestyle than anybody I've ever known. In her earlier years she was that annoying little sister who posted a steady stream of health-conscious notes, reminders, and reality checks on the refrigerator. ON THE REFRIGERATOR! There, for the certain-to-be-shamed individual to see, whenever they opened the door for a snack that did not pass her high quality standard. She was consistently exhibiting that behavior years before Post-It notes was invented. I actually believe she invented Post-It notes, but never received the patent. I guess she was too busy putting health inspiring words of wisdom on all the neighbors' refrigerators.

I hadn't seen her in more than thirty years when she arrived at my father's funeral in March of 2005. All heads turned her way as soon as she entered the viewing room at Money and King Funeral Home in Vienna. I guess she was attired in work clothes, but it looked like a full US Navy dress-up uniform, to those of us uninformed about such attire. Professional, yet stunning would just about cover it.

For the next thirteen years we stayed in touch, off and on, occasionally exchanging emails, talking on the phone, or attending more funerals. I think I improved as a person a little more each time.

Rick Duncan moved away to California with his family immediately after high school graduation at Wolf Trap in 1973. Actually, it was the next day, but as soon as the ceremony was over, Rick walked up the hill to his home and helped his parents pack the final household items. I didn't know this until many years later, but once I heard what happened I couldn't help but feel a little disappointed that he didn't hang around to celebrate with his lifetime friends. I guess it was his way of dealing with something he had no control over, and I had already accepted his fate, as well.

He briefly returned a couple of years later, then created and lived a life separate from Hicks Drive for thirty years, before returning in 2004 for a reunion hosted by Dale and his wife, Anna. We haven't seen him since our harrowing white-water rafting trip down the Gauley River in West Virginia, which was a year later. But he's welcome back any time.

Dale was an optician for most of his adult life, culminating in owning an optical shop in McLean. He, and his wife, Anna, moved to Florida in 2018 after living in Centreville, Virginia for twenty years. This is Dale's third attempt at permanent residency in The Sunshine State. Snow, ice, DC commuting, and outrageous taxes are more than enough incentives for escaping to a simpler, warmer, and cheaper life. I plan to visit as soon as they'll have me.

Peter developed a long career in water clarification and also became a pastor in 1977. He, and his wife, Patricia, have been married nearly forty years. They have remained and raised a family in the Washington metro area for the duration. I expect that is where they will eventually retire and spend those golden years with their two adult children and granddaughter nearby.

Like Rick Duncan, Mark Wood left home soon after high school and moved to Alabama, where he lived for thirteen years before returning to Virginia. While he was gone, he and I remained in close contact, and I think he did the same with the others, as well. When I moved to Texas in 1982, I stopped in Alabama to pick up Mark to help me with the relocation.

He's been in the construction and heavy equipment industries since high school, and has lived near on or near Lake Anna since the eighties.

His mother is the lone surviving parent of The Boys from Hicks Drive. All the others are gone.

Rick Speight and Karen Adams, married February 11, 1978, left Vienna and moved to Texas four years later with our first child, Matt, in tow. The Lone Star State immediately became our adopted home, and living in Austin was almost like a vacation. It was very difficult to leave there, for a job transfer to Houston, after Rick graduated from The University of Texas at Austin. Our daughter, Erica, is the only native Texan in the family. She was born in Humble, July 1986. Since then, we lived in Mobile, Alabama throughout the late eighties and nineties, then Asheville, North Carolina for sixteen years.

Matt and Erica are college graduates and live in Pensacola, Florida and Brooklyn, New York respectively. Family gatherings are now, more than ever, cherished and memorable.

Our first, and as of this writing, only granddaughter, Lily Grace was born January 2010. Moving plans began when she took her first breath, bringing us back to the Gulf Coast in 2014. And the next best thing to being part of Lily's life was moving to a beautiful town, Fairhope, Alabama, and reconnecting with our Mobile friends we hadn't seen in nearly twenty years.

Because of valuable information provided to me by John Thompson, I reached out to, and interviewed the sole surviving relative of the Fairfax Lodge Todd family, Mrs. Elizabeth Todd Ruppert. She graciously invited my daughter, Erica and I into her home in November 2018, where she hosted a lively and informative discussion of her life on the estate from 1947 until 1959. She shared her fondest memories of the mansion, the Eastern European refugees they hosted after World War II, and what it was like to travel the Vienna countryside as a young girl on her favorite horse.

I have contacted several more of the special people featured in these pages who have made life so interesting for so many—especially me—and I plan to eventually reach out to all of them. So far, every time I've summoned the courage to drop a line or pick up a phone, I have eagerly anticipated their response. And all of them did respond, at least once.

With the first note of their voices, sounds I hadn't heard in decades, I knew that the close friendships or family bonds were still there, waiting to be re-lived and enjoyed by walking down memory lane with them one more time. And in every case, I realized that it's not about living in the past, it's about the recognition and appreciation for those who are part of it.

It's never too late to reach out to someone you care about and tell them so.

It's the things we *don't* do that we regret the most.

Every Picture Tells A Story

And, that story doesn't end, but transitions into the next. With that in mind, the following are some timeless photographs that illuminate the past, create nostalgia in the present, to leave memories for the future.

Finally, I'm convinced there hasn't been written a more appropriate lyric to end this collection of adventures featuring The Boys From Hicks Drive Vienna, Virginia.

"Ticking away the moments that make up a dull day
You fritter and waste the hours in an offhand way.
Kicking around on a piece of ground in your home town
Waiting for someone or something to show you the way.

Tired of lying in the sunshine staying home to watch the rain.
You are young and life is long and there is time to kill today.
And then one day you find ten years have got behind you.
No one told you when to run, you missed the starting gun."[42]

---

42   "Time", Mason, Gilmore, Waters, Wright. 1973

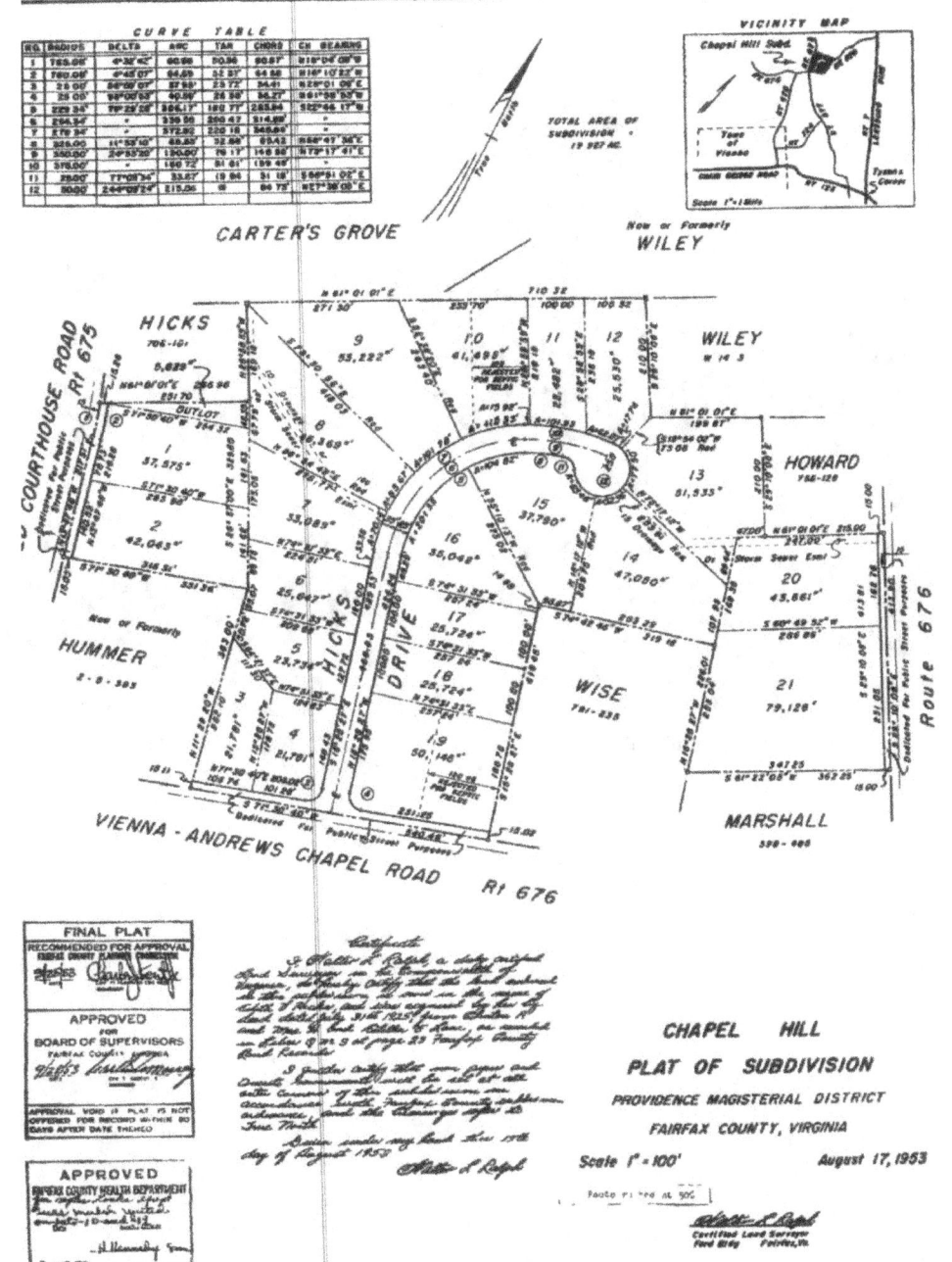

Chapel Hill Plat, birthplace of Hicks Drive, 1953.

Trap Road (Vienna-Andrews Chapel Road) across the center, dirt version of Hicks Drive to the right, Todd's field in the background. Circa 1955. Photo supplied by Eileen McCarthy Grant.

The Hall children: Carol, Dale and Ron. Circa 1956.

Mrs. Clarence Todd, Lisle A. Smith, Mrs. Ramone Eaton, Mrs. Lisle A. Smith, and Daniel Cox Fahey Jr. (on horse), 1961. Provided by John Thompson.

Cub Scouts, Pack 1128, Circa 1962
Left to right: Ricky Speight, David Finch, Roger Martin,
Pete Canciglia, Kevin Smith, Ricky Duncan.
Provided by Rick Duncan, edited by Robert I Speight.

CABIN OFFICE—Sales at The Trails, a subdivision of the Lerner Companies in the Vienna area of Northern Virginia, are made in a refurbished log cabin that had earlier been used as a hunting lodge. More than a hundred homes are being built on the former Fairfax estate. While selling new houses in the log cabin, the Lerner firm has also had an offer for the cabin.

Fairfax Lodge, the original structure on the Todd Estate, used here as a sales office by The Lerner Companies. Washington Post ad, 9/13/69. Provided by John Thompson.

The Canciglias
From left to right, back row-Linda, Mary, Angela, Peter.
Alphonse and Dora in front.
Hicks Drive late 1960s. Provided by Peter Canciglia.

1635 Hicks Drive.
George Washington's Birthday Blizzard, 1979.

Mark's home on Trap Road under construction, 1962.
Kehoe's home and their sledding hill, to the right and behind.
Photo provided by Mark Wood.

Roger explaining to Daytona Beach's finest, how that Bud got into his hand, August 1977.

Hold that dead shark, Pete, and I'll take your picture.
Hollywood, Florida. August 1977.

James Madison High School, Class of '73, 20th Reunion
Rick Speight, Alfred W Richardson, Lillian Lampman, Mark Wood.

Frances Brown and Rick Speight, James Madison High School Class of '73, 40th Class Reunion.

Rick Speight, Roger Martin, Dale Hall, and Mark Wood. March 21, 1981. Photograph provided by Mark Wood.

Rick Duncan, Pete Canciglia, Rick Speight, Dale Hall
West Virginia Rafting
Gauley River, 2005.

Rick Speight, Mark Wood, Pete Canciglia, Dale Hall
Dangerously close to Bunnyman Bridge, 2009.

Rick Speight, Pete Canciglia, and Dale Hall at my son, Matt's, wedding. Pensacola, October 2017.

Dale and Anna Hall, with Pete and Pat Canciglia.
Scotland, 2018.

The last photograph taken of The Boys From Hicks Drive, 2004.
Left to Right-Rick Speight, Mark Wood, Dale Hall,
Pete Canciglia, Roger Martin, Rick Duncan.
Camden Yards, Baltimore.

Acknowledgements

My deepest appreciation goes to my wife, Karen, for gifts too numerous to list here. But the most recent, and relevant to this book, is the experience, expertise, and sensitivity compass she provided as the initial proofreader and editor. She is living proof that sometimes you (she) *can* save people from themselves (me).

My daughter, Erica Speight and her husband Derek Misler, provided website design and marketing expertise I couldn't have handled on my own. And the value of Erica's enthusiasm for this project was extremely encouraging, as well as her editing skills, of which I took full advantage.

Hicks Drive royalty, Mrs. Elizabeth Todd Ruppert, provided key elements about her family's property, and our playground, that I couldn't have gathered from anybody else. It was more than a pleasure speaking to her about the people and places we value so dearly. Thank you so much, Betty.

Teachers have more influence on an individual's life than anybody outside the respective families. A special thanks to all of mine, kindergarten through twelfth grade, especially those below. All in Fairfax County Public Schools, except Kindergarten.

Holy Comforter Church, Vienna, Virginia: Ms. Chinn—Kindergarten

Freedom Hill Elementary: Miss Phalen—first grade, Ms. Lyons—second grade, Ms. Barufi—third grade, Ms. Botkin—fourth grade.

Westbriar Elementary: Ms. Dinsmore—fifth grade, Ms. Best—sixth grade.

Joyce Kilmer Intermediate: Mr. Alfred W Richardson—seventh grade, English, Social Studies, Guidance (ESG)

James Madison High School: Ms. Schultz—English, Ms. Crawford—Biology, Miss Mulcahey—French, Ms. Marlatt—Trig/Functions, Ms. Snuggs—Algebra II, Colonel Parker—Algebra I

John Thompson—formerly of The McGuire Court Gang, now true Vienna Historian. Reconnecting with "Johnny" was a pleasant, but unexpected surprise. Thank you for uncovering the mysteries of Todd's Farm, our childhood playground.

My editor, Ange Baker, pushed me to create beyond my skill level. Your expertise, straightforward direction, and lofty expectations inspired me to do more.

I don't know where to begin thanking The Town of Vienna, so I'll start with Councilmember Carey Sienicki for helping me look at issues from a different perspective. And, to all its citizens for making it such an enjoyable place to live.

Fairfax County offered so much. Sometimes you have to move away to realize what you miss when it's gone.

Studying state history *was* US History if you learned it while living in The Commonwealth of Virginia: Jamestown, Captain John Smith and Pocahontas, Manassas, Arlington, home to the most US Presidents, including four of the first five. Virginia is a living, twenty-seven million acre classroom.

Washington, DC; thanks to you for Broadway shows, excellent restaurants, The Smithsonian, Memorials to Everybody, Georgetown and Robert F Kennedy Memorial Stadium.

Edith V. Hicks: What if you hadn't developed those sixteen lots?

About the Author

Rick Speight is a native Virginian and a graduate of James Madison High School in Vienna, George Mason University in Fairfax, and The University of Texas at Austin.

While he has lived and raised a family in Austin, Mobile, Asheville and now Fairhope, Alabama he will always consider 1635 Hicks Drive Vienna, Virginia as that special place called home.

After graduating from UT-Austin, Rick spent fifteen years in pulp and paper chemical sales before opening a healthcare staffing agency. He and his wife, Karen, recently celebrated their fortieth wedding anniversary that began at Antioch Christian Church on Beulah Road in Vienna. Their daughter lives in Brooklyn, son and granddaughter in Pensacola, Florida.

Rick communicates with his lifelong buddies Dale Hall, Pete Canciglia, and Mark Wood on a regular basis. And when they get together, they tell the same stories over and over, keeping the laughs and adventures intact, as their own memories continue to fade.

This is Rick's first book, appropriately dedicated to best friends everywhere.

www.ingramcontent.com/pod-product-compliance
Lightning Source LLC
Chambersburg PA
CBHW071151070526
44584CB00019B/2754